The Growth of International Business

The Growth of International Business

edited by

Mark Casson

Contributors

Authors:

Peter J. Buckley Mark Casson T. A. B. Corley
John H. Dunning George Norman Robert D. Pearce
Robert Read David J. Teece George N. Yannopoulos

Reviewers and discussants:

Charles E. Harvey Neil Hood Scott Moss S. Nicholas
C. J. Sutton Louis Turner M. A. Utton
Stephen Young

London
GEORGE ALLEN & UNWIN
Boston Sydney

George Allen & Unwin (Publishers) Ltd,
40 Museum Street, London WC1A 1LU, UK

George Allen & Unwin (Publishers) Ltd,
Park Lane, Hemel Hempstead, Herts HP2 4TE, UK

Allen & Unwin Inc.,
9 Winchester Terrace, Winchester, Mass 01890, USA

George Allen & Unwin Australia Pty Ltd,
8 Napier Street, North Sydney, NSW 2060, Australia

First published in 1983

British Library Cataloguing in Publication Data

The Growth of international business.
1. International business enterprises
I. Casson, Mark
338.8'8 HD2755.5
ISBN 0-04-330333-1

Library of Congress Cataloging in Publication Data

Main entry under title:
The Growth of international business.
Bibliography: p.
Includes index.
1. International business enterprises—Addresses, essays, lectures. I. Casson, Mark, 1945–
HD2755.5.G76 1983 338.8'81 82-20750
ISBN 0-04-330333-1

Set in 10 on 11 point Times by Preface Ltd., Salisbury, Wilts.
and printed in Great Britain by Mackays of Chatham

Contents

Preface

The contributions to this book provide an integrated treatment of a new and expanding area of research. The contributors were commissioned to write upon a specific aspect of the growth of international business. Each contributor writes upon an area of which he has expert knowledge. The contributions were presented in draft form to the Annual Conference of the UK Chapter of the Academy of International Business held at Reading University in March 1982, and have been revised in the light of discussion at the conference.

Jill Turner was responsible for typing most of the papers and for administering the conference; Margaret Lewis, Barbara Wall and Christine Toms also typed some of the papers and worked very hard to meet the conference deadline. I am grateful to them all for their invaluable efforts. The Academy of International Business owes a great debt to Dr Michael Z. Brooke for setting up and running its UK Chapter; I am grateful to Michael, and to his colleague Dr Stanley Paliwoda, for support in organising the conference. I am also grateful to John Cantwell for his help. Finally, the authors owe a great debt to their referees and discussants, who put considerable effort into supplying constructive criticisms of early drafts; no specific acknowledgements are made, however, as the preparation of the book has been a truly cooperative effort.

MARK CASSON
Reading
June 1982

The authors

Peter J. Buckley is Senior Lecturer in International Business at the Management Centre, University of Bradford. He is the co-author of *The Future of the Multinational Enterprise, Going International: The Experience of Smaller Firms* and *European Direct Investment in the U.S.A. Before World War I.* He is on the editorial board of the *Journal of International Business Studies*, and has published numerous papers in this area.

Mark Casson is Professor of Economics at the University of Reading. His relevant publications include *The Future of the Multinational Enterprise* (co-author Peter J. Buckley), *Alternatives to the Multinational Enterprise* and *The Entrepreneur: An Economic Theory.*

T. A. B. Corley is Senior Lecturer in Economics at the University of Reading. He has published extensively on economic and business history, and is currently working on a major study of the Burmah Oil Company.

John H. Dunning is Esmée Fairbairn Professor of International Investment at the University of Reading. He has published extensively on international business since his pioneering work on *American Investment in British Manufacturing Industry* (1956). His most recent book is *International Production and the Multinational Enterprise* (1981). He is on the editorial board of the *Journal of International Business Studies* and has served on numerous advisory and consultative committees, including the United Nations 'Group of Eminent Persons' studying the impact of multinational enterprises on economic development and international relations.

George Norman is Lecturer in Economics at the University of Reading. He has published widely on the theory of spatial pricing. He is the author of *Economies of Scale, Transport Costs and Location* and co-author with John H. Dunning of *Factors Influencing the Location of Offices of Multinational Companies.*

R. D. Pearce is Research Economist at the University of Reading. He has co-authored numerous publications, including *Profitability and Performance of the World's Leading Companies* and *The World's Largest Industrial Companies 1962–78.*

Robert Read is a research student at the University of Reading financed by the Social Science Research Council. His work is linked to a project on multinational firms in intermediate product trade. He has made a special study of the role of multinationals in the export of tropical crops. He is a graduate of the University of Essex.

David J. Teece is Associate Professor in the School of Business Administration at the University of California at Berkeley. He is the author of several monographs, including *The Multinational Corporation and the Resource Costs of International Technology Transfer*, and has published numerous papers in learned journals.

George N. Yannopoulos lectures in the Department of Economics and the Graduate School of Contemporary European Studies at the University of Reading. He has written and edited several books and articles in the field of international and regional economics. He has also acted as adviser to the Greek Foreign Ministry and to the National Bank of Greece. He is currently preparing a book (jointly with Matthew McQueen) on the EEC and the developing countries.

1 Introduction: the conceptual framework

MARK CASSON

1.1 NEW DIRECTIONS IN RESEARCH

Ten years ago industrial economics, international economics and business history were relatively stagnant areas of research. The stagnation in industrial and international economics was particularly surprising as there were very important contemporary developments which affected both these disciplines. Prominent among these developments was the rapid growth of multinational firms and their foreign direct investments. Logically, the analysis of the multinational firm lies at the interface of industrial and international economics. Yet the growth of the multinational firm could not be explained by a straightforward synthesis of the orthodox theories of the time. As a result, the study of multinational firms remained divorced from mainstream economics.

Today industrial and international economics are amongst the liveliest areas of research. New theoretical concepts have been developed – or old concepts rediscovered, according to one's perspective. These concepts have been developed partly as a direct response to the challenge of explaining the growth of the multinational firm. They have enabled the study of the multinational firm to be absorbed into mainstream economics. As a result, the way is now clear to develop and deepen our knowledge of this subject.

The situation in business history has been somewhat different. Business historians have for a long time been plagued by conflicting research objectives (Cole, 1962; Galambos, 1966; Tucker, 1972). Is the primary function of a business history simply to record the growth of a particular successful firm? To what extent should business history involve the study of wider issues such as the growth of capitalist enterprise and more recently the emergence of the large corporation? How much emphasis should be placed upon social and psychological factors, such as the personality of the individual founder of a firm and the ethos with which he imbues it? How far should historians seek to generalise about the growth of firms; in particular, is it possible to generalise about the factors which make for a firm's success?

In scientific research the primary object is to test a theory, and the business historians' problems are largely due to the fact that until recently they had no conventional theory to test. Admittedly there was an economic theory of the firm, but this had little to say about two factors of major interest: the relationship between the strategy and the structure of the firm, and the dynamics of the firm's growth. Many business historians found the most interesting theories to be those concerned with the social psychology of the entrepreneur, but these were often too lacking in precision to permit a satisfactory test. Now at last there is emerging an economic theory of business strategy and growth which is generating hypotheses for business historians to test. The availability of this theory is a major factor in the renewed vitality of business history research.

The study of the growth of international business links the disciplines of industrial and international economics on the one hand, and of business history on the other. The documentation of the growth of international business is already well established. Like most historical research, it is hampered by a lack of data, notably by the absence of consistent economic time series on direct investment flows. There is, however, a considerable amount of archival material obtainable from individual firms, and some of this has been collated and standardised, and is available in published form (Vaupel and Curhan, 1969, 1974). A particularly valuable source is contemporary studies and reports on foreign direct investment: the most prominent of these include Frankel, S. H. (1938), Lewis (1938), Marshall, Southard and Taylor (1936), Moore (1941), Remer (1933), and Southard (1931).

The standard references on the history of international business are two volumes by Wilkins (1970), (1974a). Wilkins provides most useful bibliographies, as do Brooke, Black and Neville (1977) and Stewart and Simmons (1964). References to more recent work are available from the bibliography at the end of this book.

1.2 ORIGINS OF THE MODERN THEORY OF THE FIRM

The object of this introductory chapter is to outline the theoretical concepts which underlie the study of international business growth The relevant concepts are those of the institutional theory of the firm. The antecedents of this theory are to be found in papers written in the 1930s on the nature of the firm.

It is useful to begin with Kaldor's critique of the Marshallian long-run theory of competitive supply (Kaldor, 1934). Even today the radical implications of this paper have not been fully grasped.

Marshall deduced the upward-sloping industry supply curve from the upward-sloping supply curve of the representative firm (Marshall, 1920). In the long run, of course, the number of firms in the industry is variable. Thus before he could derive the industry equilibrium, Marshall had to assume that in the equilibrium there would be a sufficient number of firms to sustain competition. Kaldor points out that this assumption is warranted only if, as output expands, the average cost of the representative firm increases faster than the average cost of the industry as a whole. If it increases at the same rate then the number of firms would be indeterminate. When inputs are hired competitively, Kaldor's condition is satisfied only if the firm employs a fixed factor. Kaldor concludes that even in the long run the representative firm in a competitive industry has a fixed factor.

But what can this fixed factor be? Kaldor considers three possibilities: a capacity for uncertainty bearing, as defined by Knight (1921), supervision (analogous to the 'superintendence' discussed by Mill, 1848), and coordination.

Kaldor argues that joint-stock capitalisation makes uncertainty-bearing a variable factor which can be hired through the equity market. Supervision may involve indivisibilities – e.g. the full-time employment of a foreman – but the indivisible inputs can be replicated under constant returns – e.g. by appointing more independent foremen with non-overlapping spans of authority. But coordination is fundamentally fixed as well as indivisible: the coordinator must be 'one' otherwise he cannot coordinate:

> You cannot increase the supply of co-ordinating ability available to an enterprise alongside an increase in the supply of other factors, as it is the essence of co-ordination that every single decision should be made on a comparison with all the other decisions already made or likely to be made; it must therefore pass through a single brain. This does not imply, of course, that the task of co-ordination must necessarily fall upon a single individual; in a modern business organisation it may be jointly undertaken by a whole Board of Directors. But then it still remains true that all the members of that Board will, in all important decisions have to keep all the alternatives in their minds – in regard to this most essential mental process there will be no division of labour between them – and that it will not be possible, at any rate beyond a certain point, to increase the supply of co-ordinating ability available to that enterprise merely by enlarging the Board of Directors. The efficiency of the supply of co-ordinating ability can be increased by the introduction of new

technical devices, e.g. by a better system of accounting; but given the state of technical knowledge and given the co-ordinating ability represented by that enterprise, the amount of 'other factors' which can be most advantageously employed by that enterprise will be limited. (Kaldor, 1934, pp. 68–9)

Coordination, in Kaldor's view, is the essence of what is commonly called 'entrepreneurship'. It is the one factor which in the long-run is 'rigidly attached to the firm, which, so to speak, lives and dies with it'.

Coordination is essentially a dynamic function: it is the activity of adjusting to disequilibrium. It has no place in the long-run steady state. Under static conditions coordination is valueless and so the optimum size of the firm – and hence the number of firms in the industry – becomes indeterminate. What renders the size of the firm determinate is the average pace of economic change. Kaldor appears to suggest that if demand conditions in the product market or supply conditions in the factor markets change frequently, unpredictably and by large amounts, then the demand for coordination increases. Since coordination is unitary, the optimum size of firm is reduced and the optimum number of firms – and hence of entrepreneurs – increases. Kaldor concludes that:

> In relatively 'quiet' times, i.e. when tastes and the rate of saving are steady, technical innovations rare and changes in population small, we may expect the actual size of 'representative firms' to expand . . . The reverse is true in times of 'disquietude', when changes of data become more frequent and far-reaching. (Kaldor, 1934, pp. 74–5)

The concept of coordination as a dynamic activity was endorsed by E. A. G. Robinson (1931), (1934). According to Robinson, coordination is the function of the manager. The successful manager

> must see an opening where a new enterprise can be expected to succeed, he must possess or secure capital, he must choose the best site for his plant, he must decide what equipment to install, and arrange its most efficient lay-out. He must design the goods that he is to produce, and prepare the necessary drawings; he must buy materials, estimate costs, and fix his price. He must organise and supervise production, instruct his workers as to how the goods shall be made, inspect them when made for defects, arrange their packing and transport, and collect payment. He must keep the factory accounts and see where profits are being made and where losses, he

must work out the depreciation of the plant, and negotiate with the rapacious Inland Revenue authorities. He must persuade unwilling and suspicious bankers or investors to lend him money, producers of raw materials to give him credit, middlemen to buy his goods. He ought, no doubt, to have time and patience to read those outspoken articles in which journalists, politicians, even economists, tell him how to run his business. (Robinson, 1931, pp. 36–7)

Although it is very much concerned with disequilibrium, Robinson's analysis still makes extensive use of equilibrium concepts. This is not so contradictory as it sounds, for there are many different kinds of equilibrium. Robinson is not concerned with an exact deterministic equilibrium but rather with an economic system in continual movement within the neighbourhood of such an equilibrium. Spontaneous changes are continually moving the system away from full equilibrium. Without management the system would diverge increasingly from full equilibrium. The function of management is to adjust to the change and restore the system toward an equilibrium. The greater are the changes, the greater is the demand for management services to initiate a response. This demand induces more managers to enter industry and leads to a smaller average size of firm. In line with Kaldor's argument, the greater is the pace of change the greater is the number of managers that will be used to maintain the stability of the system.

Robinson himself does not, however, pursue this particular line of reasoning very far. So far as Robinson is concerned, management is just one of several functional areas of the firm, the others being production, marketing and finance. The optimum size of firm is determined not by management alone but by the interplay between the optimum sizes for each of these functions. In his discussion Robinson attaches equal weight to each of these functions, though he argues that management has a particular significance in that it sets an upper limit to the size of the firm.

Consider first the economics of production. Robinson postulates that in each industry there is a minimum efficient scale of production; below this scale the average cost of production is falling; above it, average cost is constant. Marketing and finance exhibit increasing returns to scale. Management exhibits first increasing and then decreasing returns to scale. The increasing returns are accounted for by the advantages of the division of labour between specialisms, which becomes easier as the size of the managerial unit is increased. Decreasing returns set in because of the difficulties of communication that are encountered as the hierarchy of reporting and control expands. Since management is the only function which exhibits decreasing returns, it is management which effectively sets an upper limit to the size of the firm.

One of the weaknesses of Robinson's analysis is that he relates costs to a single variable – size – although for the firm as a whole the influence of size upon costs depends critically upon other variables, in particular the structure and diversity of the firm's operations. Structure and diversity in turn reflect the degree of integration effected by the firm. Without a satisfactory theory of integration Robinson was unable to take his analysis of the optimum firm any further. This lacuna in the theory was filled a few years later in a seminal paper by Coase (1937).

1.3 THE CONCEPT OF INTERNALISATION

Coase's analysis of internalisation is a landmark in the development of the institutional theory of the firm (Coase, 1937). Coase demonstrates, amongst other things, that integration simply involves the substitution of coordination by planning for coordination by prices. The economics of integration are not primarily technological – as had previously been thought – but are organisational and contractual.

According to Coase, the firm is a planning unit which 'supersedes the price mechanism'. Without the supersession of the price mechanism there would be no firms. He quotes with approval Robertson's comment that firms in a market economy are 'islands of conscious power' in an 'ocean of unconscious cooperation' (Robertson, 1923, p. 85).

The rationale of the firm is that it avoids the cost of using the price mechanism:

> The most obvious cost of 'organising' production through the price mechanism is that of discovering what the relevant prices are. This cost may be reduced but it will not be eliminated by the emergence of specialists who will sell this information. (Coase, 1937, pp. 390–1)

Contrary to popular opinion. Coase was not primarily concerned with analysing the economics of integration. He was concerned with a still more fundamental issue in the theory of the firm – an issue which has received surprisingly little attention (though see Simon, 1957; Williamson, 1975). This issue concerns the nature and scope of management's control of the worker: an issue which is not merely of theoretical interest, but of practical social and political importance. Coase demonstrates that managerial control stems from the employment contract, which accords the employer discretion over the activities of the employee. The rationale for the employment contract is that it substitutes a single large transaction for many separate smaller transactions; by reducing the number of contracts it economises on the costs of using the price mechanism:

> The costs of negotiating and concluding a separate contract for each exchange transaction which takes place on a market must . . . be taken into account . . . It is true that contracts are not eliminated when there is a firm but they are greatly reduced. A factor of production (or the owner thereof) does not have to make a series of contracts with the factors with whom he is cooperating within the firm . . . For this series of contracts is substituted one . . . The contract is one whereby the factor, for a certain remuneration (which may be fixed or fluctuating) agrees to obey the directions of an entrepreneur *within certain limits.* The essence of the contract is that it should only state the limits to the powers of the entrepreneur. Within these limits, he can therefore direct the other factors of production. (Coase, 1937, p. 391)

Coase explains the long-term open-ended nature of the typical employment contract along similar lines:

> It may be desired to make a long-term contract for the supply of some article or service. This may be due to the fact that if one contract is made for a longer period, instead of several shorter ones, then certain costs of making each contract will be avoided. Or, owing to the risk attitude of the people concerned, they may prefer to make a long rather than a short-term contract. Now, owing to the difficulty of forecasting, the longer the period of the contract is for the supply of the commodity or service, the less possible, and indeed, the less desirable it is for the person purchasing to specify what the other contracting party is expected to do. It may well be a matter of indifference to the person supplying the service or commodity which of several courses of action is taken, but not to the purchaser of that service or commodity. But the purchaser will not know which of those several courses he will want the supplier to take. Therefore the service which is being provided is expressed in general terms, the exact details being left until a later date . . . The details of what the supplier is expected to do is not stated in the contract but is decided later by the purchaser. When the direction of resources (within the limits of the contract) becomes dependent on the buyer in this way, that relationship which I term a 'firm' may be obtained. (Coase, 1937, pp. 391–2)

It is clear that Coase has in mind the labour contract, because he goes on:

> A firm is likely therefore to emerge in those cases where a very short-term contract would be unsatisfactory. It is obviously of more importance in the case of services – labour – than it is in the case of the buying of commodities. In the case of commodities, the main items can be stated in advance and the details which will be decided later will be of minor significance. (Coase, 1937, p. 392)

According to Coase the extent to which the price mechanism is superseded is governed by the margin where 'the costs of organising an extra transaction within the firm are equal to the costs involved in carrying out the transaction in the open market'. To some writers this conclusion seems little more than a tautology. Coase did, however, attempt to formulate testable hypotheses on the basis of this result:

> it would appear that the costs of organising and the losses through mistakes will increase with an increase in the spatial distribution of the transactions organised, in the dissimilarity of the transactions, and in the probability of changes in the relevant prices. (This assumes that an increase in the probability of price movements increases the costs of organising within a firm more than it increases the cost of carrying out an exchange transaction on the market – which is probable.) As more transactions are organised by an entrepreneur it would appear that the transactions would tend to be either different in kind or in different places . . . Inventions which tend to bring factors of production nearer together, by lessening spatial distribution, tend to increase the size of the firm. Changes like the telephone and the telegraph which tend to reduce the cost of organising spatially will tend to increase the size of the firm. All changes which improve managerial technique will tend to increase the size of the firm. (Coase, 1937, p. 397)

These hypotheses are particularly valuable as they link the size of the firm to its industrial and geographical diversification. The remarks about inventions and managerial innovations are particularly relevant to the growth of a geographically diversified firm such as a multinational.

1.4 VERTICAL INTEGRATION

So far as the multinational firm is concerned, particular interest attaches to the factors influencing vertical integration. It may be satisfying to know that the internalisation of markets in highly specific labour services constitutes a rationale for the firm. But the international firm exemplifies a particular species of firm, namely the multi-plant firm. The multinational firm is simply a multi-plant firm whose plants are located in two or more different countries. The real significance of internalisation for the international firm is not that it explains the existence of the firm but that it explains multi-plant operation over space.

Vertical integration is an important factor in many multi-plant operations. Prior to the development of internalisation theory, economies of vertical integration were usually assumed to be technological. In modern terminology, vertical integration was assumed to allow the exploitation of beneficial 'externalities' between adjacent plants, e.g. the conservation of heat achieved by the integrated steel works. It is apparent that technological economies of this kind normally work against the internationalisation of production by restricting the scope for the international division of labour between different stages. To explain international production in terms of vertical integration the economies must have a very different origin. By focusing upon the contractual nature of vertical integration the theory of internalisation suggests what these economies might be.

Buckley and Casson (1976) distinguish several economies of vertical integration which are particularly relevant to the multinational firm.

First, there are economies of internalising long-term contracts. As Coase indicates, it is usually convenient to make long-term contracts contingent upon future states of the world. But long-term contingent contracts are often difficult to enforce. Williamson (1975, 1979) shows that using alternative contractual arrangements it is possible to establish a more efficient 'governance structure'. This structure internalises the transaction and thereby substantially reduces the risk of default.

Long-term contracts are particularly important in industries which make intensive use of illiquid capital assets (such as long-lived producer durables). Raw materials are purchased on long-term contracts in order to secure future supplies and so keep the assets fully utilised. This is a major factor in, for example, the economics of oil-refining and metal-refining. Internalisation of the raw material market leads to the integration of the extraction and the processing of the mineral.

Second, a monopoly of supply in an intermediate product creates an incentive to internalise the market. This is because of the difficulty of enforcing price discrimination in an external market. A monopolist maximises his profit by charging discriminatory prices based upon each buyer's demand curve (the classic reference is Pigou, 1938, who distinguishes several degrees of discrimination). The opportunities for arbitrage that exist in an external market limit the monopolist's ability to discriminate. Even if he could discriminate, efficient pricing would be inhibited by lack of information about the buyer's demand curve. He is therefore obliged to charge a uniform price, and this reduces his profit. More significantly, it reduces the profit of the monopolist by more than it reduces the profits of the buyers. In other words, there is a deadweight loss of profit on account of uniform pricing. This loss can be avoided by internalising the market. Internalisation prevents resale and also gives the seller full information about the buyer's demand (Arrow, 1975). With internalisation the monopolist can transfer the intermediate product from one activity to another at notional discriminatory prices, such that the marginal unit is priced at marginal cost. This allows both activities to operate at more efficient levels, and earns a higher profit for the integrated firm.

This analysis suggests, for example, that the integration of the extraction and use of a primary commodity will be greatest when the supply of the commodity is monopolised. Robinson (1931) reaches a similar conclusion, though by a rather different argument. He maintains that by 1930 vertical integration within the coal, iron and steel industries had proceeded further in Germany than in Britain because the degree of monopoly in coal-mining was much greater. He predicted that contemporary British legislation to 'rationalise' mines into larger groups would indirectly promote vertical integration in Britain along similar lines.

Third, there are economies of transfer pricing. The importance of transfer pricing for multinational firms has been stressed by numerous writers (for empirical evidence see e.g. Ellis, 1981). Transfer pricing can be used to reduce the incidence of *ad valorem* tariffs, to exploit international differentials in rates of profit taxation and to by-pass exchange controls. Transfer pricing illustrates an even more general phenomenon, namely the ability of internal markets to avoid many of the government regulations and fiscal interventions that are experienced in external markets. This is one of the advantages of internalisation stressed by Coase:

> exchange transactions on a market and the same transactions organised within a firm are often treated differently by Governments or other bodies with regulatory powers. If we consider the operation of a sales tax, it is clear that it is a tax on market transactions and not on the same transactions organised within the firm . . . Similarly, quota schemes, and methods of price control which imply that there is rationing, and which do not apply to firms producing such products for themselves, by allowing advantages to

> those who organise within the firm and not through the market, necessarily encourage the growth of firms. (Coase, 1937, p. 393)

Another economy of vertical integration, recently emphasised by Casson (1982b), is the ability to improve quality control. Products are sold to consumers on the basis not only of price, but also of quality. Quality reflects both the design of the product and the standard to which individual units of the product are manufactured. This standard in turn depends upon the standard of the raw materials and the components used in its manufacture. A producer who intends to retain the goodwill of consumers must have absolute confidence in the quality of the components he uses. If he cannot find a component supplier who enjoys goodwill of his own then the producer must integrate backward into component manufacture. He internalises the market for the component in order to guarantee the quality of his supplies.

The significance of quality control for vertical integration has long been recognised, even though the precise formulation of the principle is fairly recent. Lavington (1927), for example, considers a case where:

> process and product are essentially individual in character, so that the successive processes are bound together by the need at every stage for the personal supervision of the individual producer. Wedgwood and other skilled potters necessarily make for themselves the various 'bodies' from which their fine wares are shaped; in the manufacture of motor cars vertical dissociation of processes has made least progress among the firms making cars of high quality; indeed, it is evident that the condition works to maintain the complexity of a wide range of undertakings engaged upon 'quality' products and proprietary articles. It is this condition, it would seem, which forms a large part of the explanation of the sharp contrast in the Wool Textile industry between the marked integration in the making of woollens and the vertical specialisation in the making of worsteds. For success in the making of woollens depends far more than it does in worsteds on the skill with which the particular producer makes his particular blend from a very great variety of raw materials, and on his ultimate adaptation to that blend of one of the wide range of modes in which his cloth may be finished; so that at each stage process and product are individual in quality and must be united under a single control. (Lavington, 1927, p. 34)

One of the most important applications of the theory of quality-uncertainty is to the market for proprietary knowledge. The literature on proprietary knowledge has developed along a distinct but parallel path to the literature on vertical integration, and has only recently become integrated with it. It is to this literature that we now turn.

1.5 PATENTS AND PROPRIETARY KNOWLEDGE

An important feature of the theory of international business is its emphasis on the production and exploitation of knowledge. The modern literature assumes that the production of knowledge is financed by the firm, and that the discoverer or inventor is an employee. This was not always the case; in the nineteenth century the inventor was supposed to be his own boss. The relation between the producer and exploiter of knowledge was similar to that prevailing today between the author and his publisher: the author produces the 'intellectual commodity' and licenses the publisher to exploit it on his behalf.

The switch by the inventor from principal to employee can be explained by a number of factors: the increasing cost of financing invention, the incentive to increase inventive efficiency through teamwork, and the growth of accrediting agencies – universities and professional associations – which enable entrepreneurs to recruit specialist team members more easily. The exact importance of these (and other) factors has still to be established however (see e.g. Neumeyer and Stedman, 1971).

An inventor is normally rewarded by a patent for his invention. The economic role of the patent system has, however, long been a controversial subject. Few people would deny that inventors should receive some reward for their effort. Both efficiency and equity support this position. But why should this reward take the form of a patent monopoly? As Arrow (1962), Johnson (1975) and Magee (1981) have emphasised, the need for a monopoly reward arises because knowledge is a public good. The physical characteristics of a public good mean that its use by one person does not preclude its use by others. For this reason the private production of a public good is inhibited by the 'free rider' problem. Bentham (1793) and Say (1803) seem to have perceived this, and J. B. Clark (1907) is very explicit on the point:

> Why should one entrepreneur incur the cost and risk of experimenting with a new machine if another can look on, ascertain whether the device works well or not, and duplicate it if it is successful? Under such conditions the man who watches others, avoids their losses, and shares their gains is the one who makes money;

> and the system that gave man no control over the use of his inventions would result in a rivalry in waiting for others rather than an effort to distance others in originating improvements. (Clark, 1907, p. 360)

The entrepreneur's reward therefore depends upon his obtaining a right of exclusion, namely a patent.

The case against patents was outlined by Plant (1934). Plant criticises the patent system on three main counts: first, it leads to an excessive allocation of resources to invention; secondly, it misdirects inventive activity to unsuitable projects; and, thirdly, it inhibits the exploitation of an invention. It is instructive to consider Plant's objections in detail, because while some of them are valid, others reveal common economic fallacies.

To begin with, Plant argues that pecuniary reward is not the primary motive for invention; the inventor's instinctive pursuit of novelty is paramount. For this reason the level of inventive activity might be close to the social optimum even in the absence of the patent system. Now the role of pecuniary incentive is essentially an empirical question. Psychological surveys indicate that pecuniary factors are perceived as important by inventors (cf. Rossman, 1931). Moreover the increasing cost of financing invention suggests that economic calculation must now be very considerable influence on inventive efforts, even if it was not so before.

To reinforce his argument, Plant maintains that if pecuniary incentives were important, the fact that invention earns a monopoly reward while routine production earns only a competitive reward would bias the allocation of resources toward invention. In common with Stamp (1929), he is inclined to argue that this bias leads in the long run to an unwarranted rate of obsolescence and to excessive technological unemployment.

This argument that the patent monopoly stimulates excessive invention rests on a simple fallacy. It confuses the dynamic gains from improving the allocation of resources and the static gains from trade. It has been shown earlier – in the discussion of Kaldor and Robinson – that in a long-run steady state the demand for entrepreneurial services is zero. Routine producers in a steady state earn no superprofit because there is no need for change. It is only when change occurs that the opportunity for superprofit is created. When change is stimulated by invention the value of the invention is measured by the increase in social product which it effects. But because the marginal cost of diffusing knowledge of the invention is relatively small, the private competitive reward of the inventor would be very small as well. Indeed, it might be insufficient to cover the fixed costs of the invention. To ensure that a worthwhile invention is always profitable it would be necessary to allow the inventor to appropriate the entire increase in the social product. On this view, the patent monopoly is necessary in order to prevent an under-allocation of resources to invention. This illustrates the general point that although competitive theory characterises efficiency in the steady state, it is monopoly theory that characterises efficiency in a world of change.

Turning from the determinants of aggregate inventive activity to the direction of inventive activity, Plant argues that the patent system fails to channel inventors into projects of the greatest social value. He focuses his criticisms upon the way that priority is established when awarding patents. This discourages people from working on fundamental research, and from working on further applications of inventions that have already been patented. It concentrates effort on the point where basic research results are translated into applications. The system

> operates in favour of only one or one group of the many participants in the progress of an invention from the birth of the scientific discovery to the emergence of the patent monopoly. The scientific discovery itself may be the culmination of the research and of the tentative hypotheses of many scientific workers: the possibility of applying it in a particular device may occur almost simultaneously to large numbers of industrial technicians; priority in the formulation of the provisional patent application may be a matter of days or of minutes. But one application alone can satisfy the requirement of this man-made law that the patent shall be granted to 'the first inventor' . . . Lotteries in open competition there may well be; but the lottery of the patent system awards but one prize, and that a monopoly, while those who subscribe most of its value may be precluded from qualifying for the prize. (Plant, 1934, p. 50)

This is undoubtedly a valid point. Moreover the system of awarding patents by priority also induces wasteful rivalry in research. Inventors racing to register their patents may replicate one another's research. Entrepreneurs may form excessively large teams of researchers in order to complete the invention before the opposition. The strategic aspects of inventive activity are surveyed by Kamien and Schwartz (1982) and applied to the multinational firm by Casson (1979). In theory it would be more satisfactory to sell licences for research to the highest bidder, rather like licences for prospecting and exploration are sold; however the world of knowledge is very different from the world of natural resources and the practical difficulties of administering the system would be immense.

Plant's final objection to the patent system is that it inhibits the diffusion of information. This is the very opposite of the truth. First, as Bennett (1943) points out, the inventor always has the option of keeping his invention secret. In the absence of patent protection this is the logical way of maintaining a monopoly. Once the invention has been patented, it can be published and so made available for other people to develop further. The only danger is that the inventor may fear that such developments may bypass his patent and render it obsolete. In this case he may decide not to patent (or to delay the patent as long as possible) so that other people do not learn of the invention.

Secondly, Plant fails to recognise that patents promote a market in knowledge. Plant recognises that patentees can license other users, but he appears to believe that licensing will only be undertaken under duress. For this reason he approves of the Licence of Right introduced in Britain in 1919 as it involves a subsidy to licensors.

In principle, however, licensing is just as effective a disseminator of knowledge as a system which allows public access. The only qualification is that licences must be priced accurately and the law must ensure that the costs of enforcing the licensor's rights are kept to a minimum. There may be a social and political case for subsidising licensing, but the strictly economic case is very weak.

The principle of a patent monopoly, once accepted, has widespread implications. As noted above, the efficiency of the monopoly often depends upon proper dissemination of knowledge through licensing. However to appropriate the full economic value of the patent the licensee must maintain the monopoly and, as Bowman (1973) shows, this normally requires the licensor to exercise a measure of control over the licensee.

In certain cases the incentives applied through the structure of royalty payments may be sufficient to harmonise the interests of licensor and licensee (Casson, 1979). These cases are, however, the exception rather than the rule. In most cases restrictive business practices must be invoked – practices which conflict with the spirit, if not the letter, of competition policy and anti-trust law. Licensors often control either the licensor's price or output, and sometimes even the customers he supplies. Particularly controversial is the requirement that ties the licensee to buy key inputs from the licensor. Tied inputs have several functions: they are an indirect method of metering the licensor's output, of maintaining quality control and, if the inputs are overpriced, of disguising the true royalty rate (Vaitsos, 1974). While from a social point of view the unnecessary tying of inputs is a wasteful practice, it is equally clear that in some cases the practice may be justified as a contribution to the overall efficiency of the innovation process.

The interface between patent law and competition policy involves some very thorny issues. Two radically different philosophies are in conflict: the philosophy of the changing and innovative economy in which efficiency demands that the inventor receive a monopoly rent and the philosophy of the static equilibrium economy which regards the agents of change as valueless and demands a purely competitive reward for everyone. It is, indeed, difficult to exaggerate the conflict, because the dynamic approach not only supports the existence of a patent system, but suggests that its scope should be widened and that patents should be made easier to enforce. Both philosophies regard the present patent system as inadequate, but they wish to reform it in opposite ways.

Even if the patent system were strengthened, however, it is doubtful if the licensing of patents would become a universal practice. The inventor typically has much more knowledge of his invention than that embodied in the patent. The process of invention generates experience which, though not formalised, is still valuable in the commercial exploitation of the invention. This additional information is not freely available to a licensee. This means, firstly, that prior to the contract the licensee cannot value the invention as accurately as the licensor, and secondly that once the contract has been concluded there is a resource cost of 'educating' the licensee (Teece, 1976).

The first problem is an example of asymmetric information, or quality uncertainty, of the kind discussed in the previous section. The buyer (the licensee) is uncertain of the quality of the product (the invention) and so tends to value the invention less than the patentee. This tendency is reinforced by the additional resource cost incurred in communicating informal knowledge to the licensee. Under these conditions the patentee's optimal strategy may be to forego licensing and exploit the invention himself.

As explained in Chapters 2 and 3, this vertical integration of invention and exploitation has been a crucial influence on the growth of multinational firms.

1.6 ORGANISATION THEORY

Organisation theory is essentially interdisciplinary, but the present discussion is confined exclusively to its application to the firm. Some 'positive economists' consider that organisational factors have little bearing on the economic behaviour of the firm. This may be so in a world where information is freely available to decision-makers, such as a world of long-run equilibrium where everyone has had time to learn of the prevailing conditions. But in practice information is scarce and its sources are localised. Different organisational structures will channel different information to each decision-maker, and in many cases this will affect the decision that is made. In a world of change and disequilibrium, therefore, organisational factors may be a major influence on the firm's behaviour.

The application of organisation theory to the firm has been strongly advocated by Papandreou (1952) and subsequently Chamberlain (1962). It received a tremendous boost from the application of psychological theories of administrative behaviour (Simon, 1947, 1957, 1980) to production and inventory control; this led to the 'behavioural theory of the firm' (Cyert and March, 1963).

It could be argued, however, that although organisation theory has promised much, it has so far yielded few tangible results. The problem seems to lie in the complexity of the subject. It is probably on account of this that much of the literature involves taxonomy – the categorisation of possibilities – rather than a theory – predictions about which of these possibilities will occur. Analogy also has a major role in many expositions: analogies with the brain, and with social, biological, political and engineering control systems. Few of these analogies are helpful because they are rarely exact, and in any case the system with which the analogy is made is often just as complex and obscure as the firm itself.

The function of an organisation is to make decisions and implement them. In an organisation decisions are made by cooperation between different individuals. The cooperation is achieved by communication between the individuals according to an agreed procedure. The decisions are made on behalf of the institution to which the organisation is attached. The institution is a legal entity; the organisation is a social entity which decides what property rights the institution shall acquire and how these rights shall be exercised. The firm, for example, is an institution, while the managers, and indeed any workers who participate in decision-making, form the organisation. They decide what factors of production to hire, in what quantities to combine them, and how to utilise them.

The rationale for an organisation is that it economises on information costs. Costs are incurred in searching out information, in organising and communicating it, and in using it to take decisions (Marschak, 1968). A decision is taken cooperatively when the information required is too great – or too diverse – to be handled by one individual. Cooperation circumvents the problem posed by the 'bounded rationality' of the individual (Williamson, 1975).

Information costs and bounded rationality have many profound implications. The present chapter concentrates on just two aspects. The remainder of this section is devoted to implications for the decision process, i.e. for the way decisions are made. The next section considers the implications for organisational structure, i.e. for the way that cooperation between decision-makers is effected.

Consider now the decision process. The cost of processing information means that it is usually uneconomic to identify an 'optimal' decision. Efficiency may call for locating quickly and cheaply a solution in the neighbourhood of the optimum. The decision-maker may therefore terminate his search for a solution as soon as a 'satisfactory' – rather than optimal – solution has been obtained. This is termed satisficing behaviour.

Satisficing is normally achieved using a very simple decision rule. Repeated application of the same rule allows the decision-maker to become increasingly proficient in its use; 'learning by doing' gives him a dynamic comparative advantage and encourages the specialisation of the decision-maker on the use of a particular rule. For example a wholesaler may control his purchases not by using explicit forecasts of demand but by fixing a reorder level at which inventory is to be replenished automatically. Occasionally, however, the decision-making routine may have to be altered because it is no longer appropriate under new conditions. A fall in demand, for example, may lead to inventory remaining at too high a level for too long, so that interest payments may begin to deplete cash reserves. A new response is called for to maintain the 'homeostasis of the balance sheet' (Boulding, 1950).

It is difficult, however, to programme into the organisation a procedure for changing the decision rule. A common approach is for those concerned to think it through – and to talk it through amongst themselves – until either a consensus or a prevailing view emerges. This procedure calls for very different skills from those of the routine decision-maker.

Thinking through a problem may be termed a rational approach to decision-making. Once the problem has been identified it is solved by modelling the environment. The model is used to assess the probable consequences of alternative policies, and the policy with the most favourable outcome is chosen.

The rational approach is not always the one pursued, however. An alternative is the pragmatic approach. The pragmatic approach relies upon practice rather than theory – on 'experience' rather than analysis. The pragmatist focuses upon the symptoms of the problem, e.g. excessive inventory and a shortage of cash. He recalls his previous experience of these symptoms and the remedies that were tried in each case. If one remedy has been frequently successful then it is applied, and only if this turns out not to work is a new remedy investigated.

The pragmatist may draw upon experiences other than his own. In particular he may learn from his colleagues of past experiences which form part of the 'folklore' of the organisation. Such folklore may induce a very traditional – if not idiosyncratic – organisational response to problematic situations.

An individual with intellectual capabilities will normally prefer the rational approach. He may attempt to ascertain whether demand has fallen because of specific factors – e.g. the appearance of a substitute – or general factors – e.g. a fall in aggregate demand. There is no guarantee, however, that a less intellectual individual will obtain better results from a rational approach because his model of the environment may be seriously wrong.

This discussion has identified three methods of decision-making: by rule, by pragmatism and by rational thought. Different people are best suited to different methods of decision-making according to their intellectual qualities. As a result, there are gains from specialising different types of decision with different individuals. The way this separation is effected within the firm is determined by its organisational structure.

1.7 ORGANISATIONAL STRUCTURE: THE HIERARCHY AND ITS ALTERNATIVES

Organisational structures are developed in order to coordinate decisions taken by different people. Decisions may be specialised with different people according to the quality of the judgement that needs to be exercised, and also according to the kind of specialist information that they need to draw upon. The first type of specialisation leads to decisions being allocated between two different levels of the organisation, while the second type leads to the allocation of decisions to different functional areas at the same level. These functional areas include production, marketing, research, personnel, finance, etc.

The hierarchy is often used as an 'ideal type' of organisational structure. Williamson (1975) has proposed a classification of structures which emphasises two particular forms. The unitary form organises the firm into different functional departments each reporting to the firm's chief executive. The multidivisional form is built around different operating divisions, often concerned with different parts of the product range. Each division has its own functional departments, with the heads of division reporting to a general office. The general office has a staff of specialists to advise it, and the specialists are also available to consult with particular divisions. The primary role of the general office is to organise corporate budgeting; it may be likened to an internal capital market allocating funds between competing divisions.

The distinction between unitary and multidivisional forms has proved, however, rather difficult to apply in practice. It is useful in characterising broad historical trends, but not so helpful in analysing more specific issues such as the impact of organisational structure on the capital market's valuation of the firm. In response to these difficulties Williamson has expanded his classification to include various derivative, transitional and 'corrupt' forms of organisational structure.

It is doubtful, however, if 'redrawing the hierarchy' can ever succeed in capturing some of the more subtle variations in organisational structure. Some writers would reject this view on the grounds that the hierarchy is the defining characteristic of an organisation. To an economist, however, organisation is simply a method of achieving cooperation between decision-makers without an exchange of property rights between them. It can be very misleading to focus exclusively upon cooperation through hierarchy. Altogether five different principles of cooperation may be distinguished, and only one of these is hierarchical. The other principles may be termed aggregation, consultation, negotiation and anticipation. Normally all of these principles are present within an organisation to some degree.

The essence of hierarchy is that cooperation between any two decision-makers is achieved because they act within constraints set by some other decision-maker at a higher level. When the principle of hierarchical cooperation is applied repeatedly it yields the pyramid structure with which it is commonly associated. When the principle of 'unity of command' is also invoked the root, or branch, structure of an 'organisation tree' is obtained.

Aggregation and consultation are exemplified by the committee system. Decisions in committee may be made by aggregating the votes of members using a principle such as majority rule; a committee using the aggregation principle may be regarded as a political system in microcosm (Black, 1958; Mueller, 1979). In many cases, however, committees have a purely consultative role. A committee may function simply as a forum in which members brief each other about their provisional plans in order to improve the quality of their decisions.

Committees are often used in conjunction with hierarchies, e.g. the sub-committee system typical of bureaucracies. By and large the aggregation principle applies when the committee members are all drawn from the same level of the hierarchy; this case may be described as political bureaucracy. The consultative principle, on the other hand, normally applies when some members – perhaps just a single member such as the chairman – are drawn from a higher level than the others; a hierarchy built around consultative committees may be termed a consultative bureaucracy.

Some committees resemble a market place where decision-makers bargain with each other. The principles underlying this procedure are described in the literature on economic planning (Heal, 1973) and comparative economic systems (Montias, 1976). Each member of the committee is responsible for a division of the firm, which is constituted as a separate profit centre, and each member bargains to maximise his notional profit. The negotiations involve only shadow-bargaining, however, and the procedures laid down by the organisation ensure that no one stands to gain by prolonging the haggling or attempting to default. The principles of shadow-bargaining illustrate clearly the parallel between the internalisation of markets to form the institution and the problem of cooperation in decision-making within it.

Finally, it is important not to lose sight of the fact that an organisation is typically a community in which individuals have an opportunity to learn informally about one another's behaviour. As a result, decision-makers may learn to anticipate the way that their colleagues will act, and so acquire the knack of cooperating without any formal communication with them at all. This exemplifies coordination by anticipation.

Having established this taxonomy of cooperation, it is natural to inquire under what conditions each of these principles is most likely to be preferred. This question cannot be answered without reference to the environment of the organisation, and in particular without reference to the role of the institution to which it is attached. This calls for a synthesis of the institutional and organisation theories of the firm.

1.8 INSTITUTIONS, ORGANISATIONS AND THE CHANGING ROLE OF MANAGEMENT

In the analysis of organisational structure the relationship between the capital market, the owners of the firm, and the members of the organisation is crucial.

The twentieth century has seen two remarkable developments in this relationship: the separation of the ownership and control of large corporations (Berle and Means, 1932, Gordon, 1945), and the growth of conglomerate and multi-divisional firms, (Chandler, 1962, 1977). These trends are sometimes analysed separately, but there are grounds for supposing them to be linked. A link may be found in the issue of managerial discretion, and the economics of the alternative contractual arrangements to control it.

In small firms – particularly family businesses – the managers who make up the organisation are often the owners of the firm. In most large firms, however, the demand for managerial services exceeds the capacity of the family and managerial services have to be hired. Information costs and costs of enforcing contracts mean that hired managers have an incentive to underperform, e.g. by reducing their supply of effort (Leibenstein, 1976). This incentive applies to any manager whether he is a self-employed agent selling decision-making services, or an employee.

The advantage of employment to the owners of the firm is that it gives more opportunity to monitor managerial performance. This reduces the incentive for a manager who is an 'unknown quantity' to underperform; it also provides information on the manager's personal characteristics. These characteristics include not only ability, but also integrity, which, when it is present, is valuable in allowing a subsequent reduction in the employer's monitoring costs.

The only condition under which an independent agent would be employed is if he were a person of proven ability and integrity. A reputation for these qualities will reduce the owner's perception of risk. This suggests that personal reputation is an important influence on the contractual relation between the owners and managers of the firm.

An explanation of twentieth-century trends may be found in the changing role of the top management of the firm. In many large firms the executive board members have ceased to be employees in all but name. The owners take few active steps to monitor them (apart from the obvious step of watching the share price). Top managers have become agents rather than employees – indeed they are often retained as self-employed consultants. These agents appear to have assumed the owners' role of monitoring the employees and identifying investment opportunities for the firm.

This change may well be a consequence of the development of integrated capital markets as a result of improved communications systems. This has made it easier for managerial reputations to be acquired and large funds mobilised to back people who have the confidence of the market.

The role of the manager-agent is to carry out the owner's functions on his behalf. He monitors other employees and endorses or overrules their decisions on crucial matters. As a person of proven ability he established a chain of confidence between the owners of the firm and the lower-level managers of unproven ability (Knight, 1921). It is for this reason that the top manager's functions are mainly confined to personnel and finance.

The personnel function involves evaluating the integrity and ability of other employees and promoting and demoting, and hiring and firing accordingly. This policy, when successful, secures a supply of managers of proven ability to replace the present top managers when they retire. A reputable personnel policy will normally ensure that a manager who is promoted to the top will automatically have the confidence of the capital market. In this way the personnel function maintains not only the quality but also the continuity of policy in the organisation.

The finance function involves screening the investment projects identified by the unproven managers. This function is particularly important when the projects are qualitatively different from anything the firm has done before. Endorsement of suitable projects by the top management reduces the subjective risk that the owners perceive and therefore reduces the cost at which the capital market will supply finance.

The evaluation function of senior management is a key influence on the type of cooperation around which the firm's organisational structure is built. Of the five principles of cooperation identified earlier, only two – hierarchy and negotiation – provide explicitly for the retrospective evaluation of individual performance. Some of the principles actually mask individual responsibility such as the committee which decides by majority rule. In such a committee responsibility for the decision rests with the 'median voter' – and it is impossible to identify exactly who the median voter is.

The hierarchy provides for the evaluation of each decision-maker by his immediate superior, while the negotiation principle provides for evaluation on the basis of notional profits. This suggests that in an organisation where the owners do not manage, and the managers are of unproven ability, cooperation will be effected using these two principles. Consultative committees may also be employed, but decisions in committee will not be taken on a vote. The only exception to this rule occurs at the top of the organisation, where the managers already command confidence and the evaluation of individual performance is regarded as not such a crucial issue. Here the board of directors may function on a democratic basis.

By contrast, in private firms where the owners manage, or in public enterprises where the implementation of the ownership principle is relatively weak, political bureaucracy built around a committee system may function to a much greater degree. In such cases the owners either do not need to evaluate, or cannot be bothered to do so, and so the committee system is an adequate substitute for hierarchy and negotiation.

It remains to consider the factors which influence the choice between hierarchy and negotiation. The main factor here appears to be the logic of the decision problem – a logic which is strongly influenced by the technology of the resources which are being managed. It is not difficult to see that if there are many externalities between the resources then it is difficult to identify areas of responsibility which do not overlap. When there are many overlaps negotiations between decision-makers become extremely complicated, and so cooperation through negotiation is difficult to achieve. Thus the greater the complexity of interactions within the production system the more efficient is a hierarchical organisation.

The precise relationship between technology and organisational structure is an enormous subject and lies, unfortunately, well outside the scope of this introductory chapter. Suffice it to say that the technology of international operations embodies special features which favour negotiation rather than hierarchy. As a result, the exclusive application of the hierarchical concept to analyse international business organisation can generate very misleading results.

1.9 THE GROWTH OF THE FIRM

The simplest reason why a firm may grow is that it has a monopoly of a product for which there is a growing demand. Eventually however the market will become saturated and growth will cease; and even before this imitators may appear or substitutes may render the product obsolete. Long-run growth requires either a steady geographical expansion of the market area or the continuous innovation of new products. In the long run only product innovation can avoid the constraint imposed by the size of the world market for a given product.

An obvious dynamic for growth lies in organised research financed by the firm (Kay, 1979). Indivisibilities in research mean that up to a point there are increasing returns to the size of the research team. This means that large-scale research and continuous innovation are more economic than small-scale research and intermittent or one-off innovation.

It must be recognised, however, that in principle the output of research can be licensed. Licensing, though, poses problems of the kind discussed in Section 1.5. From the buyer's point of view the problem of quality control is particularly acute: 'buyer uncertainty' reduces the return available through licensing and encourages the internal exploitation of research output. To absorb all the research output the firm is obliged to expand production and sales. It is on these grounds that Buckley and Casson (1976) link the research intensity of the firm to its rate of growth.

It should be emphasised that research will only generate profitable growth if the research effort is guided by market forces. Indeed the ability to respond to market forces is crucial for it may form the basis for profitable growth even in the absence of research. Penrose (1959) has indicated the opportunities for profitable innovation which exist for those who can identify 'interstices' in the economy. In the context of consumer theory the exploitation of interstices may be related to the development of products having new combinations of characteristics (Lancaster, 1979; Iremonger, 1972). In similar vein, Leibenstein (1978) has commented on the opportunities for 'gap-filling' that exist for small firms in a world of large 'X-efficient' enterprises.

A manager's ability to identify opportunities may depend upon his gaining privileged access to information. It is more likely, though, that the ability to synthesise different kinds of information is what really matters. This ability has been likened to the possession of a watchtower, which allows the watchman to scan over a wider area than anyone else. Another possibility is that while everyone has the same information the opportunist is able to interpret it much better. He may, for example, be a rational thinker in a world where most other people are pragmatists. He may be more imaginative than other people and so evaluate options that do not occur to them (Shackle, 1979). Or he may have some quality such as 'alertness' (Kirzner, 1973, 1979).

Non-pecuniary motives may also be an important stimulus to growth: the desire for the status which large sales command (Baumol, 1959) or the satisfaction of psychological drives fired by a romantic view of business achievement (Schumpeter, 1934; McLelland, 1967). Still, these motives are not by themselves sufficient to guarantee the success of a firm; they have to be combined with the entrepreneurial abilities described above. They may explain, however, why these abilities are channelled into business rather than into some other line of activity.

Entrepreneurial abilities may exist not only at the top of the firm; they may also be latent in middle and lower management. A firm will continue to grow so long as it can harness these abilities by encouraging middle managers to put up promising projects for consideration by the directors at the top. If the directors perform their evaluations correctly they will be able to select the best projects and allocate funds to them. If middle managers are discouraged by apathy or mistaken evaluations they may leave in order to set up in business on their own account. In effect they are withdrawing from the internal capital market operated by the directors and seeking backing from the external capital market instead.

The evidence suggests that many new firms are set up by former employees who have faced discouragement – such as blocked promotion, or an unwillingness by the employer to back new projects to which they have become committed. Many of these new firms fail, of course, but a small number do succeed. The loss of key personnel to self-employment is a recognised hazard in many expanding industries. This indicates that the ability of the large employer to identify entrepreneurial ability among his employees is a key factor determining the distribution of industry growth between the expansion of existing firms and the creation of new ones (Casson, 1982a).

It is important, though, not to overlook the constraints on the growth of firms. Two major constraints may be distinguished: the limited availability of external finance, and the costs of coping with fast-moving organisational change.

It is apparent that if external finance is not readily available then the growth of the firm is constrained by the profits generated by past investment projects. The availability of external finance will reflect the capital market's confidence in the management of the firm. The greater is the management's reputation, the lower is the cost of capital to the firm. This explains why newly-formed small firms cannot borrow as cheaply as established firms (which are typically larger). It also explains why entry on a large scale into an industry by a newly-formed firm is virtually impossible. Where entry conditions demand a large scale, the potential entrant will tend to be an established firm diversifying from another industry.

The problem of the newly-established firm can to some extent be mitigated by appointing to the board of directors people who enjoy the confidence of the market. Their role is simply to approve decisions taken by the other managers. This approval or 'acceptance' function does not normally require that the person concerned be a full-time member of the board – he may be able to serve part-time on several boards as a non-executive director.

It must also be recognised that some managers may be reluctant to use external finance even when it is available. Marris (1964), in particular, has argued that managers in large corporations may be averse to financing growth using fixed interest debt. Owner-managers of small firms, too, may be reluctant to borrow if they attach considerable importance to 'being their own boss'.

It is necessary for a firm not only to organise itself for growth but also to implement changes in organisation as growth proceeds (Penrose, 1966). There may have to be changes in divisional structure when new product ranges are added, and changes in the structure of functional departments when the output of existing products expands. New posts are created and new people appointed to them; existing employees have to adjust to the new structure of formal communications; and new employees have not only to learn their jobs but also to integrate themselves into the informal social network built up by the long-serving employees. The implementation of these changes and the subsequent adjustments to them cannot easily be speeded up without disrupting day-to-day management activity. For this reason the need to cope with organisational change constitutes a major constraint on the growth of the firm.

The constraint can be mitigated to some extent by contracting out management functions at critical stages, e.g. using sales, purchasing or factoring agencies. A more creative response is to develop an organisational structure tailored for flexibility. Typical of these is the holding company structure which allows entire units of the company to be added or subtracted at will. Expansion is achieved by merging with existing firms and contraction is effected by divestiture. The feasibility of this structure depends, of course, upon the technological and contractual economies that the firm is designed to exploit. Nevertheless, where opportunism and psychological drives are important factors in growth it seems likely that the holding company philosophy of management, and its associated policy of growth by merger and contraction by divestiture, will be present to some degree.

1.10 SUMMARY AND SYNTHESIS

This section draws together the strands of the preceding discussion by identifying a number of themes which have recurred throughout the analysis.

(a) The function of management is to adjust to change. The demand for management services is a derived demand, like any demand for factor services. But the demand for management is unlike any other derived demand in that the demand is zero in an equilibrium state. Management is needed to correct a disequilibrium. Disequilibrium is a continuing state because as one disequilibrium is corrected another appears on account of further change. The faster the rate of change, the greater is the demand for management services.

(b) The rationale of the firm is partly technological but primarily contractual. Technological economies are an important influence on the size of the production plant but have little relevance to multi-plant operation. Contractual economies are a major factor stimulating the expansion of both the size and the diversity of the firm. They also influence the dynamics of growth by encouraging the internal exploitation of inventions.

(c) Organisational diseconomies are a major limitation on the size of the firm. The problem is that the complexity of the decision problem in a large diversified firm, coupled with the bounded rationality of the individual, necessitates the cooperation of several individuals in decision-making. Because each decision is, in a sense, 'one and indivisible', it is difficult to evaluate the contribution of each individual to improving the decision that is made. There are two main principles for combining cooperation in decision-making with evaluation: hierarchy and negotiation. The combination of these two principles can push back the limit on the size of firm very considerably. It requires, however, great subtlety to devise and constructively blend these principles in an appropriate way.

There remains the issue of who evaluates the evaluator. This is a tactical problem which can only be satisfactorily solved by the existence of people with reputation, who command the confidence of the owners of the firm and evaluate other employees on their behalf. The emergence of an elite of agent-managers is a major factor in attracting financial support for large scale organisations.

(d) However sophisticated their structure, organisations are inherently more rigid than a pure market system in which each individual takes his own decisions about his own resources acting upon his own information (supplied, in Hayekian fashion, by the price system). In periods of radical change the demand for managerial services will rise, while organisational rigidities will prevent many managers from receiving appropriate internal rewards. The increasing value of managerial services will attract some people into management from other occupations. But more significantly, it will encourage many existing managers to become self-employed. The size of the 'representative firm' will fall as established enterprises face new rivals. The inexperienced managers who have entered from other occupations may not survive long, but some of the experienced managers in self-employment may well thrive. As a result a new generation of firms will be born, and some of the existing generation of firms, unable to withstand their competition, will go into decline. Some of these firms may be swallowed up by merger with their newer, but more dynamic competitors.

1.11 APPLICATIONS TO INTERNATIONAL BUSINESS

The theoretical framework presented above can readily be applied to the study of international business, in conjunction with conventional theories of international trade and finance. Recent progress in this area is critically reviewed in the following chapter.

A major advantage of the framework is that it facilitates an integrated analysis of the four major trends in twentiety-century industrial organisation:

(a) the divorce of ownership and control in large companies,
(b) the growth of the multi-divisional firm,
(c) the growth of the multinational firm, and
(d) the emergence of large scale research and development as an engine of corporate growth.

We have already commented upon (a) and (b) in Section 1.8, where it was suggested that improved communications and the consequent improvement of capital markets has allowed top management to evolve an agency relationship with shareholders. The essence of this is that the management performs the evaluative function of the employer on the owner's behalf. The multi-divisional structure, it suggested, has developed to allow this evaluative function to be performed more efficiently.

The development of capital markets is also credited with stimulating the corporate organisation of R & D. There is another factor, here, however, which may in turn have some bearing on (a) and (b). It is the development of educational institutions offering qualifications which can be used in screening the organisation's recruits. The first effects of this development were probably felt in the training of scientists and engineers for recruitment to R & D. It seems, however, to have extended quickly to management, and to have become standard practice for potential managers to be recruited on the basis of their educational qualifications. These qualifications may be important also in establishing the reputation of top managers and enabling them to take on an agency role. It is important however, not to overstate this point. There are few Nobel-prize-winning scientists without a doctorate, but there are quite a few chairmen of large companies without an MBA. Entrepreneurs cannot easily be screened by academic criteria, and probably not by any method other than their 'track record'.

What relevance do these factors have, then, to the growth of the multinational firm? So far, the literature on this issue has been dichotomised. One school sees the growth of the multinational as primarily a consequence of the growth of organised R & D and its internal exploitation on a world wide basis. The other school sees it as by-product of improvements in communications and other factors which have led more generally to the growth of the managerially controlled multi-divisional firm. These views are in fact quite complementary. This chapter has, it is hoped, indicated the lines upon which these two approaches can be synthesised.

1.12 PLAN OF THE BOOK

In the following chapter Peter Buckley critically examines recent developments in the theory of international business. Because of the complexity of the subject, a satisfactory theory of international business must contain many 'degrees of freedom'. Buckley argues that, despite recent developments, many authors restrict their degrees of freedom unduly; for example, they identify an industry with its dominant firm, or the growth of the firm with the growth of demand for its principal product. In this way important variables such as market structure and product diversification are suppressed in their analysis. More fundamentally, he argues that many authors are still trying to analyse dynamic issues in the growth of the firm using an inherently static approach. They assume, for example, that firms are endowed with monopolistic ownership advantages, without examining the entrepreneurial process by which these advantages are acquired. Without some insight into entrepreneurship it is difficult to explain why some firms are continually alert to new opportunities for new products and processes – which enable them to maintain their market dominance – while potential entrants are too slow off the mark to gain a foothold in the industry. Nor can the theory explain convincingly why some nations nurture more successful innovating multinational firms than do others.

Buckley criticises the recent literature for failing to operationalise and test internalisation theory. In Chapter 3 David Teece responds to Buckley's challenge, and attempts to formulate internalisation theory in testable fashion. Teece begins with the distinction between governance costs and production costs. He relates these costs to two key industry and firm characteristics: technological complexity and asset specificity. He argues that not only governance costs but also production costs are affected by internalisation. The savings in both governance costs and production costs effected by internalisation vary directly with technological complexity and asset specificity. The production cost savings effected by internalisation may cause internalisation to be preferred in cases where the governance cost savings alone would not warrant it. Teece supports his argument by reference to the empirical work reported later in this book.

In Chapter 4 Mark Casson and George Norman respond to Peter Buckley's challenge to develop a more dynamic theory of international business. Dynamic analysis is applied to the familiar issue of the product pricing and market sourcing strategies of the multinational firm. The chapter examines the rivalry between the innovator of a product and his potential imitators. The rivalry involves a sequence of encounters between the firms in different national markets. It is shown that not only does market structure influence firm behaviour but also that firm behaviour – in particular the innovator's propensity to invest in entry barriers – influences market structure. It is shown that in many cases the innovator's optimal strategy under threat of competitive entry is not to exclude entrants, but to admit them under conditions which encourage the evolution of an international oligopoly. It is argued that oligopolistic rivalry often favours mature countries, whose markets are amongst the first to be penetrated by the new product, and is particularly disadvantageous to the newly industrialising countries whose market are amongst the last to be penetrated.

The second part of the book deals with empirical and historical aspects of international business. In Chapter 5, John Dunning reappraises the history of foreign investment and international production in the light of the most recent research. Dunning examines both the conceptual issues and the practical difficulties involved in estimating the growth of foreign direct investment since the latter part of the nineteenth century. He presents a number of new estimates which help to chart the growth of foreign direct investment more accurately than has been possible before, and interprets this evidence from a modern theoretical perspective.

In Chapter 6 Bob Pearce examines the role of industrial and geographical diversification in the growth of the multinational firm. Industrial diversification and geographical diversification are sometimes presented as alternative avenues for expansion by a firm which has excess managerial capacity. This view may be extended to suggest that some firms may specialise in expansion by one route and other firms specialise in expansion by the other. For example, it could be hypothesised that industrial diversification is best suited to firms who operate at the early stage of the product cycle – generating a multiplicity of new products spun off from an R & D programme – while geographical diversification is best suited to firms whose skills lie in the adaptation of existing products to new markets. The latter firms may seek to 'free ride' on the former type by imitating their products prior to adaptation, or they may acquire their products under licence. Whether or not the relation is strategic or contractual, however, the result is that the R & D-oriented firm is liable to be industrially diversified across new products with low volume production whose overseas markets are serviced principally by exports, while the less

R & D-oriented firm is more likely to be geographically diversified, supplying worldwide markets in a limited range of high-volume products through local production. Pearce's results afford limited support to this hypothesis, though anomalies also appear which indicate that the hypothesis has important limitations as well.

In Chapter 7 Robert Read examines the evolution of multinational operations in the banana export trade. Superficially, bananas are a very 'low-technology' product affording very few economies of integration. Read shows, however, that the perishability of the banana exerts a crucial effect on transport technology and logistics, while susceptibility to disease also makes quality control on the plantation of paramount importance. Emphasising the contractual economies that result from internalising plantation and transportation operations under conditions of quality uncertainty, Read provides a convincing account of the evolution of the multinational banana trade. He shows how improvements in quality control have enabled multinationals to introduce consumer brands, whose bananas can sell at a premium price compared to the unbranded bananas supplied on an irregular and largely seasonal basis through the arm's length export trade.

In Chapter 8 Tony Corley considers the factors in the early growth of one of the smaller multinationals in the oil industry – the Burmah Oil Company. He contrasts the company's first phase of rapid growth to 1905, when technical progress and market opportunism were paramount, with the later phase of far slower growth, in which more formal hierarchies and more stringent control from home were introduced. He critically examines the extent to which Burmah Oil conforms to current theories of corporate growth, emphasising – for instance – the perilously thin entrepreneurial structure. He shows that – in common with many other oil firms – the company's dynamic for growth owed something to the home government's desire to strengthen its strategic and military position. For example, on the outbreak of war in 1914 the British government, anxious to secure a fuel oil contract with Burmah's subsidiary Anglo-Persian, agreed to share the business risks by the unprecedented step of buying a majority stake in the subsidiary company.

Until recently the role of banking in the growth of multinational firms was a relatively neglected subject, despite widespread recognition of the importance of banking for international trade. In Chapter 9 George Yannopoulos surveys the recent growth of multinational banks, and seeks to explain the close relationship that has evolved between the multinational producers and their bankers. He argues that this relationship owes much to the confidential nature of bankers' information about the turnover, salary payments, etc., of their clients and the role of the banker as an 'honest broker' standing between the management of the multinational producer and the host-country capital market that supplies it with much of its long-term finance.

Taken together, these chapters present a new and refreshingly different perspective of the evolving role of multinational firms in the world economy. The various contributions are linked by a common thread – namely the institutional theory of the firm outlined in this chapter. Although the authors collectively discuss many different aspects of their subject, there is a unity – though not uniformity – of approach, which augurs well for future research in this area.

2 New theories of international business: some unresolved issues

PETER J. BUCKLEY

2.1 INTRODUCTION

In 1976 it was possible to claim that 'It is little exaggeration to say that at present there is no established theory of the multinational enterprise' (Buckley and Casson, 1976, p. 32). The enormous output of theoretical work on the multinational enterprise (MNE) since that date now makes this statement outdated (cf. recent summaries by Buckley, 1981, and Calvet, 1981). However, grave doubts must remain concerning the ability of the emergent synthesis to explain and predict the behaviour of MNEs.

The search for a general theory of the multinational enterprise has led to the 'stretching' of partial concepts or to an increasingly cumbersome taxonomy. Challenges to the new orthodoxy have been met by redefinition of central concepts or increasingly long inventories of classification.

This chapter attempts to review the received theory of the MNE by examining those concepts which I believe are central tenets in the hope of providing a basis for some much needed theoretical restructuring. Section 2.2 outlines some essential definitions and distinctions. Sections 2.3 to 2.5 present and criticise central concepts, the 'building blocks' of the theory, and Section 2.6 ventures into the dynamics of multinational enterprise. The conclusion suggests a research agenda.

2.2 DEFINITIONS AND DISTINCTIONS

Inputs and Outputs Let us adopt the simplest possible definition of a multinational firm – a firm which owns outputs of goods or services originating in more than one country (Casson, 1982c). The firm thus adds value by producing in more than one national economy. This addition of value may involve increasing the quantity of goods, enhancing their quality, or improving their distribution, both spatial and temporal. To achieve this the firm will be faced with decisions on at least some elements of the 'marketing mix' – price, product, promotion and distribution.

Orthodox neoclassical theory sees the firm simply as a black box, converting inputs to outputs and fully described by its production function (Archibald, 1971). Dissatisfaction with this position is historically well founded, for both the interaction of firm and market and the decision processes within firms are crucial to understanding of the real world (see *inter alia* Leibenstein, 1979; Malmgren, 1961; Moss, 1981).

Intermediate and Final Markets When a firm is envisaged as more than a black box, a whole range of wider issues is opened. In general, firms perform many more functions than routine production; amongst these are financing, marketing, research and development, labour training and building a management team (see Chapter 1). In order to effect these functions and to coordinate their activity, the firm must construct and deal in intermediate markets for knowledge and expertise.

Consequently, the firm is faced with an array of markets: for factor inputs, intermediate goods and services, and final products. However, it would be wrong to see the firm as a passive actor in each and all of these markets. Firms play a role in creating, sustaining, dominating and suppressing markets as well as merely reacting to them. Moreover, not all economic phenomena are captured by the operation of markets; such non-market pressures are encompassed in the catch-all 'externalities'.

Vertical integration – the internalisation of intermediate markets in goods and services – may be a reaction to non-competitive prices. Barriers to entry may prevent firms entering particular stages of production. Consequently a stage of production organised by a market may be internalised if cost or demand conditions alter (Oi and Hurter, 1965). The avoidance of uncertainty via an organised internal futures market in intermediate goods and services is in many situations an incentive to internalise vertically linked markets (Buckley and Casson, 1976).

Horizontal integration – the combination of similar activities at the same stage in the production process – has entered the theory via the economics of the exploitation of knowledge (or perhaps, more generally, information). Scale economies in the production of new knowledge provide the main dynamic for the growth of the firm and the arguments for the internal absorption into the firm rather than sale of the knowledge on the external market give the rationale for the parallel growth of knowledge-absorbing functions, including production (Buckley and Casson, 1976; Johnson, 1970). The returns to knowledge creation accrue when the product embodying the knowledge reaches the widest possible markets; because of the internalised link with production knowledge-creating firms are 'naturally' international.

Internal markets, however, involve costs, notably increased communication costs, costs of foreignness in the international context and management recruitment and training costs.

The multi-product firm Much of the interest in the theory of the MNE arises from its nature as a multi-product multi-plant firm. Its distinctiveness derives from differences from uninational multi-plant and multi-product firms (McManus, 1972). Lateral diversification across products may benefit from economies of scope (Teece, 1978). Where a set of products (indexed $i = 1, 2, \ldots, n$) are jointly produced according to the cost function $c(x_1, x_2, \ldots, x_n)$, where x_i is the quantity of good i, then there are economies of scope in production if the cost of joint production is less than the sum of stand-alone production costs. If $i = 1, 2$, the existence of economies of scope means that:

$$c(x_1, x_2) < c(x_1, 0) + c(0, x_2)$$

Consequently, the key to lateral integration of products within a firm is the free internal transfer of resources which enables costs to be reduced in areas other than those for which a resource was specifically developed.

The multi-plant firm The theory of multi-plant firms is addressed to the question 'Why should firms operate several plants of suboptimal size rather than a smaller number of plants which would be above minimum efficient scale?'. Scherer *et al.* (1975) gives several answers: (1) the buyer's desire for choice and variety on the demand side dictates that no one firm, or plant, shall dominate individual markets; (2) in many industries, long-run unit production cost is relatively flat and cost penalties are not imposed severely on less than optimal plant scales; (3) multi-plant operation is often a rational response to problems of manufacturing highly specialised products with volatile demand or other features requiring close managerial supervision or technologies well suited to low volume production. The plants come under common ownership because of the difficulties of coordination by arm's length contracts.

The distinctive nature of the MNE To be an object worthy of separate study, the MNE must pose theoretical problems which go beyond the multi-product, multi-plant firm. Several extra dimensions suggest themselves.

(1) Inter-country income transfers are implied by the operation of MNEs – particularly obvious here are the transfer pricing activities of MNEs; transfer prices may be 'market perfecting' if internal prices are closer than external prices to competitive equilibrium levels, or 'market distorting' if they are further away from such levels. Katrak (1981) has suggested that transfer price manipulations may affect the allocation of resources within MNEs.
(2) The firm will be faced with a variety of input prices for non-tradeable goods in different economies. These immobile location factors may encourage the international spread of firms wishing to benefit from the non-equalisation of prices of non-tradeables, such as factor inputs.
(3) The MNE operates in a world divided into currency areas and is therefore subject to exchange risk on assets so 'exposed'.
(4) The MNE must operate across socio-cultural barriers/divisions between nations. To a large extent, this is a matter of degree in that such differences also impinge on the multi-regional firm. However, differences in commercial law, fiscal and monetary regulation, and government intervention, will have operational significance in many cases for MNEs.

Foreign Direct Investment (FDI) The definition of the MNE given above does not necessarily imply that the firm is a foreign direct investor, unlike definitions which are asset- or ownership-based. As Casson (1982b) points out, using financial markets to separate functions, the firm can hire all resources, except possibly inventories. Such a definition avoids the difficulties of defining 'control' which distinguishes direct from portfolio foreign investments and helps to demistify foreign activities of MNEs.

In general, however, foreign production (in its most general sense of value added) will be facilitated by the act of FDI. FDI involves a real capital transfer and as Gilman (1981) points out, the selection of foreign assets must be logically separated in motive and extent from the financing of this real asset acquisition (the choice of liabilities).

2.3 FIRM SPECIFIC ADVANTAGE: A STATIC CONCEPT APPLIED TO A DYNAMIC ISSUE

Firm-specific advantage

The concept of 'firm specific knowhow' (Hirsh, 1976) or 'monopolistic advantage' (Lall, 1980) or 'ownership specific advantage' (Dunning, 1977, 1979, 1980, 1981b) has become central to current theoretical aproaches. In a sense, the concept has been part of the theoretical rubric since the seminal work of Hymer (1976, written 1960). Hymer's approach (heavily influenced by Bain, 1956, and by Dunning, 1958) moved the theory of the MNE into the field of industrial organisation. This section attempts to examine the difficulties which the concept raises.

The Growth Process

Essentially, the notion of firm-specific advantage arises because the growth process of the firm is (artificially) attenuated at the point where the firm first crosses national boundaries or at least has the potential to do so. The firm-specific advantage is a reflection of this cut-off point as a snapshot in time of a dynamic process.

The Hymer/Kindleberger approach (Kindleberger, 1960) made the assumption that, in order to overcome the disadvantages of foreignness, or the 'costs of doing business abroad', the foreign entrant had to possess some compensating advantage. The initial development of theory concentrated on the search for candidates: managerial and marketing skills, organisational development, product differentiation, oligopolistic practices and 'how to service a market' were all put forward. These unique assets, built essentially in the home market, were transferrable abroad at low cost, implicitly through internal markets, and provided the ability to compete successfully with host country firms.

This approach has been maintained and widened, for example by Rugman (1981): 'the key characteristic of the MNE is that it has a firm specific advantage in knowledge. Therefore, by definition, the MNE is a monopolist' (p. 61). This appears to be a confusion between the internal market, where a differential advantage may have been built up, and the final market, where the MNE competes with local firms and with other MNEs. However, it is useful to analyse the assumptions which give rise to the creation of this concept.

The existence of firm-specific advantages depend on propositions regarding:

(a) the diffusion of technical and marketing knowhow,

(b) the comparative advantage of firms in particular locations, and
(c) the existence of particular types of economies of scale.

(a) The diffusion of technical and marketing knowhow In Hirsh's model of the MNE *K* is defined as 'firm-specific know how and other intangible income producing proprietary assets' (Hirsch, 1976, p. 260). As such, *K* seems to have both a stock and a flow component. The stock, a result of past intra-firm investment in R & D, is added to by a flow of new proprietary information from continuing R & D expenditure. The intangible asset *K* is subject to obsolescence as rival firms catch up, and therefore it must constantly be renewed by investing in *K*-creating activities. The concept thus covers not only one-off innovations but also a continuing commitment to information creation. Possession of *K* confers a temporary monopoly, which yields a rent over and above competitive rates of profit. Moreover, *K* constitutes a barrier to entry to the industry because potential entrants have to incur costs in order to compete with *K*-possessing firms (Caves and Porter, 1977; Porter, 1980).

It has been suggested that the MNE is merely a device for slowing the rate of diffusion of information (Johnson, 1970). Indeed, this is the basis of the 'appropriability problem' on which Magee grounds his explanation of the growth of the MNE (Magee, 1977a, 1977b, 1981). Both Magee and Hirsh assume that the internalisation of flows of knowledge in combination with the production and marketing functions slows the rate of diffusion and maximises profits for the knowledge creator.

It is useful, following Casson (1979), to distinguish between two kinds of transferrable property right: (i) the right of access, which is the right to use an asset; and (ii) the right of exclusion, which is the right to prevent others from using the asset (analagous to a patent in technical knowledge). In diffusable assets, the second right must be upheld separately from the first. In what sense then is *K* firm-specific? What the authors have in mind is that (i) rights of exclusion are difficult to enforce in external market transactions in *K* (i.e. licensing agreements), and (ii) the returns to internal utilisation of the advantage are greater than the returns from external sales. The first of these propositions depends on the costs of designing and enforcing contracts in *K*, which leads us to transactions costs, and the second involves the view that internalisation will always be preferable to external sale. The latter proposition is by no means self-evident. There appears to be no well founded argument that the creator of knowledge is the best person to exploit that knowledge commercially, and much anecdotal evidence is to the contrary. Here the market can improve allocation by separating knowledge producers from those best equipped to be knowledge users. Scale adjustment costs, lack of complementary (production and marketing) skills and internal communications difficulties may all suggest a market solution in particular instances. 'Monopolistic advantages' auctioned competitively may well gain a better return than internalising the fruits of R & D.

The arguments for firm-specific advantages therefore rest on imperfections in the market for the sale of information which may have been pushed beyond that justified by empirical evidence.

(b) The comparative advantage of firms in particular locations Why should some firms invest in *K* when others choose not to do so? Presumably, the pressure to innovate arises from the market-transmitted forces of supply and demand. The product cycle solution (Vernon, 1966, 1974, 1979) is that firms are most likely to innovate when their immediate local environment is conducive to the creation of new techniques or products (see also Franko, 1976). However, for this to be an explanation of internationalisation, such innovations must be transferrable to other economies. In adapting to its market, the firm moves through stages, from innovation to standardisation and maturity according to the developing interactive forces of supply and demand for its product. There are difficulties of definition of the product in this approach and it requires us to believe that the firm can take strategic decisions sequentially, according to the stage the product has reached, and ignore interactions between these sequential decisions (there are other criticisms of the product cycle theory as well; see e.g. Giddy, 1978).

An alternative explanation is to regard some countries (notably the USA) as benefiting from high marginal products of learning resources, usually identified as skilled labour, scientists and engineers, relative to other countries. Such learning resources are able to transform the output of R & D into new forms of production ('new combinations' in Schumpeterian terms) and to reduce communication costs between R & D, production and marketing. Such learning resources could also be held to ease the transmission of information within firms and to reduce the costs of internationalising this information through internal markets. Thus a country-specific advantage, arising from high incomes, is transformed by internationally competitive firms into the potential to invest abroad.

(c) Economies of scale It is clear that the literature on firm-specific advantages assumes economies of scale in R & D. Such a proposition is an empirical one. From this, we move to the assumption that existing *K*-possessors face lower costs in the creation of new

K than new entrants. This is by no means self-evident. New knowledge often comes from those with no vested interest in extant practices. The 'learning by doing' literature implies economies of scale in the repeated performance of one, or similar, tasks, not in radical innovation. Consequently, it is arguable that MNEs become 'locked into' particular technologies (and products) and are unable to meet competition from outside this safe technological nexus (examples are Swiss watch producers facing competition from digital watches based on electronic technology, and the US motor car industry facing the oil price rise). Indeed it is this inability to diversify by industry and technology which limits the size of firms.

Moreover, it is not clear that firms with a comparative advantage in R & D should be the ones to control the production processes which embody the fruits of R & D. The postulate of intra-firm complementarities between production and R & D is implicit in the literature, but may be wrong. Severe cost penalties can arise from inadequate absorption of R & D. Also, it is not necessary to own a production process to control it. Many forms of information contracts such as franchising involve the control of large areas of the franchisee's business by the franchisor. There are many factors which may prevent internalisation of 'an advantage', and there are many ways of overcoming supposed complementarities between functions in the modern firm and interposing a market solution. Such separability will be achieved where returns justify it.

The level of the analysis

The above propositions on firm-specific advantages apply to the nature of the creation and intra-firm absorption of new information. They are, however, 'stretched' to become entry barriers to the industry. This switch between firm and industry is an awkward one. Lall removes this difficulty by the assumption that 'the behaviour of the leading firms in each industry is taken to be explicable only by the characteristics of the sectors to which they belong. By this assumption we can talk interchangeably about industries and their dominant firms' (Lall, 1980, p. 104).

The transition from firm-specific advantages to industry barriers to entry needs more justification than this. Again the picture is a static one. Dominant firms and the industry are only equivalent either in a static situation or in one where the industry structure is not changing over time. This is a most unusual situation to find, for new firms are constantly entering (and leaving) the industry as economic conditions change and technology develops. It is precisely in dynamically changing industries that FDI occurs. Again the analysis has to be static or short-period to justify the position taken.

The Role of Time

The notion of firm-specific advantage is essentially a short-run phenomenon because it is only in the short run when endowments of proprietary knowledge are fixed. In the long run, the assets of the firm *at a point in time* are determined by the firm's investment policy. What is required here is a reformulation of the theory of industry entry barriers (Bain, 1956).

In particular, entry barriers can be envisaged in a dynamic sense over the life of the industry (see Magee, 1977a). Investing in barriers to entry might take the form of: (a) acquiring a temporary lead by opportunism; (b) defending this lead by such practices as branding to consolidate the 'pioneer's' goodwill, product design to discourage reverse engineering and tying in retailers with long-term contracts regarding 'service arrangements' and spare parts supply; and (c) discouraging entry by price policies and segmentation strategies.

2.4 INTERNALISATION: A CONCEPT IN SEARCH OF A THEORY

The concept of internalisation has become a major synthesising and unifying concept in the theory of the MNE. However, widespread use of the concept has weakened rather than strengthened its power. At its most general, the concept of internalisation is tautological; firms internalise imperfect markets until the cost of further internalisation outweights the benefits. To have any empirical content, restrictions must be imposed on the relative size of transaction costs in internal and external markets.

A careful examination of the incidence of costs and benefits on a firm by firm, market by market, basis yields concrete propositions on the optimal scope of the firm. Even then, though, the framework of the internalisation approach is often static. This can induce a bias towards the *status quo* as the ideal solution. More serious, however, is the lack of explanation of a transition from one mode (internal or external) to the other. The beginnings of solutions to breaking this static mould to a dynamic problem are suggesting themselves.

Casson (1981) assumes two types of market-related costs. The first type of cost is a set-up cost incurred in bringing buyers and sellers together. The second type is a variable cost associated with negotiating and enforcing each transaction and so it is directly proportional to the quantity traded. Assume that an intermediate product market links two vertically integrated stages (one plant at each stage). The contribution of intermediate trade to joint profits can now be derived given the cost and revenue functions of the buying plant. This is illustrated by the curve AA′ in Figure 2.1. This curve peaks at B, so in the absence of transaction costs, the equilibrium value of trade is q_0. Under the assumptions that set-up costs are greater for internal markets but that variable costs are greater in external markets, transaction costs in the internal market are illustrated by locus CC′ and in the external market by DD′. These lines intersect at E so the minimum transaction costs of both modes is given by DEC′. At quantities below q_1, the plants will be separately owned and above q_1, trade will be internalised and the plants integrated. Profits are given

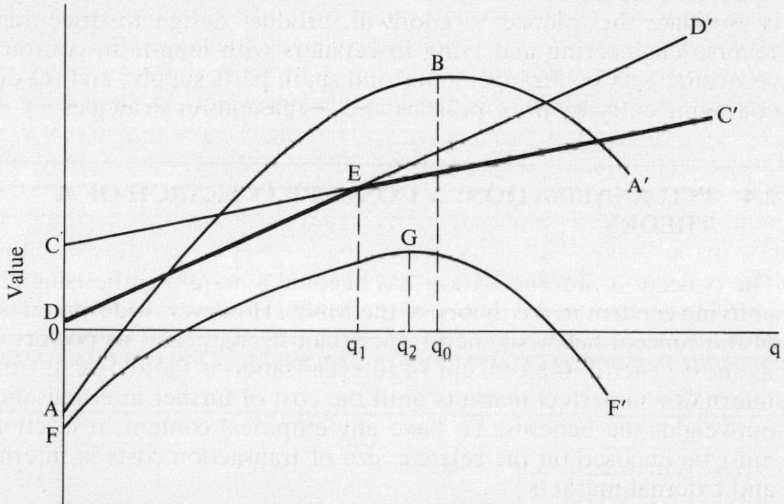

Figure 2.1 *Relation between internalisation and the volume of trade*

Notes:
AA′ – Contribution of intermediate product trade to joint profits of two plants
q_0 – ‘no transaction cost’ equilibrium volume of trade in intermediate goods market
CC′ – transaction cost of internal market
DD′ – transaction cost of external market
Minimum transaction cost locus is therefore DEC′
Profits (gains from trade minus transaction cost AA′ – DEC′) measured by FF′ peaking at G
Profit maximising output is q_2 in presence of transaction costs
If $q_2 > q_1$ market internalised
$q_2 < q_1$ there is arm’s length trading in external market

by gains from trade minus transaction costs (measured by the vertical distance between AA′ and DEC′). They are illustrated as FF′, peaking at G and giving a profit maximising output q_2. In this example, the profit maximising firm will choose $q_2 > q_1$ and the market is internalised.

The approach suggests that the propensity to internalise is greater, the higher is the volume of trade between the two plants. But this depends on a large volume of trade being associated with a high frequency of transactions in the external market. The incentive to internalise is reduced if this frequency is diminished, e.g. by long-term contracts or bulk buying.

Testable predictions can be derived from this model. It suggests, for instance, that branded product producers have an incentive to internalise backwards rather than continually buy from the same suppliers.

Another way of giving operational content to the approach is to invoke a dynamic *deus ex machina*, usually known as the entrepreneur, who spots the potential for improving situations in efficiency terms or in redistributing rewards towards himself (McGuiness, 1979). In changing situations, the entrepreneur is backing his view of an uncertain, unknown future against other people's views. In doing so he consciously undertakes risks. These risks can be reduced by the compilation and assimilation of relevant information on which to base his forecasts. This links closely the economics of information to bounded rationality and to 'learning by doing' arguments.

Because decisions are taken at a moment in time and with incomplete information (on the array of prices, markets and competitor's decisions) the concept of bounded rationality is highly relevant to entrepreneurial decision making.

Internalisation and Centralisation

It is mistaken to equate the internalisation of activities with the centralisation of those activities. Two quotes from Rugman (1981) illustrate the tendency to argue in this way: 'resource allocation processes that are internalised are those carried out in a centralised manner' (p. 29); and 'unless the R & D is centralised in the parent there is no firm specific advantage at risk through licensing, yet we know that MNEs prefer to control the rate of use of their knowledge advantage by direct foreign investment, thus they must be afraid of dissipation' (p. 105).

It is possible to envisage a situation which represents the complete opposite of 'internalisation for centralisation'. It is acknowledged that internalisation takes place in the face of imperfections in markets.

Consequently, one solution for an MNE is to operate as closely as possible to a perfect internal market. This is likely to involve decentralised profit centres transmitting shadow price signals to other decision-makers within the organisation (in cost or profit centres). The perfectability of knowledge within the organisation is increased by each decision-maker being aware of the plans of those with whom he is dealing. Scales of operation of activities can be adjusted to optimum levels on the basis of these current and forecast prices.

Internalisation and 'Markets and Hierarchies'

Recently, there has been an identification of internalisation with the markets and hierarchies framework (Calvet, 1981). It is worth emphasising certain differences. Whilst an internal market may involve a hierarchical, administrative solution, it is also consistent with an allocative system based on decentralised shadow (transfer) prices. The pure markets and hierarchies approach (Williamson, 1975) envisages the organisation as a substitute for policing and settlement of disputes: as a 'privatised legal system'. This may well be a fruitful way of introducing the cultural aspects of the firm as a management unit. It is a plausible hypothesis that some managerial cultures are more viable and progressive than others. As an example, Japanese firms may be able to draw on cultural values and behaviour unavailable to others, allowing their internal markets to be more effective than others and keeping their contractual costs lower. Consequently, the firm as an organisation exploits cultural attitudes to reduce costs through the medium of an internal market. This link between internalisation and aspects of culture seems capable of leading to several interesting testable hypotheses.

Endogeneity of market imperfections

It is a valid criticism of the internalisation rubric that market imperfections are taken as exogenous to the (internalising) firm. This gives determinacy to the theory but unduly restricts it. Many of the imperfections are the result of interaction between the firm and the market, e.g. product differentiation. One strategy of the firm can thus be typified as creating imperfections by branding or other strategies in order to advance the market penetration of the firm. This creates new information signals (perceived quality, etc.) in addition to price and quantity information so that privileged access to this information gives further cause for internalising markets in this information. Intermediate markets in quality information are thus created which affect suppliers amongst others and backward integration into previously unbranded inputs is encouraged. This involves a 'sifting' role of the internaliser in areas where price discrimination was not previously possible in the internal market. The cost of concluding and negotiating separate 'quality contracts' may be excessive and, of course, long-term contracts to maintain quality are essential. The specification of quality in the intermediate market will also be derived from the final market, hence this gives the motive power for backward internalisation. Forecasting of future quality demands will also be much easier for the final seller and thus the risk of 'quality default' in the future will be obviated if he internalises. (See Casson, 1981, and also Chapter 7 below.)

2.5 LOCATION THEORY

Dunning (1979) considers that the location theory approach to FDI was not 'wholly satisfactory' (p. 273) because for a long time it was not integrated with other theoretical approaches, notably industrial organisation theory. Rugman (1981) relegates the economics of least cost location to a footnote to internalisation theory by including 'spatial cost saving' as a firm-specific advantage. However the choice of location and the role of non-traded inputs is a vital element in the competitive stance of the firm and therefore in the firm's growth pattern.

A significant advance has been made in recent writings by examining the locational influences on different activities in the firm (R & D, finance, marketing, for instance) and the specialist literature on the location of the individual elements, e.g. on the marketing function, is liable to lead to further developments. Of great interest are the links between such areas in terms of information flow and communications costs, for these will yield a 'pull' on more distant activities (Hymer, 1971; Buckley and Casson, 1976). Such flows of expertise and information are shown in Figure 2.2 as linking R & D with two other functions of the firm. The heavier are such flows and the more difficult it is to code the signals (e.g. into shadow prices), the more will be the tendency to centralise the function. However, recent research, particularly on the international location of the research function of MNEs (Ronstadt, 1977; Lall, 1979), is beginning to show that dispersal of such functions has non-price benefits and that multinationals are developing 'dispersal skills' at a very rapid rate: witness the growth of 'offshore plants', particularly in South-East Asia (Moxon, 1974). Such developments enable MNEs to gain maximum advantage from differential prices of non-tradeables, particularly labour.

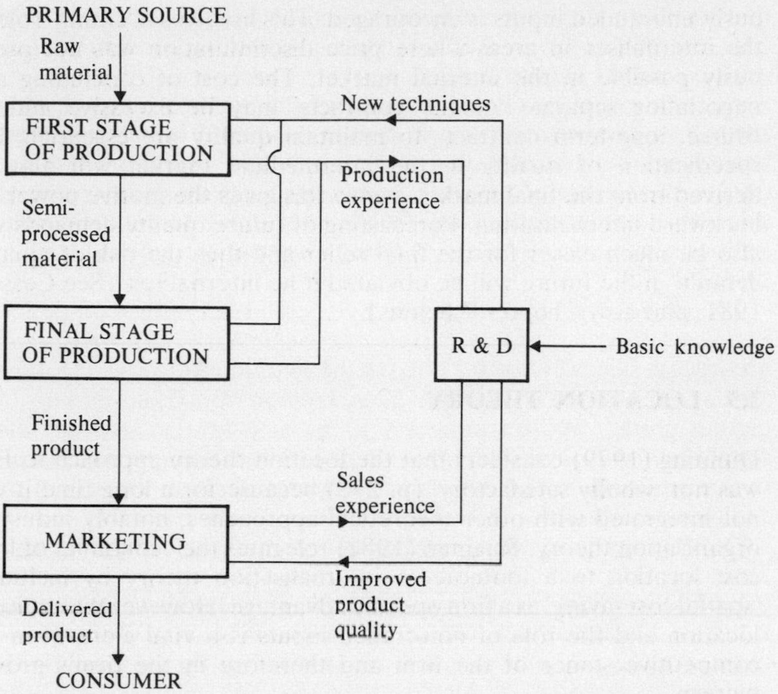

Figure 2.2 *Information flows in the multinational firm*

Notes:
Successive stages of production are linked by flows of semi-process materials. Production and marketing are linked by a flow of finished goods ready for distribution. Production and marketing on the one hand are linked to R&D on the other hand by two-way flows of information and expertise.
Source: Reproduced from Buckley and Casson (1976)

2.6 DYNAMICS

The purpose of a dynamic analysis of the growth of the firm is that it should be able to specify the timing of strategic outcomes. Consequently, not only the initial FDI, but also switches of mode of foreign market servicing (exports, licensing, direct investment) and the direction of growth of the firm are all part of its remit.

Various efforts to predict the optimal timing of FDI have been made (Aliber, 1970; Buckley and Casson, 1981). Essentially, such models specify different classes of cost which change differentially in response to exogenous factors, such as market growth. From propositions on the balance of costs and revenues faced by the firm in the different modes of market servicing, predictions on the timing of strategic moves can be derived.

Aliber's model involves a balance of the 'costs of doing business abroad' (a cost which bears on the licensing and investment modes but declines with market size), and a differential capitalisation rate to the income stream of an asset according to its nationality of ownership. At a 'certain market size' these ownership differences in capitalisation rates outweigh costs of doing business abroad and trigger a switch to FDI.

The model used by Buckley and Casson (1981) relies on defining three sets of costs; recurrent fixed cost, recurrent variable costs and a non-recoverable set-up cost of each mode of market servicing. Given assumptions on the cost profile of each mode of market servicing, on market growth and on pricing strategy in a foreign market, some simple predictions on switching can be derived. Some heroic assumptons must be made and the market servicing decision, even with such assumptions, emerges as highly complex.

Developments in the dynamics of international business growth have cast doubt on the validity of a proposition which has been fundamental from at least the time of Hymer's thesis (1976): that local firms have an advantage over foreign entrants because of local knowledge. For the case of first-time foreign investors this proposition may still have some validity. However, in the days of well established, widely diversified, efficiently managed multinational corporations we must question approaches based on such a view. Experience, skilled management and 'learning by doing' effects are all likely to make the foreign entrant a formidable competitor even in the absence of searches for 'monopolistic advantages'. Stepwise entry into markets and rational international diversification strategies add to the information on which to base investment decisions and make the established MNE a radically different competitor than a first-time foreign entrant.

This development from naive entrant to established multinational has been inadequately modelled (despite for instance Aharoni, 1966, and Newbould *et al*., 1978) and its implications for theory are as yet unassimilated.

2.7 CONCLUSION: RESEARCH AGENDA

Several unresolved issues remain in the theory of the multinational firm:

(a) The economics of research and development The arguments

for 'firm specific advantages' are founded on the creation of new knowledge and its absorption within one and the same firm. It was argued above that in many cases such an identification of knowledge producer with optimal user is unjustified. In many cases, technological breakthroughs can be too radical for the innovating firm to cope with. Such fundamental research often contains the seeds of its own destruction because the sponsoring firm cannot appropriate all the ideas. Although specialisation in R & D is possible in principle, in practice it is severely constrained. Consequently, such basic efforts have to be hived off. Firms have limited funds, limited horizons and limited absorptive capacities and often ossify at particular stages of technological development. Further investigation of the process of splintering or consolidation of R & D and its fruits are of vital importance in the consideration of the growth and size of firms.

(b) The economics of business strategy The importance of strategic models lies in their contribution to the analysis of decisions when information is restricted and interdependence between actors is recognised. A great deal of richness can be added to the behaviour of firms when the role of limited information is recognised. Limited information acts as a proprietary asset but also as an entry barrier to activities or industries. The protection of information is an activity for competitive firms. Industry structure is capable of analysis by viewing established firms as barrier builders investing in entry-deterring activities versus new entrants investing in barrier circumvention. This view of entry barriers links closely with the 'exogenous versus endogenous market imperfections' discussion above. Market imperfections are created by investment in barriers to entry, often to defend earlier types of proprietary know-how. Dominant firms may be more capable of building and perpetuating such barriers. Such a mechanism may often operate at the brand level creating a 'brand entry' problem because the costs of innovating a new brand may be less for an established firm than for a new entrant. Thus multi-brand firms have an advantage in attempts to launch profitably a new brand. Such transfers in time of entry barriers are capable of extension.

(c) Location Theory In the undoubted improvement in the theory of the multinational firm on which this chapter draws, location theory has been curiously stationary. This is partly because theorists believe that there is nothing that has not been said because the 'rational manager' in the individual firm is deemed to be able to calculate location costs, including trade and tariff barriers, and on a comparative cost basis to select the optimal location strategy. However, when non-routine production activities are included and the relationships

between R & D, marketing and production are allowed for, many new problems arise. Also, crucially, communications costs and cultural values are not fully integrated into the calculus. This lack of interest is unwarranted, and must be rectified through renewed research initiatives.

(d) A general approach The general approach of this chapter leads toward the concept of a life cycle, not only of firms and technologies but also of products and industries over economic space and time (Mueller, 1972). It is within this context that future research might attempt to map the growth of firms. To date, both theories and empirical work have reduced the degrees of freedom of analysis, for example by fixing on a point of time, by identifying 'the product' with one particular firm for all time or by equating a particular technology with a single firm. A further unwarranted simplification is to identify the industry with its leading firm. Such simplifications have led to the occasionally arid use of 'firm specific advantage', when such a concept restricts the outcomes and straightjackets the analysis.

3 Technological and organisational factors in the theory of the multinational enterprise

DAVID J. TEECE

3.1 INTRODUCTION

In recent years, the theory of the MNE has benefited from research on the economics of internal organisation by Williamson (1975), (1979), (1981) and others. Since the MNE internalises transactions which might otherwise have taken place in an external market, this theory has come to be known as the 'internalisation theory' of the MNE. However, the theory has been formulated at a rather general level, which led Buckley to comment in Chapter 2 (p. 42) that the idea of multinational internalisation, as articulated by Rugman (1981) and others, is 'a concept in search of a theory'.

The main purpose of this chapter is to indicate how this deficiency might be remedied. Building on recent work (Teece 1980, 1981a, 1981c; Williamson and Teece, 1983) and following the general approach outlined by Williamson (1981), efforts are made to dimensionalise the transactions cost properties of the MNE so that the theory predicts when and where the internalisation of economic activity within the firm is likely to be the most efficient mode for organising economic activity. By dimensionalising international transactions, and separating those which unassisted markets can handle at lowest cost from those which multinational enterprise can handle at lowest cost, the tautological nature of transactions cost or 'internalisation' reasoning can be avoided, and a contingency theory of the MNE developed. A secondary objective of this chapter is to lay out a framework which facilitates the synthesis of neoclassical trade and location theory with the theory of the MNE.

3.2 PRODUCTION COSTS AND GOVERNANCE COSTS

Throughout human history, economic activity has been governed by an immense variety of organisational forms, of which the modern corporation is perhaps the most recent. It did so in order to realise the productive potential of the technology associated with what North (1981) calls the 'second economic revolution' – the development of automated machinery and communications, the creation of new sources of energy, and the fundamental transformation of matter. This technology was characterised by significant indivisibilities, so the realisation of economies of scale required large volume continuous production and distribution. The modern corporation was a response to the need to coordinate and control this high volume throughput. 'Economies came more from the ability to integrate and coordinate the flow of materials through the plant than from greater specialisation and subdivision of work within the plant' (Chandler, 1977, p. 281).

The managerial revolution which accompanied the development of the modern corporation had two dimensions. The first was an effort to realise the productive potential of the new technology – the technological dimension. The second was the attempt to devise governance structures or organisational forms to reduce the transactions cost associated with the exploitation of the new technology – the organisational dimension.

Exploitation of the new technology required increasing specialisation and division of labour, but the greater the specialisation and division of labour, the greater the frequency and complexity of transactions. Governing these transactions uses up large amounts of society's resources, although obviously the productivity gains from specialisation have more than offset the governance costs. Some indication of the magnitude of the resources committed to this activity by a modern industrial society can be gauged from historical statistics. Between 1900 and 1970 the US labour force grew from 19 million to 80 million. While the number of manual workers grew from 10 million to 29 million, that of white-collar workers grew from 5 million to 38 million. In large measure, these white-collar workers were managers whose principal business was organising economic activity. This involved measuring the quality of inputs and outputs, regulating the use of factors of production, making resource allocation decisions, checking on contractual compliance and the like. The resources used to conduct these activities involve transactions costs which, according to Arrow (1969, p. 48), represent the 'costs of running the economic system'.

For the purposes of understanding the MNE it is useful to distinguish between production costs and transactions or governance costs. A synthesis of neoclassical trade and location theory, and the theory of MNE, can be accomplished if these distinctions are kept reasonably clear. The task of explaining FDI can thus be divided into two parts: (1) explaining the locational forces which justify spreading the production of products and services around the globe so that production activities are found in different national markets; (2) explaining the governance costs (or, equivalently, the transactions costs) associated with placing these production activities under common administrative control, rather than letting markets mediate transactions between stand-alone business units. These two aspects are not, of course, entirely separable, as the location of the firm's boundaries tends to have ramifications for production costs as well. The focus of this chapter is on the transactions cost properties of MNE, rather than locational issues, since the latter are comparatively well understood.

3.3 THE HORIZONTALLY INTEGRATED MNE

The MNE can be defined as an enterprise which manages and controls 'production' establishments located in at least two countries, where 'production' is used in a general way to encompass both service and distribution activities. It is convenient to divide MNEs into two types. The first type turns out essentially the same line of goods from its plants in each national market; this is the horizontally integrated MNE. The horizontal MNE can be equated with a multi-plant firm with production facilities located in different nation states. The second type produces output in some of its plants in some countries which serve as inputs to its plants in other countries; this is the vertically integrated MNE. Vertically integrated MNEs may make physical transfers of intermediate products from one of their plants to another, but this is not required by the definition; they need only to be producing at adjacent stages of a vertically related set of production processes. (For example, vertically integrated international oil companies may exchange crude oil with other industry participants, so that their refineries may run crude produced by others, yet by the above definition they will still be considered vertically integrated MNEs.)

Successful firms in most industries possess one or more types of intangible asset. The asset may represent technological knowhow, taking the specific form of a patented process or design, or it may be the managerial and marketing knowhow embedded within the firm. A firm-specific rent-yielding asset of this kind can provide the *raison d'être* for multinational operation if (1) the asset in question is not fully employed *ex ante*, and (2) arm's length transactions in the services of the intangible asset are exposed to high transactions costs.

Assume that the asset in question which is not fully employed is knowhow. An examination of the properties of markets for knowhow leads to the identification of several transactional difficulties. These difficulties can be summarised in terms of recognition, disclosure, and transfer costs (Teece, 1980, 1981; Williamson, 1981; Williamson and Teece, 1983). Thus if the asset is not fully employed *ex ante*, and if there are firms abroad that can profitably employ the services of this asset, then the received theory of markets indicates that trading will ensue until the gains from trade are exhausted. Or, as Calabresi (1968) has put it, 'if one assumes rationality, no transactions costs, and no legal impediments to bargaining, all misallocations of resources would be fully cured in the market by bargains'. However, one generally cannot expect this result, especially in the international market for proprietary knowhow. Not only are there high costs associated with obtaining the requisite information, but there are also organisational and strategic impediments associated with using the market to conduct technology transfer.

These impediments are normally highest when knowledge is tacit rather than explicit. Knowledge cannot always be codified; individuals often know more than they are able to articulate. When knowledge has a high tacit component, it cannot be transferred in codified form. It is, therefore, extremely difficult to transfer without intimate personal contact, demonstration, and involvement (Teece, 1981, pp. 82–4). It is well known, for instance, that the diffusion of crafts from one country to another often depended on the migration of groups of craftsmen, such as when the Huguenots were driven from France by the repeal of the Edict of Nantes under Louis XIV. Indeed, in the absence of intimate human contact, technology transfer is sometimes impossible. As Polanyi (1958) has observed; 'It is pathetic to watch the endless efforts – equipped with microscopy and chemistry, with mathematics and electronics – to reproduce a single violin of the kind the half-literate Stradivarius turned out as a matter of routine more than 200 years ago.'[1]

In short, the transfer of knowledge may be impossible in the absence of the transfer of people. Furthermore, it will often not suffice just to transfer individuals. While a single individual may sometimes hold the key to much organisational knowledge, team support is often needed, since the organisation's total capabilities must be brought to bear on the transfer problem. In some instances, the transfer can be effected through a one-time contract, which would provide a consulting team to assist in the start-up. Such contracts may be highly incomplete. The failure to reach a comprehensive agreement may give rise to dissatisfaction during execution. This dissatisfaction may be an unavoidable – which is to say an irremediable – result. Plainly, establishing a foreign subsidiary is an extreme response to the needs of a one-time exchange. In the absence of a superior organisational alternative, one-time incomplete contracting for a consulting team is likely to prevail.

Reliance on repeated contracting is less clearly warranted, however, where a succession of transfers is contemplated. It is also less clearly warranted when two-way communication is needed to promote the recognition and disclosure of opportunities for information transfer as well as the actual transfer itself. The parties in these circumstances are effectively joined in a bilateral monopoly trading relation. As Williamson (1975) explains, such contracting is full of hazards. A more cooperative arrangement for joining the parties would enjoy a greater comparative institutional advantage. Specifically, intra-firm transfer to a foreign subsidiary (which avoids the need for repeated negotiations and attenuates the hazards of opportunism) has advantages over autonomous trading: better disclosure, easier agreement, better governance and more efficient transfer result. Here lies an incentive for horizontal FDI.

The above arguments, while couched in the context of technological knowhow, are in fact general and extend to many different kinds of proprietary information. For instance, managerial (including organisational) knowhow and goodwill (including brand loyalty) represent types of assets for which markets may falter as effective exchange mechanisms. Accordingly, the existence of firm specific rent-yielding assets which are non-tradeable for transactions cost reasons can be seen as providing a driving force for horizontal FDI.

This is not to say, however, that the existence of non-tradeable assets is the sole market failure providing incentives for firms to internationalise the scope of their boundaries, although the empirical evidence suggests that it may be the principal one. Teece (1976) and Casson (1981) identify a number of other possible market failures, such as the inability of unassisted markets to protect product and service quality. In a similar vein, Williamson (1981) refers to the externality principle whereby forward integration is motivated by the objective of supporting point of sale promotion and quality control effort. These factors undoubtedly help explain other incentives for the horizontal expansion of the multinational firms, particularly in low technology service-type industries, where debasement of quality for a branded good or service by one distributor might affect another.

3.4 THE VERTICALLY INTEGRATED MNE

Historically, the emergence of the MNE has been associated with the sourcing abroad of raw materials such as oil, copper and alumina. The vertically integrated MNE internalises a market for an intermediate product, just as the horizontal MNE internalises markets for know-how and other non-tradeable assets. Intermediate product markets can be organised across a spectrum of ways stretching from anonymous spot market transactions to a variety of long-term contractual arrangements (Williamson, 1975). Generally, vertical integration will be chosen over market alternatives when a trading relationship requires the development of transaction-specific assets. Relying on arm's length contracts under these circumstances would involve exposure to recontracting hazards stemming from high switching costs (Klein, Crawford and Alchian, 1978; Monteverde and Teece, 1982).

By way of example, consider a smelter located in the home country. Assume that there are many different types and grades of ore and that to smelt the ore at the lowest cost the smelter needs to be designed to process a particular grade of ore. If this ore is found only in one or two locations abroad, then there may be recontracting hazards associated with relying on long-term supply contracts with another enterprise. Once the investment in idiosyncratic smelting facilities has been made, the enterprise engaged in smelting will be extremely vulnerable to change made by the ore supplier in the conditions of sale. The supplier of the ore may well behave opportunistically, raising the price above the previously contracted level. Judicial redress may be weak, so to the extent that alternative suppliers are not available, the owner of the smelter will be obliged to honour the new terms. In extreme cases of dependence, the supplier will be able to extract a pecuniary advantage from the owner, up to the value of the smelting facility. Backward vertical integration can eliminate this risk, for if the supplier and purchaser are one and the same, the incentive for postcontractual recontracting is attenuated, and trading relations can proceed in a fashion which is relatively smooth and efficient.

But while incentives for *ex post* recontracting may be attenuated, they are not eliminated, because very often vertical integration cannot be complete, in the sense that property rights are by no means secure in many nation states. A case in point is the extraction of Third World mineral resources by multinational firms based in the industrialised countries. While firms based in developed countries may engage in backward vertical integration in order to eliminate scope for private opportunism by raw material producers, such integration provides little protection against state opportunism, and may in fact encourage it. International contract law does not appear to ensure for the foreign investor that the initial bargain and terms will last through the term of the contract (Sornarajah, 1981). Vertical integration is thus ineffective in protecting trading relationships unless it is accompanied by other measures designed to nurture and support the underlying relationship with the host country.

3.5 INTEGRATING TRANSACTIONS COSTS AND PRODUCTION COSTS[2]

Transactions cost considerations explain why plants in different countries should fall under common ownership and control rather than trade with each other using various contractual instruments. However, the analysis so far has avoided focusing on the complex interplay between production and transaction costs. Sometimes it is not possible to keep the distinctions between location and control issues as stark as has been done above. For instance, the transactions costs associated with transferring process knowhow will determine, at least in part, the level of production cost prevailing in various locations abroad. In what follows, I attempt a partial synthesis of production and transactions cost considerations. In delineating a firm's efficient boundaries one must examine how the MNE responds to the sum of governance cost and production cost.

(a) Horizontal integration

In many circumstances, organisational boundaries impact upon production costs. Consider the licensing/FDI choice. Figure 3.1 depicts the absolute and relative governance costs associated with FDI and licensing. These costs are represented as a function of the degree to which the technology in question is complex. It is assumed that complex technologies are most likely to be proprietary (and hence need protection from disclosure to competitors) and to have a tacit dimension. Let GC represent governance costs, with a subscript indicating FDI or licensing (L). GC_{FDI} is depicted as basically invariant to the degree to which the knowhow is complex. The figure depicts the situation when *de novo* entry or acquisition is necessary should the FDI selection be made. On the other hand, the governance cost associated with licensing, GC_L, is assumed to increase with the degree to which the technology is complex. The difference curve, $GC_{FDI} - GC_L$ is accordingly downward sloping. The point A at which

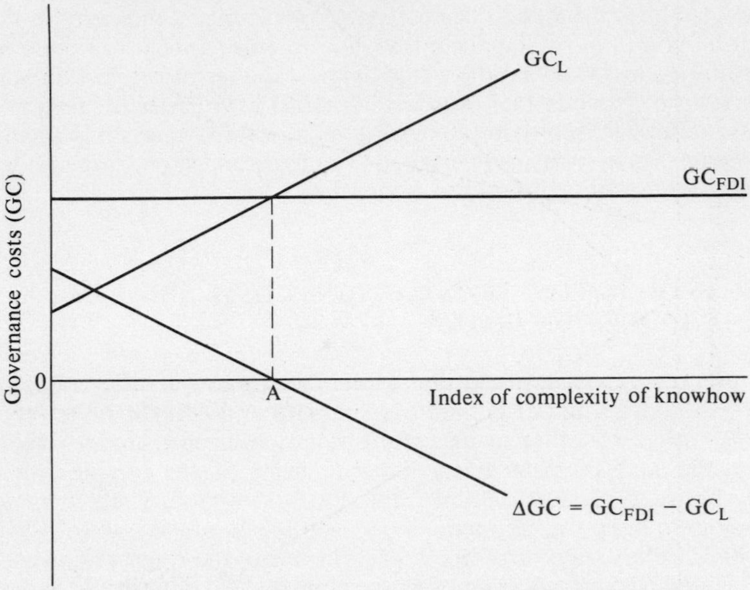

Figure 3.1 *Governance costs for horizontal integration*

it cuts the horizontal axis indicates the point at which FDI is favoured over licensing, if transactions cost were all that mattered.

Production costs (PC) must also be evaluated since the licensing/FDI choice must be made on the basis of total costs, not just governance costs. Consider, therefore, the differential production costs associated with FDI and licensing (where production costs are defined to include the non-contractual resource costs of the technology transfer). Generally, the greater the complexity of the technology the more costly it is to effect transfer and low-cost foreign production without FDI (Teece, 1977). Transfer by any mode is more costly the greater the complexity of the technology, but the costs increase faster with licensing than with FDI. These stylised characteristics are depicted in Figure 3.2.

The governance cost and production cost difference schedules from Figures 3.1 and 3.2 are brought together in Figure 3.3, and a total difference schedule ΔTC is derived. Governance cost and production cost considerations work in the same direction, serving jointly to favour FDI as technological complexity increases. Notice that, over the range A–B of the index of complexity, production and governance costs jointly may lead to a different choice between licensing or FDI than would production or transactions costs alone.

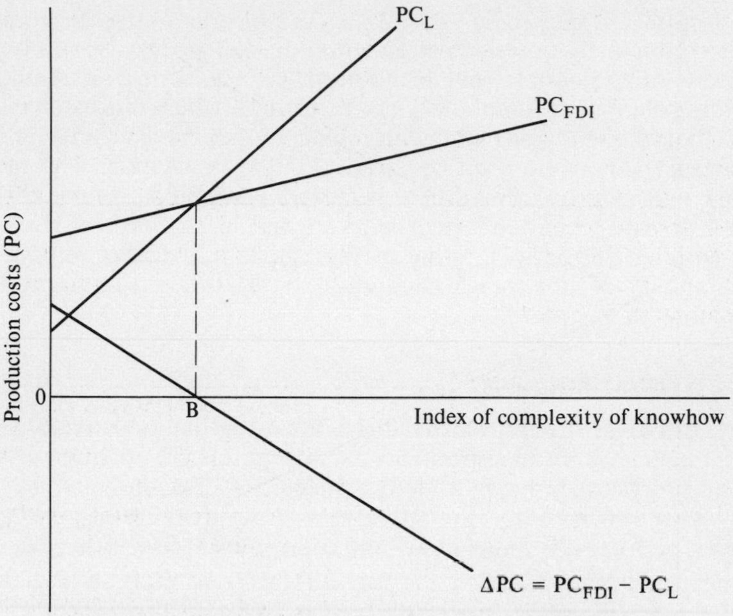

Figure 3.2 *Production costs for horizontal integration*

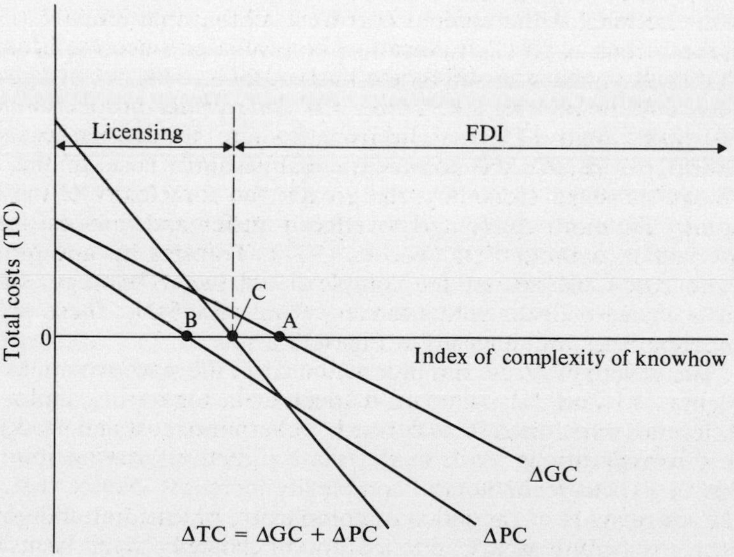

Figure 3.3 *Total costs for horizontal integration*

It must also be stressed that the choice of organisational modes is not confined to just market and non-market forms. Not only are mixed forms possible, but in addition various forms of 'relational contracts' (Williamson, 1979) can be created which redress many of the shortcomings associated with relying on faceless exchange in spot markets. This could itself constitute a separate chapter. The rather stark presentation offered here is certainly not meant to convey the idea that the choice between markets and hierarchies involves all-or-nothing alternatives. Some of the empirical evidence supporting this theory of horizontal integration by MNEs is summarised by Dunning in Chapter 5.

(b) Vertical integration

One of the most important factors influencing the incentive to vertical integration is the specificity of the physical and human asset whose services are being traded. A specific asset is one for which it is costly to switch to an alternative use; more precisely, it is an asset which earns a substantial quasi-rent in its present use, either because it has no alternative use or because it is costly to switch it to another use. A specific asset is exemplified by a purpose-designed piece of hardware which is difficult to re-jig or adapt to other purposes.

In Figure 3.4 the governance costs associated with external markets GC_M are shown as rising with asset specificity. The governance costs associated with vertical integration, GC_V, while initially higher because of set up costs, are invariant with respect to asset specificity. The result is that the difference curve $\Delta GC = GC_V - GC_M$ is a decreasing function of specificity. But the relationship is not quite that simple in the international context, as the governance costs associated with markets depends very much on the expropriation risk. While insignificant in some developed countries, the risk of expropriation without complete compensation represents an important expected cost in many foreign countries. Hence the GC_V schedule will shift according to expropriation risk. The nature of the shift will vary according to particular circumstances. For instance, the risk may be greater the more transaction-specific the investment if the host country has the leverage to 'hold up' the downstream MNE, as when the MNE has failed to 'dual-source'. Conversely, there may be circumstances where the host country has little leverage because of the flexibility of the MNE (e.g. IBM has dual internal sources for most of its components).

It is assumed that production costs are invariant with respect to asset specificity and are independent of whether there is vertical integration. In some cases there may be an internal procurement bias,

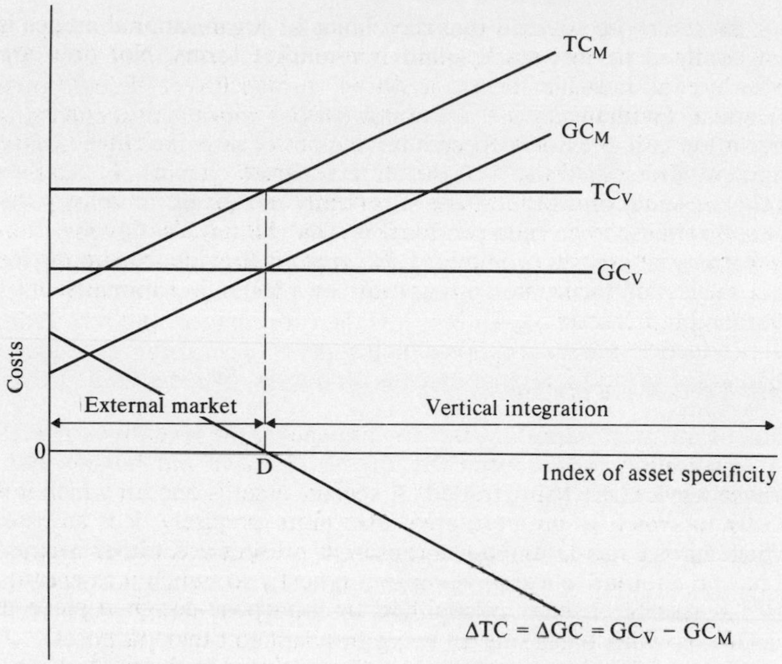

Figure 3.4 *Costs of vertical integration*

which generates a production cost differential which is a function of asset specificity, but in the present instance this possibility is ignored. The total cost functions TC_M, TC_V are thus obtained by shifting up the governance cost functions GC_M, GC_V by the same amount. The cost difference remains unchanged (i.e. $\Delta TC = \Delta GC$) and so the critical degree of asset specificity, D, at which vertical integration is just preferred, is determined by the governance costs alone.

Tests of the transaction cost theory of vertical integration in a purely international context are absent. Most of the evidence is only tangentially relevant to the hypothesis. For instance, Pugel (1978) concluded that American manufacturing industries having greater involvement with natural resources invest larger proportions of their assets abroad, and Stuckey (1981) found the international aluminium industry to contain MNEs integrated from the mining of bauxite through to the fabrication of aluminum projects; but Stuckey also found a network of long-term contracts and joint ventures. These features of the industry indicate the hesitation of firms to use spot markets for bauxite (the raw ore) and alumina (the output of the first processing stage). Stuckey also observed that switching costs are high for the ore refiner since alumina refining facilities need to be located physically close to bauxite mines to minimise transport costs, and they are also designed to handle the properties of specific ores. Alumina smelters likewise are somewhat tied for technical and transportation cost reasons to particular sources of alumina. Very similar circumstances characterise the international petroleum industry (Teece, 1976) and explain the substantial degree of integration between refining and crude production. The evidence in Chapter 7 on international banana production also appears broadly consistent with internalisation theory, but it is not the asset specificity principle which comes through loudest. Rather, it is the coordination and scheduling of production and distribution which appears to constitute the distinct advantage of multinational banana producers, like the United Fruit Company.

3.6 CONCLUSION

This chapter has attempted to synthesise a theory of multinational enterprise based on the new institutional economies advanced by Williamson (1975) and others. The theory which emerges is broadly consistent with the historical record as outlined by Wilkins (1970), (1974) and Chandler (1977), and also with the theoretical work of many others, most notably Buckley and Casson (1976). The subsequent chapters in this book are further evidence that the market failure theory of the international firm is now firmly ensconced, and promises further rich insights into the study of the international economy.

NOTES

1 This treatment is based in part on Williamson and Teece (1983).
2 The diagrammatic treatment employed in this section is a development and extension of ideas first suggested to me by Oliver Williamson.

4 Pricing and sourcing strategies in a multinational oligopoly

MARK CASSON and GEORGE NORMAN

4.1 INTRODUCTION

It is often suggested that in many industries the market structure is tending toward an international oligopoly dominated by multinational firms (Hymer and Rowthorn, 1970; Lall and Streeten, 1977). This view is strengthened by interview evidence which suggests that the managers of multinationals often perceive the decision to invest abroad in oligopolistic terms (Aharoni, 1966). Unfortunately, few authors have analysed in detail the economic rationale for such behaviour. The present chapter is an attempt to fill this lacuna in the theory by bringing to bear upon it current analysis of spatial economic behaviour (Norman, 1981; Norman and Nichols, 1982).

Sections 4.2 to 4.4 consider some of the strategic aspects of oligopolistic rivalry – in particular, the role of pricing strategy in market penetration. Section 4.5 relates pricing strategy to the market sourcing decision, i.e. to the decision on the location of production. This analysis provides a simple explanation of why the location decision is of such strategic importance to the firm. Section 4.6 analyses 'follow the leader' behaviour in the context of a sequence of oligopolistic encounters in different regions of the world market. Section 4.7 considers the implications of the analysis for international economic policy, and for future research on oligopoly.

4.2 THE DYNAMICS OF MARKET STRUCTURE

It is now widely recognised that market structure is closely related to the age of the product. The product cycle theory (Vernon, 1966, 1974) suggests that it would be useful to distinguish three stages in the evolution of market structure. These stages are listed below, together with the assumptions that are introduced to simplify the analysis. It should be noted that no prior assumptions are made about the lengths of those three stages. These will be dependent upon both product and market characteristics.

(1) Monopoly or monopolistic competition It is assumed that a new product is introduced, with different variants being marketed by rival firms. Consumers make trial purchases and one of the variants becomes the market leader.

(2) Oligopoly The other firms adapt their products to imitate the market leader. Thus the market involves a homogeneous product sold at a uniform price. It is assumed that the leader retains his share of the market because of the goodwill built up in the monopoly stage; the other firms acquire the residual market by initiating price competition. Outside entry is impossible at this stage because of the difficulty of acquiring the know-how of the established firms.

(3) Competition As production methods become standardised, so know-how becomes easier to acquire. Provided that the minimum efficient scale of plant is relatively small, once the knowhow becomes a free good new firms enter and competition prevails. It is assumed that new entrants cannot bid away buyers from established firms. Just as the leader retains his share of the market when the followers enter, so the leader and followers retain their market shares when the competitors enter.

To further simplify the analysis it is assumed that there are just two rival firms: firm 0 is a leader and firm 1 a follower. In the first stage the leader successfully innovates a new product, while the follower produces a variant for which – though it is technically very similar – there is no demand. The leader can therefore price monopolistically.

In the second stage the follower imitates the leader. The leader sets an output and the follower supplies the residual demand. The follower adopts a Cournot response, in the expectation that the leader's output will remain unchanged (Koutsoyiannis, 1979).

It is assumed that all production takes place with constant average variable cost. Thus the effect of competitive entry is simply to depress the market price to the level of variable cost. This means, of course, that once competition emerges the two established firms can no longer earn any surplus to cover the fixed cost of product development.

The market for the product is worldwide, but is divided up into distinct regions. Each region has its own particular requirements which call for special adaptation or differentiation of the product

(Caves, 1971). Thus entry by the leader into each region incurs a fixed cost of differentiation over and above any fixed costs incurred in the original development of the product. Entry by the follower also incurs a fixed cost in imitating the regionally differentiated product. Because of regional differentiations the product cannot be re-exported from one market area to another, so that international price discrimination is feasible (for the consequences of relaxing this assumption see Horst, 1971). Under these conditions marketing strategies in the different regions are essentially independent, and so interfirm rivalry can be examined in terms of the rivalry in a representative region (though see Section 4.6).

The main interdependency between regions arises in the choice of the location of production from which to service each market. To simplify the analysis it is assumed that both firms are already producing some variants of the product outside the representative market that is being studied. This assumption is not crucial, though, and can easily be relaxed. The firm can continue to produce outside the market and service it by exports (mode 0) or it can establish production within the market (mode 1). The contractual arrangement under which it produces does not concern us here; production could involve a wholly-owned subsidiary, a subcontractor, or a licensee. The essential point is that the firm can either directly or indirectly control the marketing strategy (using restrictive practices in the case of a licensee) and ultimately bears the full cost of production (Buckley and Casson, 1981).

When a market is serviced by local production it is to be expected that the fixed cost will be relatively high but the variable cost will be relatively low. It is assumed that the variable cost of local production is the same for both firms but the variable costs of exporting are different. These reflect differences in the initial location of production which affect labour costs, transport costs to the market and perhaps (in the case of a customs area, for example) the rate of *ad valorem* tariff that is applicable.

In the first part of the analysis it is assumed that each firm is committed to one particular mode of market servicing; furthermore, that the leader anticipates (correctly) that the follower will choose the same mode as himself. These assumptions are relaxed in the second part. It is shown that there is a critical level of market supply at which it is efficient to switch from exporting to local production. Below the critical level the relevant marginal cost of market supply is the marginal cost of exporting, while above this level the relevant marginal cost is the cost of local production. This creates a discontinuity in the marginal cost curve which has important implications not merely for market sourcing but for pricing and output strategy in general.

4.3 MODELLING MARKET STRUCTURE

Consider a duopoly in a particular representative market, in which firm 0 is the leader and firm 1 the follower. Let

$p \geqslant 0$ be the price of the product,
$q_j \geqslant 0$ the amount supplied by the jth firm ($j = 0, 1$),
π_j the profit earned by the jth firm,
$a > 0$ the intensity of individual product demand,
$\beta > 0$ the inverse of the price-sensitivity of individual demand,
$c_{ij} > 0$ the marginal cost of supply by the ith mode for the jth firm ($i = 0$: exports; $i = 1$: local production),
$d_{ij} \geqslant 0$ the fixed cost of entry to the market by the ith mode for the jth firm, and
$N > 0$ the number of consumers (all assumed to have identical demand).

The market demand schedule is

$$p = a - \frac{\beta}{N}(q_0 + q_1) = a - b(q_0 + q_1) \quad \text{where} \quad b = \beta/N \qquad (4.1)$$

whence the profit accruing from the ith mode is, for the jth firm,

$$\pi_j = -d_{ij} + (a - bq_k - c_{ij})q_j - bq_j^2 \qquad (k \neq j) \qquad (4.2)$$

Monopoly Firm 0 sets a monopoly price p^m by maximising profit π_0 conditional upon $q_1 = 0$. Assuming that a positive profit can be earned, the first order condition gives the familiar results

$$p^m = (a + c_{i0})/2 \qquad (4.3a)$$

$$q_0^m = (a + c_{i0})/2b \qquad (4.3b)$$

$$\pi_0^m = -d_{i0} + (a - c_{i0})^2/4b \geqslant 0 \qquad (4.3c)$$

Equation (4.3a) indicates that the leader marks up his marginal cost by a proportion $\frac{1}{2}[(a/c) - 1]$. A corollary of this is the monopolistic freight-absorption rule: when marginal cost varies just one half of the additional cost is passed on to consumers in a higher price (Greenhut and Greenhut, 1975, Norman, 1981).

Oligopoly When entry is possible the follower takes the residual market, i.e. the market that remains once the leader has sold all his output. The follower's strategy is to maximise profit π_1 conditional upon q_0. The first order condition generates the Cournot reaction function

$$q_1 = \tfrac{1}{2}[(a - c_{i1})/b - q_0] \tag{4.4}$$

which is illustrated by the line AB in Figure 4.1.

Limit pricing When entry is threatened the leader may attempt to deter the follower by setting a limit price, p^l. The price is set so that by taking the residual market the follower can at best break even, and therefore does not enter the market at all. To set a limit price the leader fixes his output at q_0^l so that max $\pi_1(q_0^l) = 0$.

Substituting the first-order condition (4.4) into the profit function (4.2) with $j = 1$ and equating the result to zero gives

$$q_0^l = (a - c_{i1})/b - 2(d_{i1}/b)^{1/2} \tag{4.5a}$$

Substituting (4.5a) into (4.1) with $q_1 = 0$ gives

$$p^l = c_{i1} + 2(bd_{i1})^{1/2} = c_{i1} + 2\left(\frac{\beta d_{i1}}{N}\right)^{1/2} \tag{4.5b}$$

Equation (4.5b) shows that the limit price is based upon the follower's cost conditions and is independent of the leader's costs. The leader marks up the follower's marginal cost by an amount which is

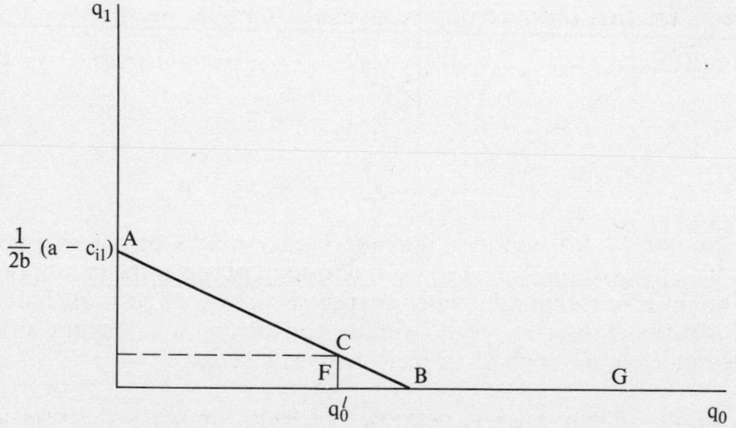

Figure 4.1 *The follower's response to the leader*

greater the lower is the price-sensitivity of demand (i.e. the higher is β), the higher is the follower's fixed cost of entering the market, and the smaller is market size (the smaller is N). The higher is the limit price, of course, the smaller is the leader's supply; thus the amount of product supplied will vary directly with the price sensitivity of demand and market size, and inversely with the follower's fixed cost of entry.

The situation is illustrated in Figures 4.1 and 4.2. The existence of a limit price truncates the operational part of the follower's response function AB at C, giving a discontinuous response function ACFG. This type of reaction function is also discussed in Dixit (1979). The same result is illustrated in Figure 4.2; DD′ is the market demand curve, so that when the leader sets an output q_0^l the residual market is only just sufficient to meet the follower's average cost, illustrated by the curve HH′, which is tangent to DD′ at J. HH′ is drawn with respect to a vertical axis translated to q_0^l. The follower, if he entered, would supply an amount $(d_{i1}/b)^{\frac{1}{2}}$, but it is assumed that he decides not to enter at all. As a result only q_0^l is supplied to the market and the price is therefore set by the leader at p^l, giving market equilibrium at E.

Alternatives to limit pricing It is often implicitly assumed that it is always better to set a limit price than to allow entry to occur, but this is incorrect. Allowing the follower into the market may be more profitable than keeping him out, provided that the leader manipu-

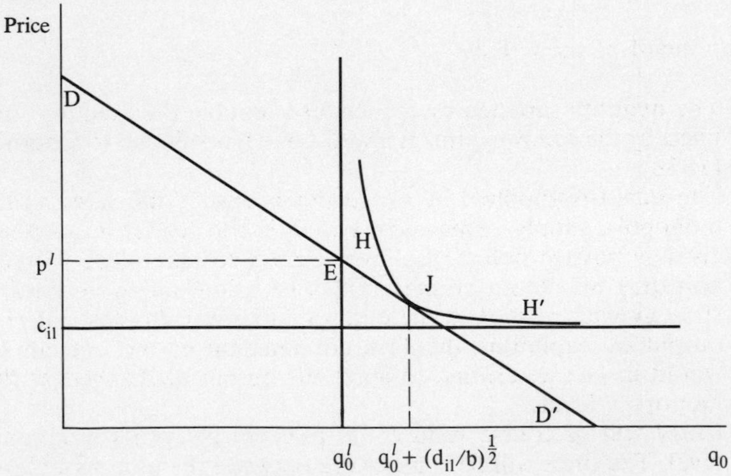

Figure 4.2 *Limit-pricing*

lates the entrant's expectations in an appropriate way. Suppose that the leader exploits the follower's Cournot response to set an entry price p^e and entry output q_0^e which maximises π_0 subject to the constraints (4.1) and (4.4). This requires the leader to supply

$$q_0^e = (a + c_{i1} - 2c_{i0})/2b \tag{4.6a}$$

to which the entrant will respond with

$$q_1^e = (a + 2c_{i0} - 3c_{i1})/4b \tag{4.6b}$$

giving an equilibrium price

$$p^e = (a + 2c_{i0} + c_{i1})/4 \tag{4.6c}$$

To interpret these results it is easiest to assume a mutual commitment to local production, in which case the marginal costs of the two producers are the same. Applying

$$c_{10} = c_{11} = c_1 < a \tag{4.7}$$

to equations (4.6) and comparing the results with (4.3) shows that

$$q_0^e = (a - c_1)/2b = q_0^m \tag{4.8a}$$

$$q_1^e = (a - c_1)/4b = q_0^e/2 \tag{4.8b}$$

$$p^e = (a + 3c_1)/4 < p^m \tag{4.8c}$$

Equations (4.8) show that:

(a) The quantity supplied by the leader is double the quantity supplied by the follower; this is a well-known result due to Cournot (1838).
(b) The quantity supplied by the leader is exactly the same as his monopoly supply. This means that if the leader follows an entirely passive policy of allowing entry to take place without adjusting his output he may in fact be following an optimising strategy with respect to the entrant. If he were to calculate his output by exploiting the Cournot reaction of the entrant he would in fact determine to leave his output unchanged at the monopoly level.
(c) Entry will of course reduce the price to below its monopoly level. The price will lie somewhere between the monopoly level and the marginal cost of production.

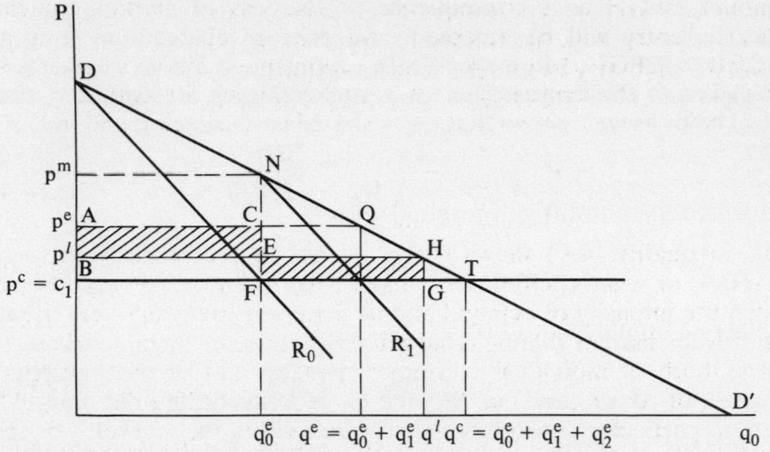

Figure 4.3 *Entry-pricing*

These results are illustrated in Figure 4.3. The leader begins with his monopoly price p^m selling an output $q_0^e = q_0^m$, set at the point where the monopoly marginal revenue curve DR_0 intersects the marginal cost curve (the horizontal line with intercept c_1). The follower faces the residual demand curve ND′ and sets his output of q_1^e where his marginal revenue curve NR_1 intersects the marginal cost curve (which by assumption is the same for both firms). Market equilibrium is at the point Q where the price is bid down to p^e. Given this price the geometry of the diagram confirms that the leader and the follower share the market in the ratio 2 : 1.

The results regarding quantities cease to apply, however, once the marginal costs of the two firms differ. If for example the follower's costs were lower than the leader's then the leader will reduce his output below the monopoly output, and the follower will increase his output, so that the market ratio will fall below 2 : 1. Conversely if the leader's costs are lower than the follower's then the ratio will rise above 2 : 1.

Accepting or deterring entry Under what conditions is it best to accept entry? Clearly, entry deterrence is always the dominant strategy if $p^l > p^e$. If, however, $p^e > p^l$, it may well be the case that profits for the leading firm will be greater if entry is allowed than if price is set to deter entry. Assume that the limit price is p^l in Figure 4.3. If the leader charges entry price p^e, his profit increases by the amount ACEB as a consequence of the higher price, but falls by amount EFGH as a consequence of the loss of market control. Clearly, entry will be accepted, and price p^e charged, so long as ACEB > EFGH. More specifically, applying equations (4.2), (4.5) and (4.6) to the inequality $\pi_0^e \geqslant \pi^l$ and assuming for simplicity that (4.7) holds as well, shows that entry should be accepted if and only if

$$\frac{d_1}{N} \leqslant [(a - c_1)/4(2 + \sqrt{2})]^2/\beta \qquad (4.9)$$

The inequality (4.9) shows that it is best to accept entry in large markets, or when the follower's fixed costs of entry are very low, or when the intensity of demand and its price sensitivity are very great. Intuitively, market sharing is more likely to arise in 'large' markets, in terms both of individual consumer demand and of the aggregate number of consumers. Further, the more sophisticated the market – and, in particular, information structures within the market – or the less appropriable the technology employed by the leading firm (Magee, 1981), i.e. the easier is imitation by followers, the more likely is it that market sharing will emerge.

If assumption (4.7) is dropped, a more complicated version of (4.9) holds, with the same qualitative conclusions. In addition, as might be expected, entry deterrence will be more (less) likely the greater (lesser) the operating cost advantage of the leading firm with respect to potential competitors.

4.4 LEADER VULNERABILITY, AND A METHOD OF OVERCOMING IT

Quitting the market So far it has been assumed that in the second stage of market evolution both limit pricing and entry pricing will at least allow the leader to break even. There is no guarantee however, that a leader who operates profitably as an unassailable monopoly can operate profitably under threat of entry. If his costs are high relative to those of the potential entrant then his optimal strategy when threatened with entry may be to cut his losses and quit the market altogether.

Once he has entered the market at the monopoly stage the leader's fixed costs of entry become sunk costs, and his decision to remain in the market depends only upon his marginal costs. Only if his follower's marginal costs are substantially lower than his own is withdrawal from the market likely to commend itself. This would be the case, for example, if the leader were sourcing the market from a more distant location than the follower, and the size of the market was not large enough to warrant local production.

Avoiding the market altogether While the fixed costs of entry cannot affect the leader's decision to withdraw from the market, they can certainly affect his decision to enter it in the first place. Although it is assumed that entry as a monopolist is profitable, the monopoly may well be a transitory one. In some markets a leader may reasonably anticipate that entry will be threatened very quickly. The returns from a short-lived monopoly may make a negligible contribution to the leader's fixed costs. In this case the fixed costs must be recovered at the second stage when the leader is constrained by threat of entry. A combination of high fixed costs and no entry constraint may make it impossible for the leader to break even. As a result he may decide not to enter the market in the first place. The follower, not having anyone to imitate, must either assume the role of leader himself or abandon his own plan to enter the market too. Since the follower is, by assumption, not so well placed to innovate the product, it seems unlikely that he will assume the leader's role. As a result the market will remain in abeyance.

The situation is illustrated in Figure 4.4. As before, the leader and follower have the same marginal costs, but now the leader's fixed costs are introduced as well. When the costs are fairly low the leader's average cost is indicated by C_1C_1. If the follower's entry cost is low, then the limit price will be low as well and the limit pricing strategy, indicated by U, may well be unprofitable; this is illustrated by the fact that C_1C_1 lies above U.

As shown, the entry-pricing strategy, which allows the leader to sell

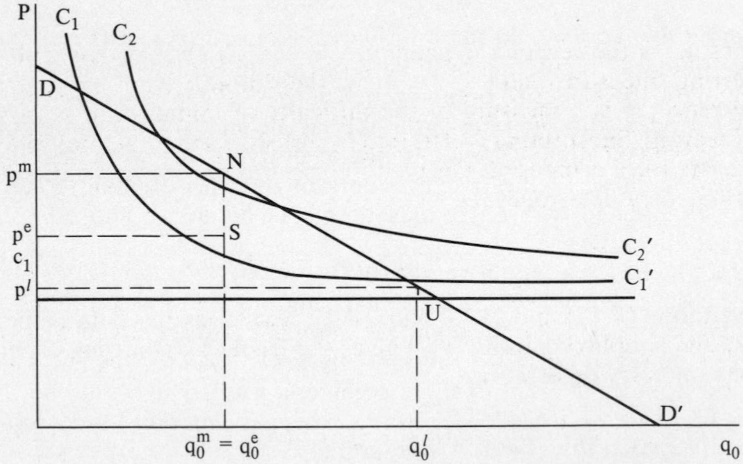

Figure 4.4 *Impact of fixed cost on the leader's profitability*

at S, is clearly preferable. If the leader's entry cost is high, however, as indicated by the average cost curve C_2C_2, then entry pricing too may be unprofitable, as indicated by the fact that C_2C_2 passes above S. Thus, although the monopoly situation, indicated by N, may well be profitable, this is insufficient to warrant entry if the monopoly is a purely transitory one.

Non-price entry deterrence It is evident that leader vulnerability arises not merely because the leader's own fixed costs are high but because they are high relative to the follower's entry costs. This suggests that if the leader could raise the follower's entry costs then limit-pricing would become more attractive. In some cases it is possible for the leader to invest in security which makes it more difficult for the follower to gain access to his knowhow. The leader's increased expenditure on security increases the follower's expenditure on imitation. Another, rather similar, strategy is for the leader to invest in a product design which it is difficult for the follower to 'reverse engineer', or for the leader to produce a range of integrated products, forcing potential imitators to produce a similar range. Strategies of this kind which raise the follower's fixed costs of entry may be termed methods of non-price entry deterrence.

The limit-pricing model is easily extended to include non-price entry deterrence. Suppose, for example, that the follower's fixed cost of entry by the mode i varies in direct proportion to the leader's initial expenditure on entry:

$$d_i = g(d_{i0} - \bar{d}_{i0}) \tag{4.10}$$

where $\bar{d}_{i0}$ is the leader's expenditure in the absence of any entry-deterring measures and $g > 1$ is the 'productivity' of entry-deterrence; it is a measure of the difficulty of imitation or reverse engineering. Substituting (4.10) into (4.5b) shows that the limit price increases (at a decreasing rate) with respect to the leader's expenditure on entry deterrence:

$$p^l = c_{i1} + 2[bg(d_{i0} - \bar{d}_{i0})]^{1/2} \tag{4.11}$$

Substituting (4.5a) and (4.11) into (4.2), maximising π_0 with respect to d_{i0} and simplifying using (4.7) gives the leader's optimising expenditure on entry-deterrence:

$$d_{i0} - \bar{d}_{i0} = [(a - c_1)/b]^2 bg/(1 + 4g)^2 \tag{4.12}$$

Equation (4.12) shows that expenditure on entry-deterrence will be greater, the greater is the size of the competitive market, $(a - c_1)/b$, the lower is the price sensitivity of demand, $1/b$, and the lower is the 'productivity' of entry-deterrence, g.

The determination of the leader's costs by (4.12) is, of course, confined to situations where limit-pricing, when augmented by entry-deterrence, dominates the alternative strategies of entry-acceptance or withdrawal from the market. Clearly, limit pricing is most likely to dominate when the productivity of entry-deterrence is high. Thus high productivity, g, makes it more likely that some entry-deterring expenditure will be made, though, as equation (4.12) indicates, the higher is the productivity the less expenditure is actually incurred. High productivity, in turn, is more likely for sophisticated technologies, or in markets in which the information systems available to potential imitators are either not particularly well developed, or afford high degrees of protection to innovating firms.

4.5 THE INTERPLAY BETWEEN PRICING STRATEGY AND MARKET SOURCING

Hitherto it has been assumed that both firms are already committed to (the same) sourcing strategy. It is apparent, however, that the least-cost sourcing strategy depends upon the volume of supplies. Local production involves higher fixed costs but lower variable costs than exporting. Assuming constant marginal costs this means that there is a critical level of sourcing

$$q^*_j = (d_{1j} - d_{0j})/(c_{0j} - c_{ij}) \qquad (4.13)$$

at which the saving on variable costs afforded by local production is just equal to the additional fixed cost incurred. Above this critical level local production is preferred, while below this level exporting is preferable.

This suggests that pricing strategy has important implications for market sourcing. For pricing strategy governs both the total volume of demand and also the allocation of the supply between leader and follower. Since pricing determines the amount supplied by each firm, it also affects the method of sourcing that the firm will choose.

Limit pricing, for example, is predicated on the leader's assumption that he will monopolise the market, while at the same time stimulating demand by setting a fairly modest price. A strategy of entry-pricing, on the other hand, means that the market will be shared; furthermore entry-pricing will only be preferred if it gives a market price above the limit price, so that the total market will be smaller than under limit-pricing. With entry-pricing both firms will source the market on a much smaller scale so that exporting is likely to be preferred to local production.

The link between pricing strategy and market sourcing involves two-way causation. For a change in sourcing strategy affects the marginal cost of market sourcing, upon which the choice of marketing strategy depends. For example, if the fixed cost of local production is fairly low then the firm may decide to assess pricing strategy on the assumption that local production will be preferred. This reduces the estimated marginal cost of market sourcing, encourages the lowering of market price and also (according to the inequality 4.9) makes limit pricing more attractive.

A full analysis of the situation would involve the simultaneous determination of prices, outputs and methods of sourcing. This is, however, a technically cumbersome exercise because of the zero-one nature of the sourcing decision. Indeed, it is not clear that such an analysis would be useful, for it is unlikely that in the early stage of entering a market a firm would have sufficient information to make its decisions in this way. It seems more likely that the leading firm will explore the market first via the export route and then evaluate the switch to local production on the assumption that existing pricing strategy and levels of supply will be sustained.

Such a 'satisficing' approach to the foreign investment decision leads to a characteristic sequence of developments. For once local production has been established, and some degree of local autonomy has been conferred, the local producer will recalculate the optimal pricing strategy on the basis of lower sourcing costs. Substituting the marginal cost of local production for the marginal cost of export sourcing will suggest a reduction of price and an expansion of output to meet the resultant increase in demand. Also the case for limit pricing will become much stronger than before. This aggressive stance by the newly-formed foreign subsidiary has often been noted, and has prompted considerable theorising. Penrose (1956), for example, developed the 'gambler's earnings' hypothesis to explain the desire of foreign managers to retain profits for expansion rather than to remit them to the parent in the way that was originally anticipated (see also Barlow and Wender, 1955). It is not suggested that the analysis above affords a complete explanation of such behaviour, but it seems likely that the factors discussed are a significant element in the subsidiary's case for autonomy in production and marketing decisions.

Local production by the leading firm may emerge not merely on the basis of cost comparisons discussed above, but also as a defensive response, or as an attempt to preempt competitors (Stobaugh *et al.*,

1976). Examination of such cases requires that profit, or 'pay-off', matrices be constructed for leading and following firms for each possible pricing strategy. A full taxonomy of all possible cases is too tedious to be presented here. One interesting case should, however, be examined.

Assume that, no matter what the sourcing strategies of leading and following firms are with respect to a particular market, the leading firm chooses not to price to deter entry, i.e. price/quantity strategy is given by equation (4.6). Further, assume that (4.7) holds if both firms choose local production, while if the export mode is chosen:

$$c_{00} = c_1 + t_0 < a \quad (t_0 > 0) \tag{4.14a}$$

$$c_{01} = c_1 + t_1 < a \quad (t_1 > 0) \tag{4.14b}$$

where t_j can be interpreted as transport costs per unit shipped by firm j from its point of production to this particular market.

Finally, assume that

$$d_{0j} = 0 \; (j = 0, 1) \tag{4.15}$$

i.e. that exporting incurs no additional fixed costs (this assumption is not crucial, but does slightly simplify subsequent analysis).

Profit matrices for the leading and following firms are then as in Table 4.1. Clearly, many possibilities may arise depending upon the parameter values. One case of particular interest is where these parameter values give rise to a prisoner's dilemma (Luce & Raiffa, 1957; Shubik, 1980). Assume for example, that the profit matrices shown in Table 4.2 apply. Given these profit matrices, it is clear that Firm 0 will choose local production: the choice of the export mode runs the risk of the following firm choosing local production. Firm 1 will then respond by local production, with the result that both firms end up as local producers although both would be better off if they exported to this market.

The parameter values for which a prisoner's dilemma is likely to arise are not particularly restrictive. It can be shown that the range of fixed costs for which such a dilemma will arise is greater in markets which are large (in either intensity of demand or aggregate demand), where price sensitivity of demand is high, and for markets which are relatively more distant from the leading firm than from the follower (i.e. for which $t_0 > t_1$).

It might be suggested that the dilemma can be resolved by collusion between the firms. If, however, this is a one-off encounter, or if the two firms are likely to encounter each other in a known limited

Table 4.1 *Profit matrices*

Matrix A: Profit of firm 0

		Market Sourcing Strategy of Firm 0	
		Export (E)	*Local Production (L)*
Market Sourcing Strategy of Firm 1	*Export (E)*	$\frac{1}{8b}(a - c_1 - 2t_0 + t_1)^2$	$-d_{10} + \frac{1}{8b}(a - c_1 + t_1)^2$
	Local Production (L)	$\frac{1}{8b}(a - c_1 - 2t_0)^2$	$-d_{10} + \frac{1}{8b}(a - c_1)^2$

Matrix B: Profit of firm 1

		Market Sourcing Strategy of Firm 0	
		Export (E)	*Local Production (L)*
Market Sourcing Strategy of Firm 1	*Export (E)*	$\frac{1}{16b}(a - c_1 + 2t_0 - 3t_1)^2$	$\frac{1}{16b}(a - c_1 + 2t_0)^2$
	Local Production (L)	$-d_{11} + \frac{1}{16b}(a - c_1 + 2t_0)^2$	$-d_{11} + \frac{1}{16b}(a - c_1)^2$

Table 4.2 *Profit matrices: a numerical example*

Profit of firm 0

$$\begin{array}{c} \\ E \\ L \end{array}\begin{array}{c} \begin{array}{cc} E & L \end{array} \\ \begin{pmatrix} 10 & 16 \\ 2 & 5 \end{pmatrix} \end{array}$$

Profit of firm 1

$$\begin{array}{c} \\ E \\ L \end{array}\begin{array}{c} \begin{array}{cc} E & L \end{array} \\ \begin{pmatrix} 10 & 2 \\ 15 & 5 \end{pmatrix} \end{array}$$

number of markets, the following firm will always gain from a 'double-cross' and the dilemma remains (Luce & Raiffa, 1957, p. 97).

4.6 GLOBAL STRATEGY

In the preceding analysis it has been assumed that it is always the leader that 'endogenises' the follower's response in making strategic decisions, and that the follower responds in the way predicted. This approach is not unreasonable in the context of a once-for-all encounter between the two rivals. But, as noted earlier, the analysis relates to just one of many regional markets for the same product. It is reasonable to suppose, therefore, that the encounter will be repeated many times in different regions. Following the product cycle approach, the initial encounters will be in the markets of the mature or developed countries and the later encounters in the markets of the newly industrialising countries.

In a sequence of encounters the follower has an opportunity to influence the expectations of the leader in order to modify the leader's behaviour in the next encounter. It may benefit the follower to behave in an unexpected – and therefore apparently irrational – way in the early encounters in order to achieve better results in the later ones. Any short-term costs incurred in the early encounters may be repaid from longer-term gains accruing from the later encounters.

Suppose, for example, that the leader were to base his expectation of the follower's output upon the follower's actual output in the previous encounter. In the first encounter, for which there is no precedent, the leader anticipates a Cournot response from the follower. But if the follower realises how the leader's expectations are formed, and seeks to exploit his knowledge, then the follower's response in the first encounter will not be the one that the leader anticipates. His confidence in his own expectations having been shaken, the leader may resort to a much simpler precept, namely to act as though the follower will supply the same output in the next encounter as he has done in the present one.

An extension of the model

Consider a sequence of regional markets, indexed n = 1, 2, . . . , N, in each of which the leader innovates a local variant of a new product and the follower imitates him. (The home market, in which both firms are supposed to be already producing, is once again excluded from the analysis.) For simplicity it is assumed that each regional market has the same demand and cost conditions and that the costs of the two firms are identical. It is also assumed that it is difficult for the leader to deter entry – so that entry-pricing is used throughout.

In each market, after the first, the leader sets his output by maximising profit π_{0n} on the assumption that the follower's output q_{1n} will be equal to his previous output q_{1n-1}. This implies that the leader now exhibits a lagged Cournot response to the follower's output:

$$q_{0n} = \tfrac{1}{2}[(a - c_1)/b - q_{1n-1}] \qquad (4.14)$$

The response function (4.14) is illustrated by the line XY in Figure 4.5.

When setting q_{1n} the follower must take account of both the impact of q_{1n} on his current profit, given that the leader's current output q_{0n} has already been set, and its impact on his future profit, given that q_{1n} will influence q_{0n+1} and hence affect π_{1n+1}.

If the follower were very sophisticated he would recognise the importance of choosing his strategies for all the regional markets simultaneously. This is because to exploit the leader's predictability fully the follower must allow for the fact that the output he sets in any one market will, through the leader's response, affect the relative profitability of his own alternative output strategies in subsequent markets. Hence the repercussions of his current output decision are felt in all the markets subsequently entered.

It is, however, unreasonable to assume that the follower will be quite so sophisticated as this. In addition, there is no reason to believe that either follower or leader has any information on the likely number of potential future encounters the firms will have. It adds realism to the analysis – and simplifies the model too – if it is assumed that the follower expects his output in the next market to be the same as in the present market. Thus as each new market is entered he plans his output strategy anew on the assumption that the impact of his current output decision will not spill over to influence his output decisions in subsequent markets.

When the follower adopts this approach, his actual output in any

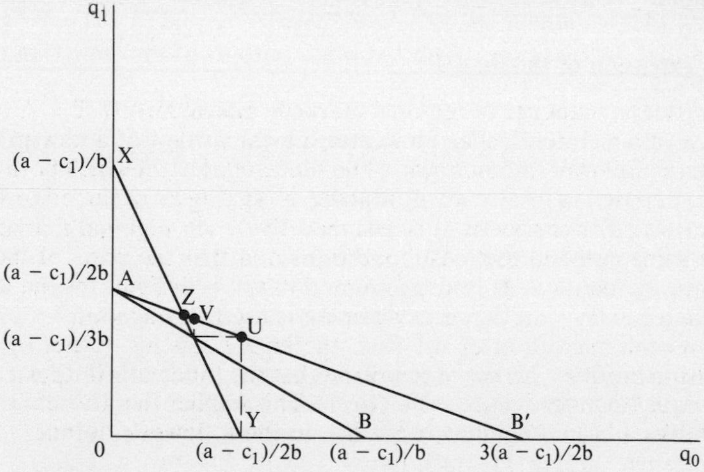

Figure 4.5 *The sequence of outputs in global rivalry*

market will not normally agree with the output he anticipated when planning his strategy for the previous market. It is assumed, however, that the follower either fails to learn from experience that his anticipations are incorrect, or that he does not consider that the benefits of more sophisticated planning outweigh the additional computational costs involved.

Maximising the undiscounted sum of present and future profit with respect to $q_{1n+1} = q_{1n}$ and setting $q_{1n+1} = q_{1n}$ gives the follower's decision rule:

$$q_{1n} = (a - c_1)/2b - q_{0n}/3 \qquad (4.15)$$

The response function (4.15) is illustrated by the line AB′ in Figure 4.5. Comparing (4.15) with the original response function AB derived from (4.4) shows that for any current output of the leader the follower's current output is larger than before. This is because the losses incurred by the follower in raising his current output are now outweighed by the gains from the reduction induced in the leader's output in the next market that is entered. The only circumstances under which the response function (4.4) remains relevant are when the final market has been entered, because then there is no point in the follower attempting to influence the leader's expectations.

The leader's supply to the first market is determined by the entry pricing rule (4.6a); then equations (4.6a), (4.14) and (4.15) together determine the entire sequence of outputs and market shares until the final market is reached, when the follower switches to the original response (4.4). If there were an infinite sequence of markets then a steady state would be reached; setting $q_{1n+1} = q_{1n}$ in (4.14) and (4.15) and solving shows that the steady state outputs of the leader and the follower are respectively

$$q_0^s = 0.3(a - c_1)/b \qquad (4.16a)$$

$$q_1^s = 0.4(a - c_1)/b \qquad (4.16b)$$

whence from (4.1) the steady state price is

$$p^s = 0.3a + 0.7c_1 \qquad (4.16c)$$

The sequence of outputs generated by this process is illustrated by the path UVZ in Figure 4.5. The leader begins, just as before, by supplying $(a - c_1)/2b$ units in the first market, which is one half of the competitive supply. He anticipates that the follower will supply half his own amount, but in fact the follower supplies $(a - c_1)/3b$ units, 50 per cent more than expected. When the second market is entered the leader reduces his output to $(a - c_1)/3b$ units, a reduction of one-third on the previous level, and the follower takes the opportunity to increase his output slightly. As a result the output combination changes from U to V. The geometry of the figure indicates that the total market supply is lower than before. This process of response and counter-response is stable, and converges upon the output combination Z.

Comparing the outputs and prices in equations (4.16) with those in equations (4.8) shows that the tactical behaviour of the follower substantially improves his market share (it rises immediately from 33 per cent to 40 per cent and increases further in subsequent markets towards a limit of 57 per cent). Although this tactical behaviour increases the total market supply in the first instance, it eventually reduces it. This has the interesting implication that in the first foreign market to be entered the follower's tactical behaviour favours consumers by increasing supplies and hence reducing the product price, but in the markets entered later these tactics damage consumers' interests by discouraging the leader from offering large supplies. The follower makes good some of this shortfall, but by no means all of it.

The analysis goes some way toward explaining the 'follow the leader' tactic which seems to be common in the early stages of foreign investment. It is not always easy to see why export-substituting foreign investment by the leading firm in an industry should induce similar investment by rival firms in the same region. In principle the leader should be able to take such a large share of the local market that he can discourage rival firms from seeking to produce locally as well. Yet rivals do not seem to be so easily discouraged, but appear willing to follow the leader even if substantial excess capacity results. In terms of the theory developed above, the leader's decision to produce abroad may be interpreted as a signal to his rivals that he plans to pursue an aggressive marketing strategy – he plans to produce abroad only because he intends to generate a large output which will cover the additional fixed cost of production. The rival's tactic is to signal in reply that he too will increase his output. He commits himself to produce abroad, even if this involves 'spoiling the market' for both of them, because he hopes to discourage the leader from a similarly aggressive stance in the future.

It is worth noting that a similar set of behavioural responses will arise once the analysis of the prisoner's dilemma in Section 4.5 is placed in this dynamic context. As was indicated in Section 4.5, if the firms know the number of markets in which they will be in competition, no resolution of the dilemma presents itself. But it is highly unlikely that such information will be available to the two firms: no 'last' market will be identifiable. In such circumstances, the advantages of a 'double cross' are much less clear-cut, and tacit or explicit market sharing is much more likely to emerge.

No matter which of these two approaches is adopted, once the initial sparring is over, the two rivals will settle down into a more stable oligopolistic equilibrium. The theory predicts that the leader will opt less frequently for foreign investment, and the follower will become less committed to match the leader's every move as more markets are entered and fewer markets remain to be tapped. According to the product cycle, the earliest markets to be entered will be those of the mature economies, and these economies will be the ones to benefit from the foreign investment and from the low prices resulting from excess capacity. The later markets will be those of the newly industrialising countries. Not only will these countries receive the product later, but their markets are less likely to be serviced by local production, and their consumers are likely to have to pay higher prices.

4.7 SUMMARY AND IMPLICATIONS FOR FUTURE RESEARCH

This chapter has analysed the interplay between oligopolistic pricing and market sourcing decisions in the context both of a single 'representative' regional market, and in a global context where regional markets are entered sequentially. It has been shown that the often paradoxical behaviour displayed by oligopolistic foreign investors can be explained quite simply by profit maximisation. There is no need to invoke models of managerial discretion or psychological theories of decision-making to account for the 'follow the leader' tactics of the parent firms or for the expansionist pressures generated by managers of foreign subsidiaries.

The analytical techniques used in this chapter are very powerful and are capable of much wider application. The discussion in this chapter has touched upon only a few of the many issues in oligopoly that can be examined using these techniques. Notwithstanding these limited terms of reference, however, some important conclusions have emerged.

Perhaps the most significant is the way that oligopolistic rivalry favours the countries whose markets are the first to be entered. For obvious reasons these markets tend to be the largest markets, which means the markets of the wealthiest countries and those with the greatest social and cultural affinity with the innovating country. Not only are these markets the easiest to enter but they also provide the most favourable climate for local production. Newly industrialising countries typically have much smaller markets and exhibit significant cultural dissimilarities, so that they are the last to be entered, and are less likely to be entered through local production. The very fact that they are the last to be entered means that they are most susceptible to oligopolistic restrictions of supply. This restriction of supply further inhibits local production. Because of this, the newly industrialising countries will have to offer much larger factor cost savings to attract local production than would otherwise have been the case.

5 Changes in the level and structure of international production: the last one hundred years

JOHN H. DUNNING

5.1 INTRODUCTION

Alongside advances in the theory of foreign direct investment and the multinational enterprise, the last two decades have seen the emergence of a wealth of new descriptive material about the activities of corporations outside their national boundaries in which they have a controlling equity stake.[1] This material ranges from macro-statistical data on the stock or flow of foreign direct investment in, or between nation states, through *ad hoc* country and sectoral case studies, to individual business histories and company profiles. Between them, these new sources of information enable us to piece together a much more comprehensive and reliable picture of the growth and pattern of international production than was thought possible even fifteen years ago. Certainly, it is difficult to think of any branch of economics or business studies which has generated so much interest, and caused so many books, articles, reports and papers to be written since 1960, as that of the MNE.

There is, however, one major snag with much of the published data. That is that they are rarely directly comparable with each other. Moreover, some of the historical facts a first-year student reading a course in international business may reasonably expect to be told are just not available. We still have only a rough idea of the number of MNEs operating in 1914 or the value of their foreign investments at that time; and even today, very few countries publish the kind of information which scholars need to evaluate properly either the causes or the effects of international production. Thus, to present a statistical portrait of the growth of MNE activity, which might enable us to test our new theories – or even the old ones – in any rigorous fashion, is not possible. Such testing must, at present, be largely confined to cross-sectional industry, firm or country data; and, certainly in the last twenty years, econometric studies of this kind have considerably enriched our understanding about the determinants of FDI.[2] But the most one can realistically expect from a broad overview of the kind presented in this chapter is an interpretation of major events, set within the framework, if not making use of the technical apparatus of recent theoretical advances. This is what the following pages seek to do.

The discussion proceeds in the following way. Section 5.2 reviews the main facts about the growth of international production over four periods in the last century, viz. from around 1870 to 1914, 1919 to 1939, 1945 to the mid-1960s, and the mid-1960s to the late 1970s. This section presents some new statistical estimates of the FDI stock in 1914, 1938, 1960, 1971 and 1978. Sections 5.3 to 5.5 attempt to explain and interpret these data, using the kind of conceptual framework favoured particularly by economists of the University of Reading; and a final section attempts to bring these strands of thought together.

5.2 THE FOREIGN ACTIVITIES OF FIRMS

(a) 1870–1914

Studies published in the last twenty or so years suggest that earlier scholars considerably underestimated the role of the MNE as an entrepreneur and as a transfer of intangible assets in the forty years prior to the First World War. By assembling widely disparate estimates of both the inward and the outward direct capital stake of countries, we can estimate that, by 1914, at least $14 billion had been invested in enterprises or branch plants in which either a single or a group of non-resident investors owned a majority or substantial minority equity interest, or which were owned or controlled by first generation expatriates who had earlier migrated.[3] This amount represented about 35 per cent of the estimated total long-term international debt at that time; a ratio considerably higher than was thought until fairly recently and, in relation to the national income of most capital-exporting countries, more significant than at any time before or since. There is also little doubt that, from the viewpoint of some home and host countries, FDI, both as a channel for the transfer of resources between countries, and as a means of controlling the use of these and complementary local inputs, played a no less important role than it has done since the mid-1950s, and a far greater one than it did in the inter-war period. There is also little doubt that several economies, particularly developing countries, and some sectors, particularly capital-intensive primary product and technology-intensive manufacturing sectors, were dominated either by affiliates of MNEs, or by foreign entrepreneurs who both financed these activities and organised the supply of technology and management for them. Indeed, the territorial compass of FDI was probably wider than it has been for most of the last thirty-five years; Eastern Europe and China, for example, were both attractive to Western businessmen in the years preceding the First World War, and there were few controls exerted on investment flows, or on the scope of the activities of foreign capitalists.

While for the first three-quarters of the nineteenth century, direct capital exports[4] mainly comprised expatriate investment or finance raised in the home country by corporations or individual entrepreneurs to purchase a controlling equity interest in a foreign company,[5] the subsequent forty years saw the infancy and adolescence of the type of activity which mainly dominates today, viz. the setting up of foreign branches by enterprises already operating in their home countries. This latter thrust began around the middle of the nineteenth century,[6] gathered pace after 1875, and, by 1914 had become firmly established as a vehicle of international economic involvement.

As revealed in Table 5.1, the UK was, by far and away, the largest foreign capital stake holder in 1914, with the USA some way behind. However, even at that time, US direct investments were more directed to growth sectors, and a much larger proportion represented the activities of affiliates of MNEs rather than absentee equity investment by individuals or companies.[7] Such country-specific differences were reflected in the structure of resource endowments, institutional mechanisms and existing international economic involvement. Thus, while Europe had accumulated a pool of marketable venture capital, entrepreneurship and management expertise, and was already a major portfolio capital exporter, the USA with none of this background was building a strong comparative advantage in corporate technology – management skills, which were often best exploited within the enterprises generating them. Table 5.1 also reveals that, in 1914, the German and French capital stakes were about the same; and that there were some Russian, Canadian and Japanese investments.

Table 5.2 shows that about three-fifths of the foreign capital stake in 1914 was directed to today's developing countries; but taking a contemporary definition of such countries to include all areas outside Europe and the USA, the figure rises to more than four-fifths. The

Table 5.1 *Estimated stock of accumulated foreign direct investment by country of origin 1914–78*

	1914		1938		1960		1971		1978	
	$m	%	$m	%	$bn	%	$bn	%	$bn	%
Developed Countries	14302	100.0	26350	100.0	66.0	99.0	168.1	97.7	380.3	96.8
North America										
USA	2652	18.5	7300	27.7	32.8	49.2	82.8	48.1	162.7	41.4
Canada	150	1.0	700	2.7	2.5	3.8	6.5	3.8	13.6	3.5
Western Europe										
UK	6500	45.5	10500	39.8	10.8	16.2	23.7	13.8	50.7	12.9
Germany	1500	10.5	350	1.3	0.8	1.2	7.3	4.2	28.6	7.3
France	1750	12.2	2500	9.5	4.1	6.1	7.3	4.2	14.9	3.8
Belgium					1.3	1.9	2.4	1.4	5.4	1.4
Italy, Netherlands, Sweden, Switzerland (combined)	1250	8.7	3500	13.3						
Italy					1.1	1.6	3.0	1.7	5.4	1.4
Netherlands					7.0	10.5	13.8	8.0	28.4	7.2
Sweden					0.4	0.6	2.4	1.4	6.0	1.5
Switzerland					2.0	3.0	9.5	5.5	27.8	7.1
Other Developed Countries										
Russia	300	2.1	450	1.7	—	—	—	—	—	—
Japan	20	0.1	750	2.8	0.5	0.7	4.4	2.6	26.8	6.8
Australia, New Zealand, South Africa	180	1.3	300	1.1	1.5	2.2	2.5	1.4	4.8	1.2
Other	neg	neg	neg	neg	1.2	1.8	2.5	1.4	5.2	1.3
Developing Countries	neg	neg	neg	neg	0.7	1.0	4.0	2.3	12.5	3.2
TOTAL	14302	100.0	26350	100.0	66.7	100.0	172.1	100.0	392.8	100.0

Table 5.2 *Estimated stock of accumulated foreign direct investment by recipient country or area*

	1914		*1938*		*1960*		*1971*		*1978*	
	$m	%	*$m*	%	*$bn*	%	*$bn*	%	*$bn*	%
Developed Countries	5235	37.2	8346	34.3	36.7	67.3	108.4	65.2	251.7	69.6
North America										
USA	1450	10.3	1800	7.4	7.6	13.9	13.9	8.4	42.4	11.7
Canada	800	5.7	2296	9.4	12.9	23.7	27.9	16.8	43.2	11.9
Europe										
Western Europe:	1100	7.8	1800	7.4	12.5	22.9	47.4	28.5	136.2	37.7
of which UK	(200)	(1.4)	(700)	(2.9)	(5.0)	(9.2)	(13.4)	(8.1)	(32.5)	(9.0)
Other European:	1400	9.9	400	1.6	neg	neg	neg	neg	neg	neg
of which Russia	(1000)	(7.1)	—	—	—	—	—	—	—	—
Australasia and South Africa	450	3.2	1950	8.0	3.6	6.6	16.7	10.0	23.9	6.6
Japan	35	0.2	100	0.4	0.1	0.2	2.5	1.5	6.0	1.7
Developing Countries	8850	62.8	15969	65.7	17.6	32.3	51.4	30.9	100.4	27.8
Latin America	4600	32.7	7481	30.8	8.5	15.6	29.6	17.8	52.5	14.5
Africa	900	6.4	1799	7.4	3.0	5.5	8.8	5.3	11.1	3.1
Asia	2950	20.9	6068	25.0	4.1	7.5	7.8	4.7	25.2	7.0
of which: China	(1100)	(7.8)	(1400)	(5.8)	(neg)	(neg)	(neg)	(neg)	(neg)	(neg)
India and Ceylon	(450)	(3.2)	(1359)	(5.6)	(1.1)	(2.0)	(1.5)	(0.9)	(2.5)	(0.7)
Southern Europe	400	2.8	621	2.6	0.5	0.9	1.7	1.0	3.4	0.9
Middle East					1.5	2.8	3.5	2.1	8.2	2.3
International and Unallocated	neg	neg	n.a.	n.a.	n.a.	n.a.	6.5	3.9	9.5	2.6
TOTAL	14085	100.0	24315	100.0	54.5	100.0	166.3	100.0	361.6	100.0

Sources of Tables 5.1 and 5.2:

The data contained in these tables have been derived from a large number of sources but the main ones have been as follows:

1914 Allen and Donnithorne (China and Japan, 1954), Bagchi (India, 1972), Callis (South East Asia, 1942), Frankel, S. H. (Africa, 1938), Hou (China, 1965), Houston and Dunning (UK, 1976), Lewis (various 1938, 1945), McKay (Russia, 1970), Pamuk (Ottoman Empire, 1981), Paterson (Canada 1976), Rippy (Latin America, 1959), Svedberg (various, 1978).
1938 Allen and Donnithorne (China and Japan, 1954), Bagchi (India, 1972), Callis (South East Asia, 1942), Conan (Sterling Area, 1960), Hou (China, 1965), Lewis (various, 1938, 1945), Svedberg (various data collected by him, 1978), Teichova (East Europe, 1974), United Nations (1949).
1960 Various government publications are cited in United Nations (UNCTC) (1981) and especially those of the United States (Department of Commerce), United Kingdom (Department of Trade), and Canada (Dominion Bureau of Statistics). See also Conan (Sterling Area, 1960) and Kidron (India, 1965).
1971 OECD (various dates), United Nations (UNCTC) (1978), (1981) and various government publications as cited therein.
1978 OECD (various dates), United Nations (UNCTC) (1978), (1981).

distribution among recipient nations was quite diffused, with the combined Russian and Chinese share exceeding that of Western Europe and only slightly less than that of North America. About 55 per cent of the total capital stake was accounted for by the primary product sector, 20 per cent by railroads, 15 per cent by manufacturing activities, 10 per cent by trade and distribution and the balance by public utilities, banking and the like. The manufacturing investments, which were largely oriented towards local markets,[8] were mainly concentrated in Europe, the USA, the UK Dominions and Russia; while, apart from iron ore, coal and bauxite, almost all mineral investments were located in the British Empire or in developing countries.

Of especial significance in this era were the raw material and agricultural investments; this was the heyday of the plantations, e.g. rubber, tea, coffee and cocoa; of cattle raising and meat processing, e.g. in the USA and Argentina; and of the emergence of the vertically integrated MNE in tropical fruits, sugar and tobacco. Indeed apart, perhaps, from some transnational railroad activity in Europe and Latin America, it was in the agricultural sector, more than any other, where the international hierarchical organisation first made itself felt, particularly in economies whose prosperity rested mainly on a single cash crop, the production and marketing of which was controlled by a few (and sometimes only one) foreign companies, e.g. Cuba (sugar), Costa Rica (bananas), Ceylon (tea) and Liberia (rubber).[9]

Even in those early days, there were distinct geographical and industrial patterns of FDI which varied with the home country of the investor. Some details of the location of manufacturing subsidiaries of 187 and 226 non-US based MNEs which existed in 1968 or 1971 are given in Table 5.3.[10] Language, cultural, political and trading ties, as well as geographical distance, played a more important role than they do today. Thus, 72 per cent of US investment was in other parts of the American continent; while there was a strong colonial content in British, French and Belgian involvement in developing countries (Svedberg, 1981). For the most part, French and German manufac-

Table 5.3 *Percentage Breakdown of Number of Manufacturing Subsidiaries of MNEs by Country of Location*

(a) Subsidiaries Established pre-1914

	US Based MNEs	*UK Based MNEs*	*Continental European Based MNEs*
Developed Countries	*87.7*	*73.7*	*81.0*
North America	27.0	15.3	6.6
of which: USA	—	3.3	5.4
Canada	27.0	15.0	1.2
Europe	57.5	41.7	73.2
of which:			
Western Europe	51.7	21.6	61.8
Northern Europe	5.8	11.7	5.4
Southern Europe	0.0	8.4	6.0
Australia and New Zealand	1.6	8.4	0.6
Japan	0.8	3.3	0.0
South Africa	0.8	5.0	0.6
Developing Countries	*12.2*	*26.3*	*19.0*
Latin America	8.1	16.2	1.2
of which: Mexico	0.0	1.7	0.0
Brazil	2.5	1.7	0.0
Middle East	4.1	3.3	15.4
Africa (other than South Africa)	0.0	3.4	0.6
Asia	0.0	3.4	1.8
of which: India	0.0	1.7	0.0
TOTAL	100.0	100.0	100.0
Number of Subsidiaries	122	60	167

Source: Compiled from data first published in Vaupel and Curhan (1974)

turing investments were sited elsewhere in Europe, while UK firms accounted for the great bulk of capital exports to the British empire outside Canada.

However, of the home countries, the UK was, perhaps, the most cosmopolitan foreign investor; *inter alia*, this reflected the diversity of her overseas possessions, her earlier technological lead and her established trading links. Her initial industrial investments were no less broadly based although, by 1914, UK MNE manufacturing activity was strongly oriented towards the production of consumer goods and heavy engineering equipment. The USA, by contrast, was developing a comparative investment advantage in the newer technology-intensive industries and in those supplying standardised products and/or consumer goods with a high income-elasticity of demand; while the Germans – as in trade – led the world in chemical investments.[11]

The pattern of involvement by the leading capital exporters in resource-based sectors was much the same, though in different territories. However, there were some exceptions, which reflected differences in consumer tastes and distance of markets; for example, whereas the US MNEs dominated tropical fruit production, UK MNEs owned most of the foreign tea plantations. While US MNEs probably pursued a more systematic policy of vertical integration, there was, nevertheless, some backward integration by UK manufacturing companies to secure supplies of raw materials, e.g. by Cadbury in cocoa, Lever in vegetable oils, Dunlop in rubber. Trade and service investments followed the main commercial arteries of the home countries.

(b) 1918–38

The First World War and the years which followed saw several changes in the level, form and structure of international production. The war itself caused several European belligerents to sell some of their pre-war investments, while subsequent political upheaval and boundary changes further reduced intra-Continental European corporate activity, and eliminated it altogether from Russia. Only the USA remained fairly unscathed by these events but she, along with other countries, subsequently suffered from the collapse of international capital markets in the late 1920s and early 1930s. Nevertheless, because her foreign investments largely took the form of branch plant activities by MNEs, and were directed to sectors supplying products with an above income-elasticity of demand, her share of the world capital stock rose from 18.5 per cent in 1914 to 27.7 per cent in 1938.

Overall, as Table 5.1 shows, the international capital stake rose quite substantially in the inter-war years.[12] There were also some changes in its geographical distribution; these are illustrated in Table 5.4, the data for which are derived from a similar source to those contained in Table 5.3.[13] In spite of some sizeable West European investments in Central Europe (Teichova, 1974),[14] the Americas, north and south of the USA, continued to attract more than

Table 5.4 *Percentage Breakdown of Number of Manufacturing Subsidiaries of MNEs by Country of Location*

(b) Subsidiaries Established 1920–38

	US Based MNEs	*UK Based MNEs*	*Continental European Based MNEs*
Developed Countries	*78.0*	*71.5*	*74.4*
North America	24.9	12.4	9.7
of which: USA	—	5.0	9.4
Canada	24.9	7.4	0.3
Europe	43.2	39.2	61.7
of which: Western Europe	38.4	29.5	47.6
Northern Europe	2.2	6.9	5.8
Southern Europe	2.6	2.8	8.3
Australia and New Zealand	6.2	15.7	1.9
Japan	0.8	—	1.1
South Africa	2.9	4.2	0.0
Developing Countries	*22.0*	*28.5*	*25.7*
Latin America	17.3	9.2	8.6
of which: Mexico	4.2	—	0.6
Brazil	2.6	1.8	2.8
Africa (other than South Africa)	—	5.1	1.9
Asia	3.2	11.0	3.0
of which: India	0.8	6.0	1.1
Middle East	1.5	3.2	11.3
TOTAL	100.0	100.0	100.0
Number of Subsidiaries	614	217	361

Source: Compiled from data first published in Vaupel and Curhan (1974)

two-thirds of the US direct investment stake; the role of intra-European and US participation in Europe fell in the 1920s and recovered somewhat in the 1930s, as did European investments in the USA. There was also some retrenchment of European economic involvement in Latin America – particularly in the railroad sector; this was partly compensated by a slight increase in the export of capital to the UK Dominions and, prior to the Sino–Japanese War, a sharp rise in Western business activity in China (Hou, 1965).

There was also quite a lot of new MNE participation in the developing world in the inter-war years; this included new oil investments in the Mexican gulf, the Dutch East Indies, and the Middle East; copper and iron ore in Africa; bauxite in Dutch and British Guyana; nitrate in Chile; precious metals in South Africa and, perhaps most noteworthy of all, non-ferrous metals in South America. Indeed, in 1929, two experts on mining observed that 'the bulk of productive mineral resources of South America are owned by American interests' (quoted by Wilkins, 1974a, p. 106). Outside the mineral sector, the growing industrial demand for rubber led both US and European manufacturers to invest in plantations in Liberia, Malaysia and Dutch East Indies; while rising real incomes at home prompted a further flurry of activity by MNEs in sugar, tropical fruit and tobacco. There was also a sizeable expansion of public utility investments in Latin America by US firms. Both US and UK MNEs extended their foreign sales and marketing ventures into production in these years.

Yet though the number of new subsidiaries set up by MNEs continued to rise throughout the period, it was only in the 1930s that the *value* of the direct capital stake exceeded its pre-war figure. During this period, investments by Continental European firms went mainly to other parts of Europe and the USA, while US firms were strongly oriented to South America, Canada and the larger European countries.[15] The first four Japanese manufacturing affiliates of the largest Japanese MNEs existing in 1970 were set up between 1920 and 1938 (Vaupel and Curhan, 1974).

(c) 1939–60

If the inter-war years witnessed a deceleration in the expansion of international business, the thirty-five years since the end of the Second World War have been ones of almost uninterrupted growth. The period may be conveniently divided into two phases. The first, up to around 1960, was one in which the USA dominated the international investment scene; of the increase in both the capital stake since 1938 and the number of new manufacturing subsidiaries (covered by the Vaupel and Curhan, 1974, study), the USA accounted for about two-thirds. The second, spanning the following two decades, witnessed the increasingly important role of first European, then Japanese and finally some Third World countries as international direct investors. Between 1960 and 1978, of the $318 billion increase in the world direct capital stake, the USA accounted for 48 per cent and West Germany and Japan for 18 per cent; between 1971 and 1978 the respective ratios were 46 per cent and 22 per cent.[16]

The effect of the Second World War was similar to that of its predecessor, in that each of the main European belligerents was forced to divest many of its foreign assets; however, unlike the first war, the second generated major technological advances, while its aftermath produced an international economic and political climate particularly favourable to foreign business activities. Also, it was not too long before the UK and the leading Continental European nations, apart from West Germany, began to renew their foreign investments. By 1960, for example, the French and Dutch capital involvement had more than matched its pre-war level.

As a percentage of both world output and trade, the international direct investment stake rose modestly between 1938 and 1960. During this period, there was a continuation of the pre-war trend for the MNEs to favour developed countries for new venture activity. In 1914, something like two-thirds of the capital stake was directed to developing countries; by 1938 this had fallen to 55 per cent, and by 1960 it was nearer 40 per cent. Partly, this reflected another major structural change, viz. the increased interest shown in market- *vis à vis* supply-oriented investments, which was designed to overcome trade barriers of one kind or another. In 1960, about 35 per cent of the US and UK accumulated investment was in manufacturing, compared with about 25 per cent in 1938 and 15 per cent in 1914. By contrast, interest in agricultural and public utility activities declined markedly, while – taken as a whole – mining investments recorded about average rates of growth. Yet, some of these latter, notably those made by UK and US MNEs in non-ferrous metals, e.g. copper in Chile and Peru, bauxite in the Caribbean etc. and oil in the Persian gulf, grew very rapidly.

Although this was a period which saw the start of enforced divestment or nationalisation of some primary product investments and the setting up of international producers' cartels, it was not until the 1960s that the thrust of these expressions of host country economic power was fully revealed.[17] Apart from state-owned oil MNEs, European firms were not very active in raw material exploration; the major capital exporters in the 1950s, viz. the Netherlands, France and Switzerland, preferred to invest in manufacturing, trade and service activities (including finance and insurance). As in the inter-war years, UK MNEs directed their attention mainly towards Commonwealth countries. Indeed, such countries increased their share of the total capital stake from around one-half in the 1930s to over 70 per cent in 1960. During the early post-war period, first South Africa and Australia and then Canada attracted the bulk of new UK direct investment; contrast this pattern with that of US MNEs where the focus of interest was strongly directed to Canada and Western Europe. Some details are set out in Table 5.5.[18]

Unfortunately for this, as for other periods, there are no comprehensive statistics on the entry or exit of MNEs; it is, therefore, not possible to estimate how much of the growth of the international capital stake was accounted for by firms existing at the beginning of the period and how much by new entrants. Even the Harvard data (Vaupel and Curhan, 1974) do not distinguish between subsidiaries

Table 5.5 *Percentage Breakdown of Number of Manufacturing Subsidiaries of MNEs by Country of Location*

(c) Subsidiaries Established 1946–61

	US Based MNEs	*UK Based MNEs*	*Continental European Based MNEs*	*Japanese Based MNEs*
Developed Countries	*63.2*	*79.5*	*65.4*	*0.7*
North America:	14.9	15.9	16.0	0.2
of which: USA	—	3.2	10.7	0.2
Canada	14.9	12.7	5.3	—
Europe	35.9	26.6	41.8	0.5
Japan	2.6	0.3	1.5	—
Australasia and South Africa	9.8	36.7	6.1	0.0
Developing Countries	*36.8*	*20.5*	*34.6*	*99.3*
Middle East	1.4	2.6	3.0	0.6
Africa	1.4	4.6	6.6	0.3
Asia	3.4	6.9	5.8	66.1
Latin America	30.6	6.4	19.2	32.3
TOTAL	100	100	100	100
Number of Subsidiaries	2009	684	609	65

Source: Compiled from data first published in Vaupel and Curhan (1974)

set up by established MNEs and new entrants; all that they tell us is how many affiliates the 413 MNEs studied had at different periods of time. However from these and related facts two things seem perfectly clear. First, over that part of the last century for which they had been operating as MNEs, something like 800 enterprises had set up affiliates in at least 10 countries. But second, of the total number of MNEs in 1973, nearly one-half operated only in one country and 70 per cent in three or less (Commission of the European Communities, 1976). These figures, coupled with other knowledge about the post-war entry of new Japanese MNEs[19] and of some high-technology MNEs from the USA and Europe, suggest that any explanation of international production must deal with the question 'Why is the number of MNEs growing?' as well as 'Why do MNEs grow?'

Two other points might be made about this era of international business expansion. First, the proportion of new subsidiaries of the MNEs surveyed by Vaupel and Curhan (1974), which were established by green field ventures (as compared with acquisition, merger, or reorganisation) fell from 55 per cent in 1946–52 to 48 per cent in 1959–61; the corresponding figures for the pre-1914 period and 1919–39 were 67 per cent and 58 per cent respectively. Second, in the case of both US and non-US based MNEs, the proportion of affiliates in which they had a 95 per cent or more equity stake fell from 60 per cent in 1946–52 to 54 per cent in 1959 –61.[20]

(d) 1960–78

The rate of growth of the international capital stake reached its peak in the late 1960s, decelerated in the early and mid-1970s, but picked up again in the last few years of the decade. But the continued fall in the UK and US share and the increase in that of the West German, Japanese and Swiss[21] is the most striking feature of Table 5.1. This is also confirmed by an examination of the growth of 483 of the world's largest industrial enterprises (Dunning and Pearce, 1981). Between 1962 and 1977 the number of those of US origin dwindled from 292 to 240; while that of Japanese companies rose from 29 to 64; and that of developing countries from 2 to 18. In terms of investments flows, the West German share in 1979 and 1980 was scarcely less than that of the UK; the Japanese contribution was about 60 per cent of the UK, but was (and is still) rising.

There have also been changes in the geographical distribution of the capital stake. Of an estimated $293 billion invested by the seven leading home countries in 1978, (United Nations – UNCTC – 1981), 26.5 per cent was in developing countries, a figure slightly higher than that in 1971, but below that recorded (at least by US and UK

MNEs) in 1960. Most of the forced divestment in natural resources and public utilities occurred in the decade ending in 1975; these were mostly located in developing countries.[22] On the other hand, the 1970s saw a major surge in Japanese investment abroad which, more than its US and UK counterparts, is concentrated in developing countries. In 1978 such countries accounted for 56.5 per cent of all Japanese cumulative investment compared with 27.4 per cent of US and 19.8 per cent of UK investments (Kojima, 1980). Moreover, the decline in extractive investments has been largely counteracted by the growth in manufacturing and service industries; for example, the share of the total US capital stock in these two sectors located in developing countries rose from 21 per cent in 1971 to 26 per cent in 1978.

Within developed host countries, the last twenty years have seen a marked shift of interest by MNEs to Western Europe and the USA. In 1960 about 32 per cent of the foreign capital stock of developed market economies was located in Western Europe or the US; by 1970 this percentage had risen to 38, and by 1978 to 47. By contrast, the share of the British Commonwealth, which attracted so much investment in the early part of the post-war period, fell from 45 per cent in 1960 to 27 per cent in 1970 and to 17 per cent in 1978. This reallocation of activity has been particularly marked in the case of UK investors. In 1978 Western Europe accounted for 31 per cent of the UK direct capital stake (excluding oil), compared to 13 per cent in 1962; the share going to developing countries, however, fell from 37 per cent to 20 per cent. Japanese investment has also grown rather more rapidly in other industrialised countries, especially in the manufacturing and service sectors.

The industrial structure of the outward capital stake of the leading investing countries continues to reflect their factor endowments and market structures, though there is some suggestion of a convergence in patterns over the last two decades (Dunning, 1981a). However, US, West German and Swedish MNEs continue to dominate the high-technology and information-intensive industries, while those of UK and Japanese origin are more represented in consumer good sectors. In Japan's case, however, her investments up to the mid-1970s were in the traditional industries in which she once had a comparative trading advantage, e.g. textiles, or those in which she has always had a comparative trading disadvantage, e.g. primary metals; in the case of the UK, her strength appears to lie in branded goods, e.g. processed foods and cigarettes, where consistency of quality is an important competitive advantage, and in financial services.

Three other features of recent direct trends in MNE activity might also be mentioned. The first is the growth in two-way investment by countries. For example, not only has the USA's share of the outward capital stake fallen; her share of the inward capital stake has risen. In 1960, the USA's outward/inward capital stake ratio was 4.0, in 1970 it was 5.7, but by 1980 it had fallen to 3.3; by contrast, the West German ratio has risen from 0.40 in 1960 to 0.80 in 1970 and 1.09 in 1978, and the Canadian ratio from 0.19 to 0.23 and 0.31. Moreover, as has already been mentioned, in the later 1970s several developing countries, e.g. Hong Kong, Singapore, Brazil, Korea and India, also began to export capital on some scale (Kumar and MacLeod, 1981).

The second trend has been the shift away from traditional import-substituting and resource-based FDI to that designed to promote an integrated structure of production by MNEs and their affiliates. The rationale for this will be discussed later in this chapter, but the two fastest growing areas of MNE activity in the 1970s have been in export platform investments in the newly industrialising countries (NICs) and in horizontal intra-firm trade among affiliates, and between affiliates and parent companies with a regionally integrated area, e.g. EEC, LAFTA.[23]

Thirdly, the last twenty years has seen an increase not only in the importance of joint ventures and non-equity resource flows[24] but of liquidations and voluntary divestments by MNEs. According to Curhan, Davidson and Suri (1977) there were 3152 divestments by US MNEs between 1951 and 1975, while the ratio of divestments to new investments rose from 0.23 in 1968–9 to 0.56 in 1974–5. These divestments have been of two kinds, both underlining the dynamic character of MNE involvement. The first is in low or mature technology sectors in which entry barriers are falling; the second is in response to the move towards global or regional rationalisation, and, in the later 1970s, to domestic economic recession.

There were other developments of the late 1970s which space precludes us from discussing. These included the opening up of regions – notably parts of Eastern Europe and mainland China – previously closed to international business; the more ready acceptance by Japan of majority-owned foreign affiliates; the growth of MNE activity in several service sectors, notably banking, insurance, advertising and tourism; and the increasing use of cross-border arrangements not linked to equity investments.

Most of the data so far presented in this chapter relate to the aggregate FDI stake or to the numbers of the affiliates of large MNEs existing in 1970 (or thereabouts). Only *en passant* have this chapter touched on the growth of particular MNEs, or groups of MNEs as dealt with in the writings of Wilkins (1974a, 1974b), Wilson (n.d.), Franko (1976), Stopford (1974), Nicholas (1982a) and others. Nevertheless, if the statistical profile has been more macro- than micro-oriented, the analytical insights of these scholars will later be drawn upon very considerably. However, this part of the chapter concludes by illustrating, in Figure 5.1, some of the main historical landmarks in the genealogy of the contemporary MNE and indicating where some of today's international giants fit into this picture.

5.3 EXPLAINING CHANGES IN INTERNATIONAL PRODUCTION

Though several economists have been interested in explaining the phenomena of FDI *per se*,[25] most students of international business tend to view it as the vehicle by which resources are transferred and allocated across national boundaries without any change in their ownership. In Chapter 2 Peter Buckley summarised the state of our knowledge and areas of lacunae on theoretical issues. This section will just add our own particular gloss which will form the basis of the analysis which follows.

Changes in the level and pattern of international production may reflect both changes in the *number* of MNEs and/or their affiliates, and the growth or decline of established MNEs and/or their affiliates. Strictly speaking, the theory of the growth of the MNE, as a special case of the growth of the firm, is concerned with the second phenomena rather than the first; and, therefore, it cannot be expected to explain a lot of *de novo* foreign production, and particularly that which replaces domestic production.

Let us start with a few generally accepted propositions. A firm engages in two interrelated functions. First, it organises the production of individual goods and services. Second, it engages in transactions, i.e. it buys inputs and sells outputs. Some of these transactions will be with external buyers and sellers, e.g. households and other firms; others will be made within the same firm. A firm will then grow when it either increases the output of the products it is already producing (or replaces these by new and/or improved products), or internalises transactions which would otherwise have been undertaken via the market, i.e. by redistributing output from other producers to itself.[26]

While, in practice, the production and transaction functions of firms may not be easily separable, conceptually the distinction is a useful one, as is that between those transactions of a firm which are capable of being externalised and those which are not (Dunning, 1981a).

In performing these two activities, a firm may find it desirable to set up production units in more than one location, either in the country of its incorporation or elsewhere. How much output and how

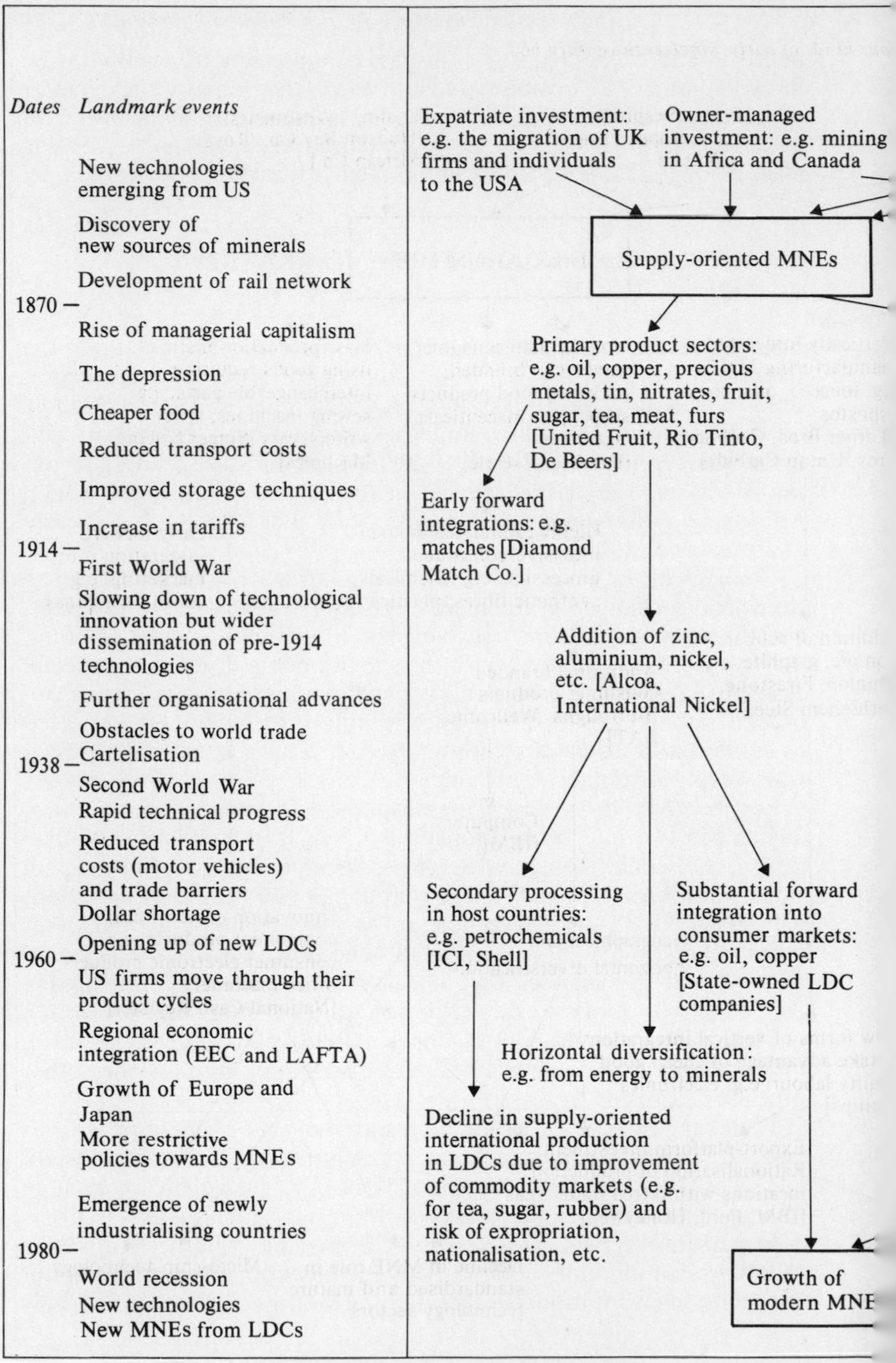

Figure 5.1 *Evolution of the Modern Multinational Enterprise*

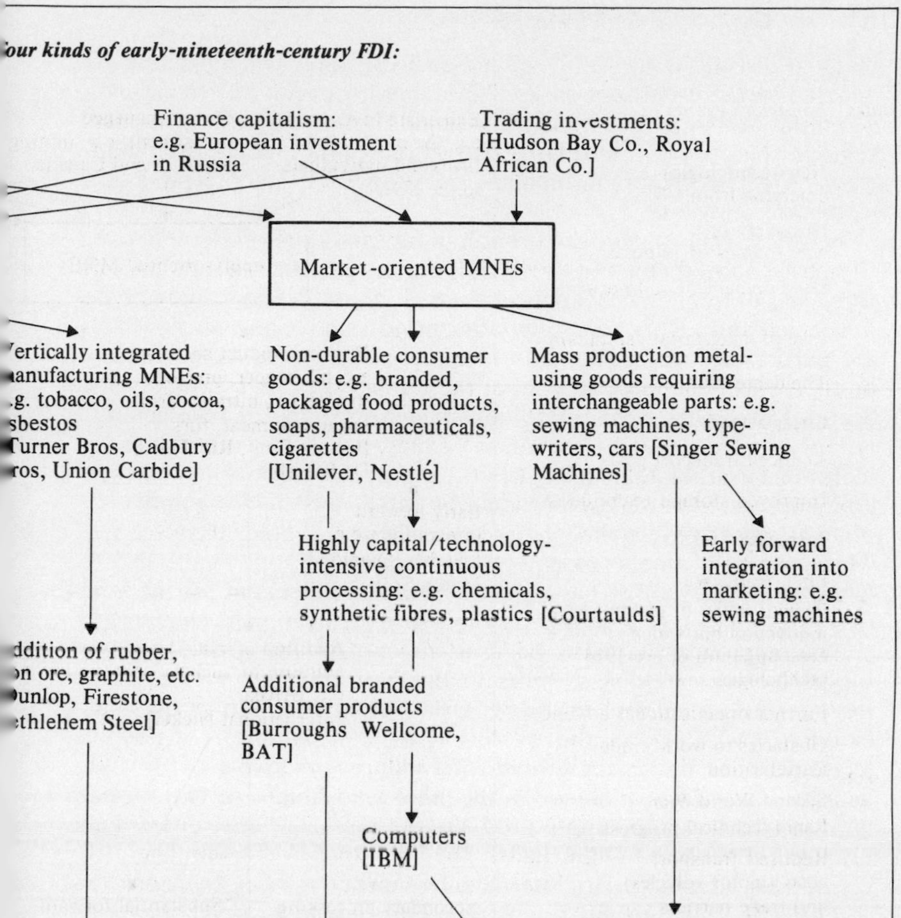
'our kinds of early-nineteenth-century FDI:
Finance capitalism: e.g. European investment in Russia
Trading investments: [Hudson Bay Co., Royal African Co.]
Market-oriented MNEs
'ertically integrated anufacturing MNEs: .g. tobacco, oils, cocoa, sbestos Turner Bros, Cadbury ros, Union Carbide]
Non-durable consumer goods: e.g. branded, packaged food products, soaps, pharmaceuticals, cigarettes [Unilever, Nestlé]
Mass production metal-using goods requiring interchangeable parts: e.g. sewing machines, type-writers, cars [Singer Sewing Machines]
Highly capital/technology-intensive continuous processing: e.g. chemicals, synthetic fibres, plastics [Courtaulds]
Early forward integration into marketing: e.g. sewing machines
ddition of rubber, on ore, graphite, etc. Dunlop, Firestone, thlehem Steel]
Additional branded consumer products [Burroughs Wellcome, BAT]
Computers [IBM]
Innovation of new multi-component products: e.g. consumer electronic products, office machinery [National Cash Register]
Geographical and horizontal diversification
ew forms of vertical integration take advantage of cheap good ality labour: e.g. electronics ilips]
Export-platform investment Rationalisation of production locations within free trade areas [IBM, Ford, Honeywell]
Decline in MNE role in standardised and mature technology sectors
Micro-chip technology

many transactions are assigned to each location will normally be decided on the usual economic criteria, but in considering the growth of output of that part of a multilocational firm produced in *particular* regions or countries, the relative attractions of these regions or countries, as well as factors influencing the growth of the enterprise *as a whole* are relevant.

In seeking reasons for the growth of international production over the past hundred years, it is possible to suggest that an amalgam of three sets of forces has been at work. First, there has been an increase in the demand for the type of goods, services and rights which MNEs are particularly well equipped to supply, and/or an enhanced ability on their part to supply and market these relative to their competitors. Second, there has been a proliferation in the type of transactions, notably of intermediate products, which are best undertaken by hierarchies rather than by markets, and/or an improvement in the efficiency of hierarchies, particularly MNE hierarchies relative to other forms of governance, to organise these and other transactions. Third, the inducements to enterprises to produce goods and services from a foreign location have grown; and/or the demand for the type of output which is best supplied from a foreign location has increased.

This approach may also be used to explain the widening geographical origin of MNEs, shifts in the industrial and geographical pattern of FDI, changes in the size distribution and product diversification of MNEs, and the evolution of new kinds of ownership strategy. Thus the faster growth of Japanese relative to US MNE activity might be explained by the improved ability of the former *vis-à-vis* the latter to supply products the market wants; or by their greater propensity to internalise their competitive advantages (or create new advantages by internalising markets); or by their greater incentive to switch production from a domestic to a foreign location. Similarly, the expansion of MNEs in high-technology and information-intensive industries, relative to that in some resource-based sectors, might be explained by a growing failure in the international market for technology and information in the former case and/ or by less market failure, or more government fiat in the latter. Finally, the increase of FDI in Hong Kong and Singapore relative to India over the last twenty years might be put down to the different types of foreign production attracted to the two groups of countries or to the very different locational attractions, e.g. attitudes of host governments, labour availability and efficiency, access to markets afforded by them.

Elsewhere (Dunning, 1981a) the kind of framework outlined above has been formalised by use of the ownership, location and internalisation (OLI) paradigm, which identifies and classifies particular competitive advantages to enterprises and countries, which are hypothesised to influence the extent and character of a firm's international economic involvement. It has been suggested that the values of these variables will vary according to certain structural parameters, such as the characteristics of home and host countries,[27] the nature of productive and transaction activities of firms and other firm-specific attributes. Except perhaps for size, these latter attributes have been generally neglected by mainstream economists; however, in the last decade, with more attention being given to the economics of the MNE *per se*, and a welcome revival of interest in the firm as an organisational unit, these are now moving towards the forefront of discussion.

A great deal of work has been done on evaluating the determinants of particular types of international production. But it now seems generally accepted that, because of the very different motives for FDI, a single predictive theory of international production is just not possible, any more than it is realistic to expect that a general theory of international trade can explain all types of trade. But as in trade theory, there are some well established guiding principles, e.g. the importance of the distribution of factor endowments between countries and the nature of markets, which have stood the test of time, so it may be possible to identify similar principles which are fundamental to an understanding of international production. And if the OLI paradigm serves to do anything at all, it is to provide such an analytical framework. Clearly *which* OLI variables are the relevant ones will depend on the type of FDI and the kind of structural parameters earlier described. It would be unrealistic to suppose that the OLI advantages which explain investment by Standard Fruit in the banana industry of Costa Rica are the same (or have the same value) as that by NV Philips Gloeilampenfabrieken in the electrical appliances industry of Greece, or that of Trust House Forte in the hotel industry of the USA; but, in each instance the basic principles are the same. More than this: it may be possible to identify sets of key variables (as is done in trade theory where different types of labour and capital are grouped) which come close to providing the OLI paradigm with operational substance. In the present context, it should be possible to see how changes in the values of these might usefully explain changes in international production.

The following sections of this chapter focus on three such sets of interrelated factors. First, the state of knowledge (including information and organisational technology) is a key variable influencing the capacity of firms of different nationality of ownership to produce and market particular goods and services, independently from where, or by which means they are supplied. Second, market failure (as proxied by the costs of a market transaction and the externalities associated with it) is the key variable influencing the administrative mode of exploiting the capacity. Third, a group of locational variables such as transfer costs (including tariff barriers), size of markets and resource availability, affect the choice of firms of where to locate their activities.[28]

5.4 TECHNOLOGICAL CAPABILITY

(a) 1870–1914

From Schumpeter onwards, several economists have asserted that innovations and technological advances have been the major cause of economic growth of industrial societies.[29] According to this view, given the size and character of the market for a particular product, the share of that market enjoyed by any one firm rests primarily on its entrepreneurship, technological prowess and organisational strategy relative to that of its competitors. It may, then, be reasonably hypothesised that, in so far as international production is part of the total production of firms, its growth is likely to be positively rather than negatively related to world technological capacity; and for its geographical origin to be similarly related to the distribution of that capacity between countries. Moreover, in so far as it is possible to identify particular areas of activity in which MNEs are likely to participate, then the more technological advances stem from these activities, the more international production might be expected to grow.

Though innovations continued throughout the nineteenth century, they varied greatly in significance and character, by country of origin, sector and type of firm, and by their speed of international dissemination. Up to around the 1860s, most discoveries were based on the comparatively elementary technology of the industrial revolution, the results of which were fairly easily transferred across national boundaries and assimilated by their recipients. While these advances were accompanied by important organisational and institutional changes, e.g. the introduction of the factory system and the emergence of the joint stock company, for the most part in this era, firms remained small, were single product and owner-managed, and supplied local markets.

The last half-century before the First World War heralded a new wave of technological advances which, in many ways, were more profound and far reaching than their predecessors. These stemmed largely from the USA, and very much reflected both its particular factor endowments and its market characteristics. They were stimulated and supported by the creation of new transport and communications networks, which helped shift both the demand and the supply curves for goods to the right. Electricity and the internal combustion engine, the interchangeability of parts, and the introduction of continuous processing were the main technological lynchpins of the second industrial revolution.[30] They combined to make possible economies of scale in production which, however, required a regular flow of inputs and assured markets if they were to be profitably exploited.

Such technological, organisational and financial changes fundamentally affected the production functions of firms, their capacity for and strategy of growth, and the market environment in which they operated. They also introduced new kinds of competitive advantage, which affected both the ability of firms to exploit foreign markets and the form by which advantages were exploited. For unlike those which preceded them, these advantages created many more barriers to the entry of firms not possessing them, and to their transfer to other countries. These included the growing cost effectiveness of large plants, the economies of process, product or market integration, and the protection offered by the international patent system. They encouraged further technological and organisational changes, which eventually led to more concentration of industrial output and to the transformation of country-specific advantages into the proprietary rights of enterprises.

There are several statistical pointers to the acceleration of technological advances during this era. By the turn of the century the rate of major inventions and discoveries was twice that of the first quarter of the nineteenth century (Streit, 1949). More impressive, from a total annual application for new patents in the USA (from both US and non-US residents) of less than 1,000 in the 1840s and 5,000 in the late 1850s, the number rose substantially to more than 20,000 in the late 1860s, to 40,000 by the turn of the century and to nearly 70,000 by the outbreak of the First World War.

No less significant was the change in the geographical origin of such advances. As Table 5.6 shows, of some 322 major innovations recorded between 1750 and 1850, 37.9 per cent originated from Britain, 23.9 per cent from France, 11.8 per cent from Germany, 16.1 per cent from the USA and 10.3 per cent from other countries.[31] In the following 64 years, during which there were 453 innovations, the corresponding percentages were 15.9, 16.8, 20.5, 34.9 and 11.9. From a dominating position in the late eighteenth and nineteenth centuries, the UK's share fell, while that of her continental competitors and the USA rose: after 1870 the USA took the lead, although its hegemony did not reach its zenith until just after the Second World

Table 5.6 *Major Inventions, Discoveries and Innovations by Country, 1750–1950 (as a percentage of total)*

		Inventions, discoveries and innovations				
	Total	*Britain (%)*	*France (%)*	*Germany (%)*	*USA (%)*	*Others (%)*
1750–1775	30	46.7	16.7	3.3	10.0	23.3
1776–1800	68	42.6	32.4	5.9	13.2	5.9
1801–1825	95	44.2	22.1	10.5	12.6	10.5
1826–1850	129	28.7	22.5	17.8	22.5	8.5
1851–1875	163	17.8	20.9	23.9	25.2	12.3
1876–1900	204	14.2	17.2	19.1	37.7	11.8
1901–1914	87	16.1	8.0	17.2	46.0	12.7
1915–1939	146	13.0	4.1	13.0	58.6	11.3
1940–1950	34	2.9	0.0	6.7	82.4	8.8

Source: Calculated from Streit (1949); see also Pavitt and Soete (1981)

War. Allowing for the time lag between innovation and foreign production, this pattern of technological advance mirrors fairly well the distribution of the stock of foreign investment set out in Table 5.1. Data on non-resident patents registered in the USA suggest a similar decline in the proportion originating from the UK. They also show that, in the period between 1883 and 1914, Germany was a more important patentor than France; and, as one might expect from its geographical proximity, Canada.[32] In the mid-nineteenth century, the proportion of the population which had some kind of tertiary education was highest in the UK and Germany. By 1914, the USA had overtaken both countries, with the UK second, Germany third and France fourth.

Changes in the character of the new technologies were no less important. Those coming from Europe tended to reflect the region's earlier pre-eminence in the basic industries, e.g. iron and steel, shipbuilding, heavy engineering and chemicals. Moreover, both in the UK and on the Continent, where most businesses were family owned, there was comparatively little vertical integration. By contrast, in the USA innovations were more directed towards light engineering, electrical goods, motor vehicles and consumer durables.[33] US firms also tended to pioneer labour-saving and/or capital-intensive production processes, while European companies scored relatively well in materials-saving innovations.

The innovations of the later nineteenth century were different in another sense. Although the earlier discoveries in metallurgy, power generation and transport were interrelated and mutually reinforcing, such interdependence rarely extended across national boundaries. The later advances were truly trans-continental; by drastically reducing transport costs and preserving quality, the railroad, the iron-steamship and the introduction of refrigeration and temperature controlling techniques opened up new sources of food and raw materials from distant countries. *Inter alia* these developments led to an increase in the size of the foreign trade sector in most European economies and of inter-regional US trade. But whereas the UK's comparative advantage was most clearly seen in the products which it had pioneered a half-century earlier, that of Germany, France and the USA was in the products first produced in the later nineteenth century, e.g. motor vehicles, electrical equipment and light chemicals. Indeed some economists assert that changes in the structure of a country's trade is a better indicator of its competitiveness than its share of world trade. Viewed in this perspective, and measured in terms of the rate of growth in world exports in the twentieth century, the USA, Germany and, to a lesser extent, France, consistently outperformed the UK.

Two other features about the sectors embracing the newer technologies should be mentioned. First, they demanded a higher and more consistent quality of inputs, e.g. technology, management, skilled labour, than their predecessors; at the same time, the materials they used were more widely found. Often the possession of these inputs generated advantages to firms which were not only exclusive (at least for a period of time) but which were transferable across national boundaries via FDI or licensing. Second, they tended to be more complex, in that their products needed a larger number of divisible production processes, both lateral – in the case of fabricating industries – and vertical – in the case of continuous processing industries. Yet to be fully effective, these separate processes needed to be coordinated within the same firm. Hence economies of scale and specialisation went hand in hand with economies of joint production. This integration extended beyond production to the purchasing of inputs and the marketing of outputs (Chandler, 1977). Teece (1981b) has argued that those economies which encouraged, by one means or another, the vertical integration of their industries in the nineteenth and early twentieth century, were those which exhibited the greatest technological advances and improved competitive position in world markets. Kindleberger (1964) has suggested the same thing, particularly in the context of the reluctance of UK firms to integrate production and selling operations. He compares the case of the UK woollen industry, which moved to direct trading in the nineteenth century and maintained its rate of technical change, with that of the cotton industry which preferred to separate selling and production activities[34] and fared less well. Frankel (1955) asserts that it was the inability of the organisational and ownership structure in the UK to adapt to the needs of new technologies which caused the UK to slip behind in the competitive race; Teece (1981b) cites the UK iron and steel industry as a case in point, although a number of the large manufacturers, e.g. Consett, expanded overseas to secure ore supplies after 1870.

An examination of the two hundred largest firms in the USA, UK, Germany and Japan at the time of, or shortly after, the First World War, as set out in Table 5.7, reveals that in the newer and/or faster growing industrial sectors of chemical, petroleum, machinery, transport equipment and measuring instruments, there were 99 US firms, 56 UK, 91 German and 53 Japanese. By contrast, in the traditional

Table 5.7 *Percentage Distribution of Two Hundred Largest Manufacturing Firms in Selected Countries by Industry at the Time of the First World War*

	US (1917) %	*UK (1919)* %	*Germany (1913)* %	*Japan (1913)* %
Newer or Mainly Producer Good Industries	49.5	28.0	45.5	25.0
Chemical	10.0	5.5	13.0	11.5
Petroleum	11.0	1.5	2.5	3.0
Rubber	2.5	1.5	0.5	—
Machinery	10.0	4.0	10.5	2.0
Electrical Machinery	2.5	5.5	9.0	3.5
Transport and Equipment	13.0	10.0	9.5	4.5
Measuring Instruments	0.5	—	0.5	0.5
Older or Mainly Consumer Good Industries	50.0	70.5	54.1	74.5
Food and Tobacco	18.0	33.0	12.0	16.0
Textiles and Apparel	4.0	13.5	6.6	28.0
Lumber and Furniture	1.5	—	0.5	1.5
Paper and Printing	3.5	4.5	0.5	6.5
Leather	2.0	—	1.0	2.0
Stone, Clay and Glass	2.5	1.0	5.0	8.0
Primary Metal	14.5	17.5	24.5	10.5
Fabricated Metal	4.0	1.0	4.0	2.0
Miscellaneous	0.5	1.5	0.5	0.5
TOTAL	100.0	100.0	100.0	100.0

Source: Derived from data in Chandler (1981)

sectors which led the industrial revolution a century earlier, viz. textiles and apparel, primary metals and fabricated metals, the respective figures were 45, 64, 70 and 81 (Chandler, 1981). Partly, of course, these statistics reflect comparative resource endowments of the countries in question; but, in retrospect, in the UK's case at least, they also suggest a failure of the economy to adapt its resource allocation to market needs and/or an inability of UK firms in the new sectors to organise themselves efficiently.

(b) 1919–38

During the inter-war years, the pace of technological advance slowed down, and what progress there was strongly favoured the US economy. For example, while patent applications in the USA doubled in the twenty years before 1914, between 1919 and 1939 they fell slightly. Major inventions, discoveries and innovations held up rather better; there were 148 in the former period and 127 in the latter. But of these later advances, the USA accounted for 60 per cent – while those originating from the UK fell to 12.5 per cent, those from France to 8.5 per cent and those from Germany to 13.0 per cent. Of the patents registered in the USA, those of UK residents rose from 1,288 in 1919 to 1,347 in 1939; the corresponding figures for Germany were 131 and 2,480; for France 363 and 634; and for Japan 56 and 57. The impressive growth in non-resident patenting in the USA at a time when the number of major innovations was falling may be explained by the growing interest of foreign firms in the US market, and the fact that many post-1918 patents were based on pre-war discoveries.

In spite of some notable inventions of the inter-war period – television, radar, the jet engine, colour photography, several manmade fibres and some antibiotic drugs, for example – these were mainly years of the development, adaptation and dissemination of the technological and organisational breakthroughs of the late nineteenth and early twentieth centuries. In consequence, one sees the most substantial increase in the share of the largest firms concentrated in these sectors; at the same time, the events of the 1920s and 1930s not only forced traditional industries to rationalise their structures and diversify into new lines of activity, but also prompted the growth industries to reorganise themselves around the new process innovations such as semi-automated production. For example, the number of vehicle and other transport equipment firms in the top 200 companies of the USA, UK, Germany and Japan fell from 74 in 1914–19 to 62 in 1930. This obviously reflected a more pronounced growth in the output of some firms than in that of the industry as a whole. Many companies in this era were moving through the later stages of their product cycles initiated several years earlier, and were paying more attention to reducing production costs, standardising product quality and promoting new sales, particularly at the lower end of the market where price sensitivity tends to increase as the product becomes available to a larger number of consumers (the introduction of the Model T by the Ford Motor Company in the UK is an example). The growing threat from European MNEs to US technological hegemony in some newer industrial sectors also led to more international cartel arrangements than in pre-war days, e.g. in aluminium, electrical equipment, and chemicals, which – in part at least – reduced the incentive for FDI.

On the purely technological front then, the inter-war years saw some restructuring of European industry but, for the most part, the US continued to retain its advantage in the newer sectors. Throughout this period the proportion of investment in non-manufacturing personnel and facilities by manufacturing firms grew as increases in hierarchical efficiency and/or market failure enabled the boundaries of the firm to be pushed further out. The need to gain control of materials to service an industrial machine increasingly vulnerable to disruptions in production flows, and the growing role of oil-based products substituting for natural materials, also combined to prompt further backward integration.

(c) 1945–60

The Second World War proved an important watershed for technological advances; indeed, it also speeded up the exploitation of certain discoveries in the 1930s, which later provided the mainspring of commercial expansion. Between 1945 and 1965 the number of patents granted in the USA trebled, with the proportion awarded to foreigners rising from 8.2 per cent to 19.9 per cent. However the increase in patenting by foreigners occurred mainly in the latter half of the 1950s; in the years immediately following the war the proportion hovered around the 10–12 per cent level. After a dramatic fall in its share of non-resident patenting, West Germany made a no less impressive recovery, and by 1960 had replaced the UK as the leading grantee. By this time France had also regained her pre-war position, while Japan was just emerging as a technological force. Most other European nations had also recovered or surpassed their pre-war shares.

No comparative data on R & D expenditure (as an alternative proxy for technological capability) are available until the mid-1960s. In 1967 the USA still accounted for 68.7 per cent of the R & D undertaken by OECD countries, with the UK (7.3 per cent), West Germany (6.3 per cent), France (6.0 per cent) and Japan (4.7 per cent) a long way behind. One imagines that in 1960 the percentages for the first three countries would have been higher and that of Japan lower. The proportion of R & D expenditure to GNP was also higher in the USA than in other OECD countries in that year, as was the percentage of the population receiving tertiary education.

(d) 1960–78

The last two decades have seen the rate of innovation falling back again. The number of new patents granted in the USA remained more or less constant in the later 1960s, moved up in the early 1970s, slackened off in the mid-1970s and recovered at the end of the decade. In most industrial countries – Japan and West Germany being two exceptions – the share of GNP allocated to R & D fell in the late 1960s and 1970s; at the same time the US share of R & D in OECD countries dropped substantially, so that by 1977 it accounted for 49.5 per cent. By contrast, all European countries increased their shares – especially West Germany from 6.3 per cent to 11.9 per cent – but the most spectacular gain was that of Japan, from 4.7 per cent in 1967 to 13.6 per cent in 1977. Germany and Japan were then the leading foreign patent grantees in the USA with shares of 23.9 per cent and 27.7 per cent of all non-resident recipients; by contrast, the UK's share had fallen to its lowest point of 10.1 per cent. Most other European countries also lost out in the 1970s to Japan. However, as a whole, non-US sources accounted for two-fifths of all patents granted in the USA in 1979 – a three-fold increase since 1960 compared with only a 9 per cent increase in US patenting. The late 1970s also saw a sharp increase in patenting by some NICs, e.g. Brazil, Mexico, Hong Kong and Korea.

More recently, some researchers have attempted to compare the trade and innovatory performance of OECD countries. One of the most interesting findings is that not only is there an apparently close correlation between those manufacturing sectors in which there is a revealed comparative trading advantage (RCA) and those in which there is a revealed innovatory advantage – the latter being proxied by number of patents granted in the USA – but also that, in those industries in which both indices are greater than one, the propensity to engage in FDI is above average (Pavitt and Soete, 1981). Further, the patterns of the two sets of RCA differ between the leading industrialised countries in a way that is consistent with variations in their revealed comparative advantage of foreign direct assets, as has been demonstrated elsewhere (Dunning, 1981a).

Other data confirm that since the early 1960s the share of the leading US industrial enterprises in world output has fallen relative to that of other countries (Dunning and Pearce, 1981; Franko, 1978). Only in computers, measuring instruments and aerospace have US firms retained their dominance; elsewhere, the erosion of the USA's position has been generally greater in the technology-intensive sectors. It is also worth recalling that it is these industries which have increased their non-manufacturing personnel the most – both absolutely and relative to manufacturing personnel – and where the average size of firm has risen the most. On the other hand, product diversification has been no less pronounced in some of the non-research-intensive sectors.

Finally, statistics on the technological balance of payments of countries tell a similar story.[35] They point to a relative decline in the USA's position as measured by its rate of growth of payments for technology to foreigners (in the form of royalties, fees, etc.) exceeding that of its receipts, while in the case of Japan and Germany the reverse phenomenon has taken place. It should be observed, however, that these data are subject to many errors, and, in part at least, reflect the propensity of companies to invest overseas.

In summary, the last hundred years have seen an ebb and flow of technological advance with major changes in the distribution of technological capacity between countries. It would seem that the main thrusts of such advances have generally preceded those of FDI and that, although the time lag between many kinds of invention and their commercialisation is probably increasing, that between their embodiment in domestic and foreign production is falling (Mansfield, Teece and Romeo, 1979). The evidence also suggests that the changing geographical origin of the foreign direct capital stake mirrors fairly well changes in the distribution of technological capabilities. Innovations in information, and in organisational, transport and communications technologies have sometimes followed and sometimes preceded changes in product, process and materials technologies, but these too have been discontinuous. Here there have been three main breakthroughs: the first was necessitated by the new manufacturing technologies of the third quarter of the nineteenth century, including those of the railroad and the telegraph; the second was brought about by the advent of the jet aircraft and the computer immediately after the end of the Second World War; and the third by the advances in satellite communication, micro-chip technology and bio-engineering of the mid-1970s, the results of which are only just being felt. These initially benefited the economies which introduced them, but via FDI and other modalities of transfer quickly spread to impinge on firms of other nationalities. On the whole, however, large firms – and large MNEs in particular – seem to have been both the main instigators and the main beneficiaries of such advances.

5.5 MARKET FAILURE AND ORGANISATIONAL FORM

However much advances in technology may be a primary cause of the growth in world production over the last century, except in a most indirect sense they cannot satisfactorily explain the changes in the distribution of that output. In particular, they cannot explain, first, the increase in the average size of firms and the extent of product or process diversification and, second, the greater propensity of some firms to produce their output from a foreign rather than a domestic location. It is now generally recognised that the answer to the first question lies in the extent to which the market or administrative fiat is the preferred mechanism of resource (or property right) allocation. In the absence of any kind of market failure (in the sense that transaction costs in the intermediate goods market are zero and there are no externalities), the function of any firm would be limited to the production of a single and indivisible product, service or right. On the other hand, if market failure was complete, then only one firm (or a government agency) would produce all products, services and rights: apart from buying factor inputs from, and selling its final output to, households, all other transactions would be internalised.

In practice of course, both markets and hierarchies coexist, and most transactions are neither pure spot or pure administered. Richardson (1972) has emphasised that many activities between firms are cooperative rather than competitive; this is borne out by the growth of a wide variety of non-equity contractual arrangements concluded between firms of different nationality. For the purpose of this chapter, however, we shall consider these intermediate organisational forms as market transactions, even though *de facto* they have many of the characteristics of internalised cooperative agreements (Nicholas (1982b)).

In applying these concepts to explaining the growth of international production, it may be argued that, in the absence of intercountry transaction costs, all firms would conduct their buying and selling with firms producing in another country via the market; i.e. there would be no incentive for FDI. Therefore, *pari passu*, the growth of international production must be associated with increased market failure of the type of output and inputs in which firms wish to trade.

The literature surveyed in Chapter 1 suggests that firms may wish to internalise transactions for two reasons. First, they may believe that this is the best way to appropriate the economic rent in whatever property right is being bought or sold. Thus a firm might internalise the transfer of technology rather than license it, because it believes this organisational route will yield a greater net benefit (or the same benefit at less risk); or it may engage in international vertical integration in a resource-based sector so as to capture the full benefits of resource exploitation for itself – rather than share them with its seller. Second, the internalisation of a particular transaction may confer benefits to the internalising company external to that transaction. Most economies of joint production and lateral diversification arise in this way. In both cases, a firm will embrace new transactions as long as the marginal cost of so doing is covered by the marginal revenue derived from the two advantages of internalisation just outlined.

In the pages which follow, the analysis will be confined to the factors influencing the choice of organisation for engaging in transactions in or between a *given location*. The next section will discuss the appropriate location of production, given the organisational form. In other words, unlike some writers, e.g. Rugman (1981), I prefer not to consider the choice between exports and FDI as one primarily involving matters of governance.[36]

The proposition following from these observations is that the growth in international production is likely to be positively rather than negatively associated with market failure and the growing incentive of firms to internalise transactions for one or two of the reasons stated above. As in the case of ownership advantages arising from the possession of a superior intangible asset, so internalisation advantages will vary according to country-, sector- and firm-specific characteristics.

(a) 1870–1914

The period up to 1870 was one in which, for most international transactions undertaken by firms, and given the environment in which they were undertaken, markets operated reasonably well, while the costs of internalising such transactions were generally prohibitive. The former situation reflected the relative simplicity, homogeneity and easy transferability of most kinds of knowledge and technology, and the comparative ease at which most raw materials and foodstuffs could be obtained; the latter manifested the diseconomies of operating distant branch plants, as well as the technical and organisational limitations on the growth of hierarchies. During this period the ratio of the number of external transactions to gross output produced by a firm was generally high. Where market prospects abroad were favourable and exports were uneconomic, then, rather than set up branch plants, enterprises found it preferable to migrate, lock, stock and barrel. Examples assembled by Coram (1967) and Buckley and Roberts (1982) include the migration of Dundee capitalists and mill superintendents to Paterson, New Jersey in 1844, that of the Clark family from Lancashire to set up the machine-making of cotton thread in Newark, New Jersey in 1850, and that of Irish hosiery manufacturers establishing knitting mills in Needham, Massachusetts in the 1850s. Later, as a direct result of rising US tariffs and difficult trading conditions in the UK, there was a substantial exodus of the tin-plate industry from South Wales, the silk industry from Macclesfield, the lace industry from Nottingham and the cutlery industry from Sheffield.[37]

In the period after 1870 several events occurred which dramatically affected the organisation of business. These included the evolution of managerial capitalism, the opening up of the US and European Continents by the railroad, improvements in intercontinental sea transport and advances in communication techniques. These events made possible the translation of single-unit into multi-unit enterprises, which in turn caused the number of transactions undertaken within firms to increase, and those between firms to decrease. At the same time, partly as a consequence of these developments, partly as a result of the increasing cost and complexity of new technology and the widening disparity of the technological capabilities between countries, and partly because of their growing need to protect themselves against the risk of disruptions to supplies of inputs affecting efficient scheduling and distributor efficiency,[38] firms found the market a less attractive mode of exchange. The latter years of the nineteenth century saw an increasing ability of firms to cope with, and a greater need to initiate, hierarchical methods of organising transactions.

From the perspective of the foreign activities of firms, it may be expected that companies which find it economic to internalise transactions in their home country would also do so abroad, i.e. those producing high technology or branded consumer goods where quality control is important. But in some cases, especially with supply-oriented direct investments in primary products, there was little experience of domestic production, e.g. investment in tropical fruits by companies located in temperate climates, and in minerals by manufacturing companies in the consuming countries. In such cases the choice between licensing (or sub-contracting) a foreign supplier or backward integration rests on the ability of the supplier to supply the product at the right price and quality at the right time, the risk of being dependent on an external source of supply, and the competitive strategy of the purchasing company. In these and other respects, primary product markets in the nineteenth and early twentieth centuries were becoming increasingly imperfect; hence the growth of FDI in mines and plantations.[39]

But country-specific factors are no less important in influencing the modality of international resource transfer (Dunning, 1982). As a general rule, market failure is likely to be greatest when one of the parties to the exchange is located in a poorer country. Partly because of this, and partly because most MNE activity in developing countries was directed to the primary product sector, non-resident resource transfer tended, even in the late nineteenth century, to be more internalised than in developed countries. The only exception was where host government policy was directed against inward investment, and this was unusual at the time. It has been shown that, in some cases, metropolitan governments deliberately tried to limit the ability of their own foreign colonies to develop markets for certain goods; in other words, imperialism fostered its own form of internalisation.

Unfortunately, data limitations do not enable us to test these ideas systematically. We do know, however, from the work of Svedberg (1978) that the proportion of the total investment accounted for by direct investment was higher in developing than in developed countries in 1914. It would seem also, from business histories, as well as case studies of particular sectors and countries, that externalised technology and managerial transfers were more common within Western Europe or between Europe and the USA than between the USA and Europe and the USA and the rest of the world. One other relevant fact is that almost all the cartels and cooperative agreements concluded prior to 1914 (i.e. where ownership advantages were traded between independent firms) were concluded between European firms – although sometimes these had very similar characteristics to internalised resource transference.

There is also some suggestion that the motives for internalisation differed between home countries. The UK manufacturing MNEs, for example, which were strongly oriented towards the supply of consumer goods (Stopford, 1974), were prompted more by the advantages of vertical selling than the US MNEs whose particular internalising needs were less to do with the protection of the quality of branded products and the assurance of adequate distributive outlets, than with the problems of international technology markets. According to Nicholas (1982a), of 119 UK MNEs giving reasons for their direct investment abroad between 1879 and 1939, 21 per cent stated 'to sell vertically', only 3 per cent less than those who put 'technology' as a factor.[40] Backward integration was mentioned by 15 per cent of UK firms, and the tariff factor, or market protection, by 23 per cent of firms. A cursory examination of the list of 50 large US MNEs established before 1914, contained in Wilkins' classic work (1970), would suggest that the internalisation of technology and the economies of synergy already gained through domestic multiplant operations were a more important consideration.[41]

(ii) 1919–38

Comparatively little change in the conditions affecting the form of international involvements occurred in the inter-war years. What data we have suggest that direct investment weathered the economic vicissitudes of the period much better than portfolio investment. We also know that the growth of foreign production by established MNEs increasingly took the form of product, process or market diversification. As a result, the typical foreign affiliate was translated from a monocentric to a polycentric entity (Wilkins, 1974a). During these years foreign affiliates began to assume an identity of their own. Sometimes this was largely autonomous of the parent company, but in other cases it was a direct consequence of further internalisation of markets by the parent company. At the same time, a lot of new MNE entrants appeared on the scene. Continual improvements in the organisation and management of firms[42] and in transport and communications technology also aided hierarchical transactions, as did the growth of markets for the kind of goods which MNEs, as a result of their integrated network of international activities, were best able to supply. This was a period in which both the average size and the number of internal transactions of firms increased sharply. It was also one which saw the growth of international cartels in the secondary sector. Although some of these associations were of pre-war origin, they flourished in the less robust economic climate of the inter-war years. The outcome was that to prevent destructive competition between oligopolists – particularly the inter-penetration of markets via international production – some kind of market sharing mechanism was thought desirable. These were also years in which governments, on the whole, chose not to exercise strong anti-trust or anti-monopoly policies.

It is worth observing that the propensity of firms to choose one form of involvement rather than another again varied by sector, country and enterprise. There were, for example, few cartels among motor vehicle producers; this was a rapid growth industry in which the technological and marketing advantages of US MNEs were particularly strong. Each firm produced a limited range of products, there were substantial economies of scale, and the need to closely schedule the flow of inputs and outputs were especially noticeable.

By contrast, in the electrical equipment industry and some branches of the chemical and heavy engineering industries, where cartels were more common, these conditions were less in evidence. Moreover, contractual technological exchanges were favoured by the recovering large companies of Western Europe – particularly those of German origin – as a way of penetrating USA markets without a substantial capital investment (which also explains why joint ventures were more common among European firms investing in the USA than *vice versa*). During this time there was also a reduction in some kinds of vertical direct investment as new international commodity markets were set up. On the other hand, in those primary sectors in which large indivisible costs and high barriers to entry kept the number of firms small, and the need to protect against variations in output was especially marked (e.g. oil, tropical fruit, rubber and several non-ferrous metals), MNEs tightened their hierarchical control.

(c) 1945–60

The conditions in the third period covered by our study were dramatically different. First, as we have seen, the USA dominated the supply of new technology for much of the period. Second, it was a period of substantial economic expansion – or recovery in the case of Europe and Japan. Third, these were years when a lot of new idiosyncratic and non-codifiable technology was produced, the market for which was extremely imperfect (see Chapter 4). Fourth, antitrust policy – particularly in the USA – made both domestic and international mergers or agreements much more difficult to conclude than in pre-war days. Fifth, the advent of the jet plane and the computer initiated a new generation of organisational advances which reduced hierarchical transaction costs. Sixth, while for the early part of the period at least international markets of almost all kinds were in disarray, the underlying environment for direct investment and trade, created at Bretton Woods and Havana, was both more congenial and stable than that which guided policy makers in the inter-war years. Add to these factors the type of sectors in which world output was expanding the fastest, the countries which were most eager to attract foreign entrepreneurship, technology and capital, and/or offered the best prospects to MNEs, and the relative unattractiveness of alternative routes of resource transfer, and it is not surprising that international production rose so markedly in these years.

This period also saw a continuation of the pre-war trend to a more integrated product and market structure on the part of established MNEs. At the same time, a reading of many country studies of FDI, published in the late 1950s and early 1960s suggests that rationalised production as we know it today was still the exception rather than the rule within the manufacturing sector. Certainly intra-firm manufacturing imports and exports by MNEs were a small fraction of what they are today and, for the most part, there was little specialisation between parent and subsidiary. Indeed the early field studies of Dunning (1958), Safarian (1966) and Brash (1966) all suggest that, in the main, US manufacturing subsidiaries were truncated replicas of their parent organisations, and, after a learning period, tended to operate with the minimum of parental interference. In other words, the benefits of foreign production to the investing company were perceived in terms of the economic rent earned on the assets transferred rather than in any synergistic gains to the parent system. Because of the very rapid growth of new affiliates – often set up to overcome tariff barriers or other import controls – monocentric foreign production flourished. Even in 1973, 62 per cent of over 9,400 MNEs surveyed by the European Commission had only one foreign affiliate, compared with less than 3 per cent which had more than 20 affiliates (Commission of the European Communities, 1976).

This leads us to a general observation. While the setting up of a foreign affiliate may be likened to that of a branch plant of the parent company in the home country, it has also some of the characteristics of a *de novo* firm. This being so, a purely Chandlerian explanation (e.g. Chandler, 1977) of the growth of a large enterprise within a country may not be wholly pertinent to the decision to undertake foreign production. This is not only because many MNEs are quite small firms,[43] but because a foreign investment decision, unlike its domestic counterpart, is often prompted by the need to protect an *existing* market, i.e. to relocate rather than to expand output. If, then, we include all kinds of barriers to trade associated with traversing space between two countries, quite a lot of manufacturing investment over the last hundred years – but especially in the inter-war and early post-war periods – originated in this way. For example, some 75 per cent of the UK and US MNEs operating in the mid-1970s first set up outside their home countries in the post-1945 period. The proportion is probably nearer 85 per cent in the case of German firms and 95 per cent in the case of Japanese firms.

Both in the capital-intensive resource-based and technology-intensive manufacturing sectors there is some evidence of the bunching of new activities by rival MNE oligopolists in this period (Knickerbocker, 1973). Vernon (1981) argues that this behaviour reflects a form of risk-minimising strategy, which in a wider context helps to explain much of the integrating imperative among MNEs. At the same time, capital investment entails a risk of its own, which, when it outweighs the risk-reducing aspects of internalisation, may lead firms to prefer a cooperative or contractual route of exploiting foreign markets.

(d) 1960–78

The last two decades have seen a further considerable change in the organisation of international resource transfer, the net result of which has been to decrease the role of multinational hierarchies in some sectors and in some countries, and increase it in others. Supporting the former tendency has been a marked improvement in some international markets for transacting resources. Reinforcing this fait has been the voluntary divestment by MNEs or enforced use of the market route by host governments in many primary industries and some key secondary and tertiary industries. So international production, initially designed to exploit a unique technological advantage which has eroded over time, has tended to fall, except in countries where user capacity is still inadequate. By contrast, in fast innovating sectors, where technology is idiosyncratic, complex and not easily codified, the MNE continues to flourish. However, both these phenomena are parts of the same story and fit in well with the ideas contained in the product or industry technology cycles. Where MNEs act primarily as a transferor of assets and a tutor in the use of these and other inputs, their role in supplying any particular asset is likely to be a temporary one. In such cases, their permanent presence can only be explained by the continual innovation of new ownership advantages. Hence, as was said earlier, one would expect the outward direct investment of a country to be related to its rate of innovation, both absolutely and compared with that of its competitors. It is also likely to be allied to the technological capacity of the countries which it services. Thus it is quite consistent for US MNEs to reduce their stake in the French pharmaceutical sector, while Hong Kong investors increase theirs in the Sri Lankan textiles industry.

At the same time, changes in environmental risks have influenced the propensity of firms to internalise their international markets. On the one hand, the threat of interruption to oil and other raw material supplies has encouraged supplying MNEs to cut off the unintegrated processors they previously supplied. On the other, the added uncertainty of a loss of sunk capital (through nationalisation) has prompted partial or full divestment of 100 per cent affiliates (Vernon, 1981).

But quite apart from the ebb and flow of these kinds of international production, the most marked development of the last fifteen years has been the growth of the multi-divisional form of affiliates of MNEs. This is what Wilkins (1974) calls the third phase in MNE development: the motive for foreign production is not to gain the economic rent which marketable advantages can earn, but to capture the economies of integration and diversification arising from such production. Such ownership advantages are different in kind from the first type, partly because they accrue to the parent system rather than any one of its affiliates and partly because they are not transferable outside the MNE, i.e. there is no market for them.[44] This multi-divisional form may result in rationalised production between a group of affiliates within a region, or between parent companies and a number of affiliates.

Such rationalisation tends to take two main forms. The first is a reorganisation of a group of largely import-substituting activities in a number of countries which were initially designed to meet domestic needs. If and when the markets are large enough and/or become integrated, then the MNE may find it economic to pursue a different strategy, based upon the economies of product specialisation and intra-group trading; e.g. instead of each affiliate replicating the other's products, it specialises in only one product with which it supplies the markets of all countries. Secondly, corporate integration may take the form of export platform manufacturing investment or downstream processing of primary products, where the division of labour tends to be between stages of production and between parent and subsidiaries, and is based on international cost differences.

The expansion of these and similar forms of MNE activity has been made possible both by a reduction in trade barriers between particular countries and by the continued improvements in hierarchical efficiency. However, in some cases (particularly within the EEC) what, in fact, has happened is that the MNE has transferred a system of organisation to the group of affiliates located in a particular region. It is less the prospective gains from internalised transactions between parent and subsidiary which has led to new foreign production and more the gains from internalised transactions between the individual subsidiaries and their regional headquarters. In this case, synergistic advantages gained in the multi-divisional form in the parent company may be usefully replicated at a regional level; examples include the benefits of centralised purchasing, the use of sophisticated accounting systems, the reduction of exchange risks, and the ability to move top personnel between affiliates.[45]

Again, one notices differences in the forms of international economic involvement both between home countries and between home and host countries. Very often these reflect industry- or firm-specific characteristics. Reference has already been made to the interdependent behaviour of MNE oligopolists. In the latter 1960s and early 1970s this was noticeable in the way in which technology was diffused in the semi-conductor industry and the drug industry

(Lake, 1979). Davidson and McFetridge (1979) have suggested that international transfers of technology are more likely to be internalised if the transferor already operates an affiliate in the recipient country, and if previous transfers have been internalised. *Inter alia*, this might explain the greater propensity of Japanese firms to conclude licensing agreements with foreign motor vehicle firms, rather than establish their own manufacturing affiliates. On the other hand, the preference of US manufacturing firms for 100 per cent ownership of their affiliates may be due to their much greater degree of international product and process integration. This, in turn, may be a function of the extent of MNE manufacturing activity; Japan is still mainly at the monocentric stage of its international production. Moveover, as Mason (1980) has suggested, the main synergistic advantages between Japanese parent and affiliate companies are captured via the 100 per cent stake of the major trading companies in their foreign subsidiaries which, in turn, often have close financial and operating ties with foreign manufacturing companies.

It would seem, then, that in the last twenty years or so, US and some European MNEs have come of age; and that, at least in some areas of the world, their foreign operations have increasingly come to resemble their domestic operations and their growth patterns to follow broadly similar paths. The convergence of international consumer and producer tastes is accelerating this trend.

It is noteworthy that, although since around the mid-1960s the share of US direct investment has been steadily falling, it is the established US MNEs that have most pursued a Chandlerian strategy towards international production. And in the 1970s there was some evidence that European firms, particularly with respect to their activities in the US, were undertaking growth for similar reasons, although here the associations sought were often of a conglomerate rather than a horizontal or vertical kind. In a study of the growth of US FDI between 1962 and 1968 based on Internal Revenue data, Kopits (1979) estimated that the share of conglomerate diversification rose from 14.1 per cent to 22.3 per cent. It is possible, of course, that such diversification may be undertaken to exploit imperfections in the capital and foreign exchange markets. However, such opportunities, which do not normally occur within a country, may also open up new channels for investment, and thus be viable organisational avenues of growth. At the same time, the new MNEs which accounted for an increasing share of international production in the 1970s did not, in general, integrate their foreign and their domestic operations (although at a macro level there is reason to suppose Japanese foreign and domestic investments are more interrelated than, for example, their US counterparts (Kojima, 1980). Finally, with innovations in trans-border information flows, some of the obstacles to hierarchical growth are being further reduced. Such innovations of course, do not only benefit MNEs. For example, the introduction of international reservation systems for hotels has meant that this particular advantage may be sold on a contractual basis rather than within a multinational hotel system, thereby reducing the need for MNE systems (Dunning and McQueen, 1981). This is an example of where a particular ownership advantage has become widely codified and specialist companies established to sell it; some management consultancy firms operate in the same way.

The previous paragraphs suggest that changes in the advantages of alternative organisational forms for transferring ownership advantages across national boundaries have played a significant role in affecting the level and patterns of international production over the last hundred years. In particular, the internalisation model explains why in those sectors where the market for transacting either inputs or the outputs (including intermediate outputs) has improved the contribution of the MNE *qua* MNE,[46] has fallen. But in other sectors, where ownership advantages have become more idiosyncratic or dependent on the integration of interrelated activities, it has become even more important.[47] We have also argued that, while Chandlerian-type theories may not always be the most useful explanation of the initial foreign investment decision by firms, the growth of established subsidiaries of MNEs, and particularly those located in large integrated markets, is increasingly following the pattern of large domestic firms. Indeed, the generally faster rate of growth of international production *vis-à-vis* domestic production may be reasonably attributed to the additional incentive to integration which is consequential upon the diversification of production facilities outside national boundaries.[48]

5.6 LOCATIONAL DETERMINANTS

Even accepting the superior ownership advantages of firms of one nationality over those of another and the incentive to internalise these advantages, it is a prerequisite for international production that it must be more profitable (or otherwise in their best interests) for firms to undertake at least some of their productive activities outside their home countries. Similarly, a growth in international production might (though not necessarily will) reflect a shift of the locational advantages in favour of foreign countries *vis-à-vis* the home country, or an increase in the type of production which favours a foreign rather than a domestic location.

The determinants of the siting of international production have been well set out in the literature (e.g. Vernon, 1974). They include all those variables likely to influence the location of activities within a country, and others which specifically arise as a result of producing in different sovereign territories and/or currency areas. Considering, then, a particular siting decision in isolation from the rest of its activities, a firm contemplating foreign production may behave differently from one considering setting up a new plant within its home country, either because the values of the first group of variables (e.g. transport, labour, material, etc. costs, market characteristics, behaviour of competitors, etc.) are different in the two cases, or because the second group (e.g. tariffs, tax rates) are more significant.

This much is fairly straightforward. Where it is possible to supply a market from alternative sites, the entry of firms into foreign production may be solely explained by a shift in the relative attractions of these sites.

In the context of the OLI paradigm, changes in the value of locational variables have other effects. For example, international diversification of activities may itself offer its own ownership advantage. For example, an MNE, by its presence in different countries may be better able to monitor inputs and outputs or to engage in international specialisation and risk spreading (Rugman, 1979). On the other hand, differences in the efficiency of markets, e.g. for technology and primary products, and the uncertainty attached to market failure and changes in government fiat, may lead a firm to internalise activities in a foreign country that it may not feel it necessary to do at home. But it should be noted that the interaction between O, L and I variables is not involved in all locational decisions – particularly those involving *de novo* international production. Neither is it helpful to think of transfer costs as a kind of market failure associated with distance which firms internalise by switching from exports to local production.

The contention of this chapter is that the growth of the MNE has seen a gradual shift in locational determinants from those associated with the production and transfer costs of a single activity to those to do with economising transaction costs or maximising benefits external to that activity, but internal to the MNE, through the appropriate deployment over space of a group of interrelated activities. In such cases, the variables likely to influence MNEs in their selection of international sites will depend less on the effect which they have on the profitability of the affiliates, and more on that of the enterprise as a whole.

While investment incentives, tariffs, differences in labour costs, economies of plant size, etc. may effect *de novo* FDI, as the degree of multinationalisation intensifies, so the role of other locational variables becomes more decisive (Dunning, 1972). These include the general climate for international investment and trade (e.g. the extent of regional integration), the efficiency of markets for intermediate products transferred across national boundaries, the international market structure in which MNEs compete, and the presence, or otherwise, of economies of plant scale. One result of such a shift is seen in the growth of both intra-firm and intra-industry trade and FDI (Dunning, 1981b; Krugman, 1979, 1981). Let us now review some of these changes in an historical context.

(a) 1870–1914

Earlier in this chapter it was shown that before the First World War FDI was mainly directed either to natural resource exploitation (particularly so in the non-industrialised countries) or import-substitution (mainly in Europe, the USA, China and Japan). Obviously a necessary condition for the former kind of investment is the presence of the resources, but other variables (e.g. exploration and extraction costs, the extent to which it is economic to engage in secondary processing, marketing – including internal and external transport costs – host government policy towards the foreign ownership of natural resources, and the demand for the products incorporating the resources) might be no less important, particularly in the case of ubiquitous primary products. Most of the early expansion in MNE activity in mines, oil wells and plantations was prompted by the prospects of market growth in home countries,[49] together with a gradual reduction in the production and marketing costs of the primary product. And, as stated in the previous sections, the fact that the ownership of these facilities in the host country was in foreign hands reflected both the superior access to technical knowledge, capital and marketing facilities possessed by the foreign firms and their belief that by internalising the use of their knowledge they could best capture the economic rents on these assets. The early vertical integration of the banana industry (see Chapter 7) is an excellent example of how MNEs dominated the development of this sector. But it is also worth observing that for a variety of reasons, including the colonial domination of many host countries, there were few restrictions placed on the ownership of natural resources by foreigners. The conditions for the growth of such investment, the end products of which were usually free of tariffs or import controls by recipient countries, were then exceptionally favourable in the years leading up to the First World War.

The literature suggests that import-substituting investment is determined by such variables as the size of the local market, the relevant stage of the product cycle, comparative input costs, transport costs, government policy, plant economies of scale, and the extent to which the firm needs to be close to its input or finished goods markets (e.g. because of differences in the availability of raw materials, customer tastes, local laws, etc.) *Ceteris paribus*, because of additional communication costs between parent and subsidiary (Hirsch, 1976), firms may have a natural preference for exporting rather than for foreign production; this is enhanced when there are additional political and economic risks in producing abroad. However, some of these costs are incurred mainly at the time of entry, and the marginal costs of expansion may be small. Moreover, as we have seen, there may be compensating risk-spreading benefits from foreign investment. Further, it cannot be assumed that a foreign environment is always less uncertain (or the behaviour of affiliates more constrained) than that of domestic affiliates; this, for example, is the case of some investment by Third World MNEs today.

The history of foreign manufacturing production before the First World War strongly suggests that artificial barriers to exports, in the form of tariffs and other import controls, were perceived at the time to be the most important locational determinant for the initial foreign investment by MNEs; but that, with the benefit of hindsight, many firms would accept that these affected the timing of foreign participation rather than its form, as, even in the absence of trade barriers, this could be justified on other grounds. It is quite clear that there was a perceived threshold for FDI in the nineteenth century, which was probably higher than was justified due to lack of information on the part of firms of the economics of producing outside their home environment; also that the fear of losing an existing or prospective market, rather than any aggressive marketing strategy, was the main stimulus for such investment.

Contrary to popular belief, the forty years prior to the First World War were not ones of undiluted free trade; indeed, both in Continental Europe and in the USA the infant industry argument dominated international economic policy. At the same time, many world markets were expanding rapidly and offered attractive prospects to firms possessing the ability to supply them. Often too, for reasons described earlier, the newer industries of the era soon became the growth sectors dominated by international oligopolists, whose defensive strategy undoubtedly accelerated the switch from exports to foreign production (Knickerbocker, 1973; Graham, 1978). In due course the innovations of the last quarter of the nineteenth century were disseminated and the products arising from them became more standardised and price elastic. Differences in production costs, and transfer costs between home and host countries then became a more important determinant of corporate strategy.

The product cycle theory of international production is an excellent explanation of this kind of investment and why its extent and pattern varies between countries. *Ceteris paribus*, such production is likely to originate from wealthy industrialised countries and be initially directed to well populated economies following one or two steps behind in the development process. The pattern reflects the comparative innovating advantages of the home countries, their psychic distance from other main markets, the size of the domestic relative to the export market, and the strategy and organisational approach adopted by firms to their foreign activities and international production in particular. Thus, even before 1914, the overseas production/export ratio was considerably higher for US firms than for European firms, and varied considerably between industrial sectors.

We conclude that locational factors were important in explaining the growth in international production relative to exports in the forty years before the First World War, in spite of the reduction in transport costs and the economies of centralised production made possible by new technologies.

(b) 1914–38

In the inter-war years locational advantages continued to shift in favour of international production; indeed, in the case of import substituting investment they were probably *the* main factor leading to what growth there was in FDI. Between 1914 and 1939 the ratio of the stock of FDI to the value of world trade rose substantially. Although part of this rise was accounted for by foreign subsidiaries existing in 1914, there were a large number of new ventures set up, particularly in the 1930s.

During these years, too, an increasing proportion of MNE activity was accounted for by US firms; in the manufacturing sector this more than quadrupled in the years 1914–43, and more than four-fifths of US MNE activity was located in Canada and Europe. There was also some syndicate direct investment in Europe – especially in the 1920s (Teichova, 1974; Franko, 1976). Contemporary empirical studies, e.g. by Southard (1931), Marshall, Southard and Taylor (1936) and the Royal Institute of International Affairs (1937), suggest that most market-oriented investment in developed countries was defensive in character; in Canada, Marshall, Southard and Taylor regard tariffs as 'of overwhelming importance in the branch plant movement' (p.

201). By contrast, the same writers estimate that only between 15 per cent and 20 per cent of Canadian–American branch factories owed their existence 'in any measurable extent to transportation savings' while the factory costs of US companies in Canada were 'in most cases definitely higher than those in the parent company' (p. 207).

In Europe, Southard (1931) concluded that US firms were prompted to establish branch plants mainly by the need to customise goods (particularly consumer goods) to local tastes, by savings on transatlantic transport costs, especially for bulky or fragile articles, and by non-tariff barriers, e.g. local government purchasing policies and 'buy at home' sales pitches. They also sought to forestall the entry of European firms into US markets through the takeover of European companies. These, and other reasons were to figure in the motives influencing post-Second World War investors, as recorded by Brash (1966 – Australia), Safarian (1966 – Canada), Stubenitsky (1970 – Netherlands), Deane (1970 – New Zealand) and Forsyth (1972 – Scotland) and summarised by Dunning (1973).[50]

It is perhaps worth repeating that, rather more than its national branch plant counterpart, the foreign plant may simply replace part of the domestic production by the parent firm.[51] However, beyond a certain point, foreign production may lead to additional growth, particularly where MNEs already ensconced in foreign countries are instrumental in persuading their hosts to introduce or increase import controls. Research also reveals that once abroad – and indeed in the act of going overseas – US MNEs may have substantially different policy objectives to American exporters (e.g. *vis-à-vis* their domestic operations). In other words, foreign production may bring with it internalising economies which exporting does not. Other studies reveal instances when exports and foreign production are directly complementary to each other (Horst, 1974).

Supply-based investments (in mining and plantations) recorded a mixed performance in the inter-war period. Due to the rapidly increasing demand for oil, both US and European MNEs expanded their investments in crude oil production. Due also to the growing popularity of tropical fruits, US investment in banana and pineapple plantations rose sharply, but in the recession of the 1930s these were cut back sharply. Mining investments rose only slightly, however, except in some of the newer metals, nitrates, etc. As mentioned earlier, the inter-war years saw the establishment of several mineral cartels, although the non-members of these cartels tried to develop alternative materials (e.g. French and German producers switched to aluminium and developed their own bauxite interests in France, Italy and Eastern Europe). There was also some mineral investment in European colonies, while investments in rubber plantations in

Malaysia and Liberia also expanded. Generally speaking, there was little secondary processing activity by MNEs in the developing countries in this period and few attempts by governments to disinternalise investments in resources. But in the later 1930s new commodity and futures markets began to emerge, which were later to erode the advantages of vertical integration, e.g. in rubber and tea. Reddaway, Potter and Taylor (1968) observe that by the late 1950s there was very little backward integration by UK firms in the raw materials sectors which they had dominated half a century earlier.

(c) 1945–60

The early post-war period favoured the expansion of all kinds of international commerce, and international production in particular. The reasons were both 'defensive' and 'aggressive', and market- and supply-oriented investments were similarly affected. By 1960 it was estimated that the value of international production was approaching that of world trade; and in the case of some countries, e.g. the USA, UK, Switzerland and the Netherlands, it was considerably higher. In the following decade the growth in the FDI stake outpaced that of trade by half as much again. During the 1950s the USA reached the peak of her economic hegemony, but, because of a world shortage of dollars, US firms were obliged to produce overseas to sell their products. There were also push factors at work – such as the growing differential in labour costs between the USA and other industrialised countries, and a revival of American antitrust policy which checked one avenue of domestic growth. Anxious to be the leaders in exploiting their new ownership advantages in foreign markets, US oligopolists in the pharmaceutical, electrical goods, computer, industrial instrument and other industries were quick to establish branch plants in Europe, Canada, Australia and some wealthier Latin American economies. Again, investing firms initially perceived these ventures less as an expansion of their domestic activities as a replacement for part of them.

Much post-war UK direct investment in Canada and Australia was of this kind and there was a certain pattern to it. First a sales and service facility was set up to promote exports; then came local production using imported materials and components, and this was followed by production with some local components, and so on. This process was frequently observed in the 1960s in both UK and US manufacturing investments. Again, rising markets, often protected by import controls, were the main inducements, together with the fear of losing markets to competitors. The abandonment of international cartel arrangements led several UK firms to set up in the USA, while others saw such investment as the best way to obtain access to American technology.[52]

The recovery of Western Europe, the move towards economic integration there and in Latin America, and the introduction of export processing zones heralded a new era for manufacturing MNEs and fundamentally affected their production and locational strategies. In the later 1960s and 1970s rationalised investment was the fastest growing sector of MNE activity, and the one which caused host countries almost as much concern as resource-based investment had done previously.

The rapid growth in industrial output following the end of the Second World War led to an unprecedented demand for raw materials to sustain that output, and increasingly the main industrial countries were forced to seek new outlets of supply. For reasons exactly parallel to those prompting backward integration in the nineteenth century, large firms purchasing primary products for processing and fabrication sought to internalise their outlets. So the surge outwards to supply-oriented investment was in direct proportion to the growth in manufacturing output and domestic incomes in the industrialised North. At the same time, there was growing concern among the supplying countries, on both political and economic grounds, about the increasing presence of foreign firms in key natural resource sectors. This was not just a matter of the ability of such firms to extract monopoly rents; much more important was their control over the way in which local resources were used, their rate of exploitation and to whom, on what terms, and by what means they were sold. There was also disquiet about the ways some MNEs earned (or were thought to earn) their economic rent, e.g. by manipulation of transfer pricing, which were not always possible to detect or control. Many of these costs of FDI were attributed to the internalising of transactions between MNEs and their affiliates.

The story about the reactions of host countries to these events is well known. In the present context, the main effect was to encourage or enforce divestments by MNEs in many resource-based sectors, and to change the terms in which others – particularly new investors – were allowed to be involved. Public fiat replaced firm fiat, while at the same time, due to the increasing competition among MNEs and the growth of indigenous firms, markets for many products became less imperfect. The consequence was a decline in the relative importance of supply-based foreign investments in the 1960s and 1970s, except in certain resource-rich developed countries, e.g. Canada, Australia and the UK (for North Sea Oil), and in countries in the Far East which appeared to have the same political persuasion as the main investors. It was in this region that Japanese investors made their first major thrust in the 1960s, and even today they have a much larger stake in resource-based investment than either their US or European counterparts. These investments are closely controlled, either directly or indirectly, by Japanese industrial or trading companies.

(d) 1960–78

Let us now turn to the major locational development of the past two decades. Partly as a result of the enlargement of markets, occasioned *inter alia* by rising living standards and regional economic integration, and partly as a consequence of changes in production and marketing strategies on the part of MNEs, the factors influencing the spatial distribution of MNE activity in manufacturing and associated activities has dramatically changed. It now rests less on the kind of determinants associated with either a single import-substitution or supply-oriented investment and more on the appropriate locations for a group of interrelated activities. In this respect there are considerable similarities between inter-regional specialisation within a large market area and international specialisation of activity. There are also parallels with the explanation of the location of similar activities across national boundaries but under separate ownership which give rise to intra-industry trade.

The best illustration of this form of FDI is that of US MNEs in the EEC since around 1960. To capture the economies of scale and centralisation of production, but to take advantage of a free trade area, firms which previously were truncated replicas of their parent companies, each producing similar products for individual markets without trade, have found it economic to specialise in particular products and processes for all markets in the region, and to trade these products across national boundaries. The choice of location and the effect of the rationalisation on the totality and distribution of the capital stake is partly determined by the disposition of existing capacity, partly by production and transaction costs, and partly by country-specific variables, e.g. the availability of skilled labour and materials, transport and communication costs, consumer tastes, government regulations, and so on (Dunning, 1972; Hood and Young, 1980). The result is a balance of activities which is based as much on the comparative resource endowments of a country as on the absolute advantages offered by particular locations. In this respect, companies may behave as countries. The allocation of the activities of companies like N. V. Philips, Honeywell, Ford and International Harvester, in the EEC is based upon this type of strategy. It helps create substantial economies of integration, and can usually only be successfully achieved through internalisation of resource transfers. This, in turn, is only viable if there are no restrictions on trade in goods, and policies towards international direct investment are reasonably harmonised.

In Europe, and to a lesser extent in Latin America, the kind of trade associated with this kind of rationalised investment is not obviously based upon differences in the distribution of factor endowments in the classical or neoclassical sense. But in other parts of the world, another type of rationalised investment – the export platform type – is of this kind. Perhaps the most rapidly growing activity of manufacturing MNEs in East Asia, Mexico and some parts of Southern Europe is to take advantage of cheap, plentiful and well motivated labour to produce those products or processes which require such a resource. The main locational impetus giving rise to this has been the growth of manufacturing capacity in a number of NICs, and the generally liberal attitude of these countries to export oriented FDI. It is here where fiscal incentives have been the most generous and most significant in influencing locational choice.

It is worth observing that much of the first and some of the second kind of rationalised production reflect a form of *growth* of foreign participation rather than an *initial* means of entry. Essentially they embrace 'specialisation within diversification', and the benefits realised are entirely those of scale and integration. Some of these economies may be specific to geographical diversification, i.e. those to do with intra-firm trade, and those arising from imperfections in exchange and capital markets and differences in the tax treatment of corporations. These strongly suggest that the common ownership of spatially separated production units *does* influence the way in which resources are allocated.[53]

The way that economic integration affects the structure of ownership of firms in a common market as well as their location has not been fully explored in the literature. Like other influences on a firm's growth to which we have given scant attention in this chapter, it underlines the interdependence between the different elements of growth. Neither a purely technological nor an organisational approach to growth is sufficient in itself, and the significance of each varies very greatly according to structural factors. And while in some cases locational theory may be used to explain why a firm chooses to internalise its ownership specific advantages across rather than within national boundaries, in many cases – and especially with rationalised production – there are additional integrative gains which affect the extent and pattern of its activities.

There is one other point which should be made. The 1970s have seen a gradual liberalisation of the attitudes of many governments toward both outward and inward direct investment. At the same time, as a result of the learning process of the previous two decades, policies with respect to entry, performance and exit conditions of foreign firms have become more enlightened. Partly too, the world recession has made countries more aware of the potential gains of inward investment; but it has also caused MNEs to cut back on some of their foreign operations to protect their domestic interests. This has been particularly noticeable in the case of US MNEs and, in part, is a reflection of the devaluation of the dollar. By contrast, the expansion of European direct investment in the USA illustrates the increasing profitability of producing in rather than exporting to the USA. Again, this shift in the pattern of international production is a location-substituting kind rather than growth-oriented. To make things more complicated, part of the investment classified as FDI in official statistics may not really be that at all but rather portfolio investment, as there is no *de facto* supervision exercised over the capital exported.

It may be concluded then, that for most of the past one hundred years, foreign production has been of an import-substituting or resource-exploitative kind. As far as the initial entry decision is concerned, quite a lot of the former was a response to changes in the profitability of supplying a foreign market from a foreign rather than a domestic base, and quite a lot of the latter a response to the inability of markets to guarantee a regular flow of inputs of the required quality and at the right price. Once established, however, the growth of affiliates of MNEs became influenced by other factors to do with exploiting the economies of geographical diversification. In the last fifteen or twenty years, the integrated manufacturing and service MNE has come of age, and the strategy of international location now includes the optimisation of integrative gains and production opportunities. These changes have been due to factors both endogenous and exogenous to MNEs; the resulting economies in transaction costs suggest that, as an organisational unit, the MNE may well claim to be 'first and foremost an efficiency instrument' (Williamson, 1981). *Inter alia* they are demonstrated by the growing quantity of intra-group and intra-industry trade among MNE affiliates and between affiliates and their parent companies (Dunning, 1981b).

5.7 SUMMARY AND IMPLICATIONS FOR FUTURE RESEARCH

This chapter began by describing some of the changes in the FDI stake of countries since the 1870s. While recognising that the most widely published data are often a poor proxy for the foreign operations of MNEs, they nevertheless give a fairly clear cut picture of how the major investing and recipient countries have fared over the years.

What however, such macro data – even at sectoral level – do not show is the extent and pattern of the growth of individual MNEs. Instead one has to turn to the growth in the size of firms in general, and see how far this is related to their propensity to engage in foreign production. And here the data strongly suggest that, when one has isolated other variables, such as industry, size, country of origin, etc., the firms which are the most multinational are also the largest and fastest growing.

This chapter has attempted to explain the growth of international production using the framework of the OLI paradigm (also referred to as the 'eclectic theory'). First, it has examined the role of technological advances backed by appropriate institutional change in creating proprietary production, marketing and transactional advantages for firms of particular nationalities; second, it has examined the organisational framework by which these advances are disseminated across national boundaries; and third, it has looked at some of the reasons why, given their technological capacity, firms of a particular country of origin should choose to locate their production activities outside rather than within their boundaries.

While this chapter has sought to identify the main factors, it has not attempted to quantify their individual significance. But what can be said is this. The growth of international production reflects a composite of interrelated forces at work. Viewed from a macroeconomic standpoint it is impossible to predict which of the OLI variables is likely to be the most important in motivating such production, in the first place, and in expanding it, in the second. Basically, it is possible to contend that at least one of each of the OLI variables must be present before foreign production takes place, though it is true that a discriminatory policy in favour of foreign compared to domestic firms may be the only ownership advantage which the former may have over the latter.[54] In some cases the technological superiority of the investing firm may be the primary force, in others the need to internalise, and in others locational forces.

Once in existence, however, it may be that only one of the components of the OLI paradigm may be necessary to explain the further growth of a foreign affiliate. It is very likely that the concentration of international production in the hands of a relatively few MNEs[55] is witness to the growing significance of hierarchical advantages which themselves follow from the growth of foreign production prompted by market forces. In some years over the past century, expansion has mainly occurred through *new* MNE entrants; such was the period immediately before and after the First World War, when technological progress was particularly rapid and locational forces encouraged a re-siting of plants outside home countries. In other periods, the pressures of existing firms to grow through integration have been particularly strong; this has always been the case in some resource-based industries, and over the last two decades has become especially pronounced in some branches of manufacturing and service industry. In the inter-war years, there was less technological advance and less powerful reasons for firms to internalise markets; but the pursuance of import-substitution policies on the part of many governments led many exporting firms to react by setting up plants in the countries in question.

It may be that this kind of analytical framework explains much the greater part of FDI over the last hundred years. Obviously, according to home and host countries, sectors and firms – not to mention time *per se* – the configuration of the OLI variables will alter a great deal. But with a little ingenuity and imagination, it should be possible to construct a matrix of OLI values and structural determinants, and then apply a time period to each to produce a reasonably comprehensive and persuasive explanation of the major changes in international production over the last century. But only when a lot more data are available will it be possible to do this.

NOTES

1 This chapter adopts the 'threshold' definition of the MNE as an enterprise which engages in production financed by foreign direct investment. According to *Who Owns Whom*, the number of such enterprises was over 12,000 in 1978.

2 A selection of these is listed in Dunning (1981a) pp. 42–5, 70–1 and 103–108.

3 I recognise that the foreign direct capital stake (a partial input measure) may not always mirror accurately foreign production (an output measure). But until fairly recently, apart from some details of numbers of the leading MNEs and their affiliates, these were the only data available. Note, too, that part of the foreign capital stake, particularly of European countries, took the form of expatriate, entrepreneurial or syndicate investment rather than branch plant activity of firms.

4 The definition of FDI – in so far as nineteenth-century investment is concerned – is still a matter of dispute among economists. But current thinking, as articulated especially by Svedberg (1978, 1981), Stone (1977) and authors of industry and country studies, suggests that quite a large part of investment originally classified as portfolio by the statisticians of the day was, in fact, managed or controlled by non-residents; while contemporary estimates of direct investment often excluded reinvested profits.

5 This was the modality chosen by many European mining companies – e.g. Rio Tinto, originated by a group of UK entrepreneurs purchasing a mine of that name in Spain in 1873 – and also for some railroad investment. In such cases, there were often two boards of directors – one in London mainly concerned with the invest-

ment management, and the other in the host country which dealt with immediate organisational and operational matters (Wilson, n.d.).

6 For some examples of British and Continental European investment in the US see Coram (1967). For a more general account of the early activities of MNEs see Wilson (n.d.) and Wilkins (1974b).

7 According to Vaupel and Curhan (1974), some 122 manufacturing subsidiaries of 187 large US-based MNEs in existence in 1968 were set up prior to 1914; the corresponding number of subsidiaries for 48 UK MNEs (including Unilever) was 60; and that of 88 Continental European MNEs (including Royal Dutch Shell) was 167. There were no subsidiaries of 67 Japanese large MNEs in 1971 which were set up prior to 1914.

8 Included among these were a whole range of new consumer industries supplying branded goods, e.g. cigarettes, soap, margarine, chocolate, glass, preserved milk, etc., which companies like Nestlé, Levers (the Dutch margarine makers) and Cadbury, were able to take advantage of: Wilson (n.d.) links the origin of this kind of MNE to the fall in living costs (and hence rise in real incomes) which occurred as a result of the Great Depression between 1873 and 1896.

9 Although there were also instances of such dependence in the mining industry, e.g. copper in the Congo, gold in the Gold Coast, etc.

10 As derived from data presented in Vaupel and Curhan (1974).

11 Using data derived from business histories and company archives, Nicholas (1982a) has set out details on the industrial structure of 119 UK MNEs which made a foreign direct investment between 1870 and 1930, and has compared this with that of a sample of pre-1914 US MNEs and of the largest 50 UK firms in 1919 and 1930. His findings about the structure of large UK and US firms at that time correspond to those of earlier writers, e.g. Chandler (1977); but perhaps of greater interest in the present context is the considerable similarity revealed between those sectors which 'dominated' the UK corporate economy and those which dominated UK direct investment.

12 Deflating the data set out in Table 5.1 by the British price indices, the real value of the foreign direct investment stake rose by at least 50 per cent between 1914 and 1938.

13 See Vaupel and Curhan (1974).

14 It is difficult to disentangle how much of these were branch plant investments. But, as in the case of the pre-war investment in Russia, one suspects that the majority were undertaken by foreign capitalists acquiring a majority equity shareholding in indigenous companies; and by foreign entrepreneurs mobilising and allocating capital and technology from their home countries.

15 For further details see Table 5.4.

16 Data on the number of new manufacturing affiliates of MNEs collected by the Harvard researchers are not available for non-US enterprises after 1970, but by that date the number of new US affiliates was falling below its peak in the mid-1960s while that of parent companies of other nationalities was rising.

17 For example of 1369 instances of nationalisation recorded by United Nations (UNCTC) (1978) between 1960 and 1976, 67 per cent were recorded in the final six years. Of some 19 producers' associations existing in 1976, only one (OPEC) was operating in 1960.

18 This table is also extracted from data compiled by Vaupel and Curhan (1974).

19 For example Sekiguchi (1979) estimates that of 1271 Japanese companies with foreign direct investments in March 1975, 482 had a paid up capital of less than 100 million yen (about $0.5 million). The great majority of these were first set up after 1960. See also Tsurumi (1976).

20 The corresponding figures for pre-1914 and 1919–39 were 62 per cent and 63 per

cent respectively. Throughout these years, the propensity of US MNEs to operate wholly-owned subsidiaries was greater than that of non-US MNEs.

21 In the case of Switzerland, one suspects a large proportion of this increase is accounted for by an outward re-channelling of investment by foreign MNEs in Switzerland, prompted by tax and/or exchange rate advantages. In several other countries, however, foreign affiliates themselves engage in outward direct investment. Examples include Australia, Canada, Bermuda, Hong Kong and the UK. Sometimes this is for administrative or tax convenience, e.g. where the responsibility for running a group of affiliates is allocated to a regional office; in others, an affiliate may be better able to serve and/or produce in some foreign markets than its parent company.

22 By contrast, most US *voluntary* divestments or liquidations of manufacturing affiliates occurred in Europe (see Boddewyn, 1979).

23 In 1975 some 59 per cent of total sales by majority owned affiliates of US MNEs were intra-company.

24 We shall not be concerned with these latter flows in this chapter.

25 For a review, and suggested integration of these approaches see Casson (1982).

26 Imagine, for example, an economy which produces a given quantity of 10 separate products, the production of each of which involves 6 different inter-firm intermediate transactions. The maximum mumber of different kinds of firm which might produce these goods is then 60, but by internalising the transactions the number could be reduced even to one firm producing the entire output.

27 These comprise the economic environment, system and policies of government – the so-called ESP combination.

28 These factors are not necessarily sequential in the decision-taking process. Moreover other writers express them rather differently. For example, David Teece in Chapter 3 of this book suggests that an understanding of the MNE involves an answer to two sets of questions, first 'what determines the location of productive activities across the globe', and second 'what determines the governance of these activities'. One may, however, reverse the order of these questions by asking 'what determines whether companies headquartered in one country are able to supply markets independently of where they are located', and 'what determines where they locate their productive activities to supply these markets'. I prefer this latter format, believing the organisational mode of MNE activity is more likely to be influenced by the extent and nature of that activity, than by its spatial distribution. But see Section 5.6, p. XXff.

29 For a recent review of the literature see Kamien and Schwartz (1982).

30 By the 1880s, continuous processing machinery and plants had been developed in the production of such products as cigarettes, matches, breakfast cereals, flour, soap and a wide variety of canned goods (Chandler and Daems, 1974). See also Wilson (n.d.). However, a working paper by James (1981) suggests that in the USA over the period 1850–90, technological arguments do not explain firm size. See also Wilkins (1976), (1977a), (1977b).

31 Mostly other European countries and Russia.

32 Between these years the UK was responsible for 31.3 per cent of all foreign patents granted in the USA, Germany for 26.2 per cent, France for 10.1 per cent and Canada for 15.3 per cent.

33 It is noteworthy that there were several inventions in Europe that were later adapted and commercialised with greater success in the USA, e.g. the internal combustion engine, the fluorescent lamp, photo-lithography.

34 And in so doing imposed barriers of communication between the ultimate customer and the producer (Kindleberger, 1964, p 148).

35 As set out, for example, in United Nations (UNCTC) (1978).

36 But see Section 5.6, p. XXff.

37 For a discussion of such exports of technology from the perspective of the product cycle theory of international investment, see Dunning (1971).

38 This was one of the key motives for the internalisation by the Singer Sewing Machine Company of its selling outlets. For a fascinating discussion of the move from agency to direct selling organisations by UK firms in the 1870–1939 period, see Nicholas (1982a).

39 In some cases, e.g. in the early non-ferrous and precious metal ventures by UK firms, the original thrust outwards was essentially an entrepreneurial one, in which it was intended to sell the mined product on the open market, or by contract. Out of this kind of investment, many of todays mining giants, e.g. Rio Tinto Zinc, emerged.

40 It should be noted that some of these motives are interdependent. In most cases, vertical selling implies a technological advantage on the part of the integrating company, while most kinds of technology exploited via FDI imply forward integration.

41 In an extremely perceptive article, Chandler (1981) has pointed out that in the UK the invisible hand of the market worked more effectively than in the USA. He puts this down to the early dominance of the family firms in Britain which were reluctant to surrender their autonomy, and to a tightly organised distributional network. By contrast, the growth of US firms coincided with the development of managerial capitalism and the railroad; and from the start hierarchies became a more attractive way of organising production and selling activities.

42 Such as the Dupont/GM financial control system and the organisational innovations made within the Bell system which helped free businesses from the diseconomies of scale inherent in the military form of organisation; see Quirin (1980).

43 For an analysis of the factors influencing the investment of smaller MNEs, see Newbould, Buckley and Thurwell (1978).

44 In other words, at a price at which the MNE could recoup the gains of internalisation.

45 Put in another way, the common ownership of productive facilities generates particular advantages to the owner quite apart from those which might have arisen through the rationalisation of these activities by independent entities. This proposition negates the prediction of the so-called separation theorem; see Caves (1980), and the next section of this paper.

46 In some cases, host government policy towards inward direct investment has been the crucial factor determining the organisational form by which foreign resources are imported. The two examples which come most readily to mind are Japan and India, but, throughout the developing world, there has been a general preference of governments for joint ventures and/or contractual resource flows relative to a 100 per cent foreign equity stake.

47 There is a good deal of evidence about the ownership strategies of MNEs and other firms with non-equity foreign interests to back this up (see e.g. Stopford and Haberich, 1976).

48 For an analysis of the differential risks involved, see e.g. Rugman (1979).

49 This was especially notable in the case of agricultural products at the time of the Great Depression (1870–95), when both raw material and transport costs fell sharply. This, together with improved methods of quality control, raised consumer demand and encouraged further investment in both food products and in several types of raw materials which were ingredients of processed goods which had a high income elasticity of demand, e.g. cocoa (for chocolate), tobacco, sugar, palm oil (for soap) and many canned foods.

50 Some authors, e.g. Forsyth (1972), distinguish between factors prompting outward investment by US firms in general and those which favour one host country rather than another. It is in this latter group that investment and labour availability are shown to be of some relevance.

51 But of course a foreign affiliate may act as a sales agent for the export of goods not produced by itself.

52 For a survey of research on FDI in the US see Arpan, Flowers and Ricks (1981).

53 This suggestion counters the proposition that administrative links between multi-production units, and particularly among affiliates of MNEs and between them and their parent companies, do not affect the allocation of resources. In a study of US direct investment in Canada, Caves (1980) finds 'appreciable although incomplete support' *against* this proposition.

54 In other words, I agree with those who argue that monopoly advantage on the part of a particular firm is a necessary condition for FDI. For a view of international trade which preserves the role for the traditional sources of comparative advantage, yet also takes account of economies of scale and imperfect competition see Krugman (1979), (1981).

55 Even though in particular sectors concentration ratios may be falling (Dunning and Pearce, 1981).

6 Industrial diversification amongst the world's leading multinational enterprises

ROBERT D. PEARCE

6.1 INTRODUCTION

The purpose of this chapter is to provide some evidence on the industrial diversification of the world's leading multinational companies. Our sample of enterprises is the 430 firms reported upon by Stopford, Dunning and Haberich (1980). This includes all the world's major $1 billion-turnover industrial corporations that had significant international investments during 1978, excluding firms in banking, insurance, commodity broking, retailing, engineering contracting and other service industries.

This chapter is organised into six sections. Section 6.2 describes the basic data and the methods used to measure industrial diversification. Section 6.3 considers some of the motives for industrial diversification and, in the light of this, analyses differences between industries in the degree of diversification and the extent of their penetration by firms from other industries.

Section 6.4 uses multiple regression analysis to analyse the determinants of industrial diversification. It is shown, perhaps rather surprisingly, that size of firm has little relation to diversification, once other factors have been allowed for. Neither does the nationality of the firm appear significant. It is possible to detect signs of a 'trade-off' between industrial and geographical diversification, though only for firms in the most research-intensive industries.

A major limitation of this analysis is the absence of data on the research-intensity of the individual firm (as opposed to the research) intensity of the firm's principal industry). Section 6.5 repeats the multiple regression analysis for a reduced sample of 221 firms for which data on research intensity is available. The results are somewhat unexpected, for while the research intensity of the industry tends to increase industrial diversification, as one would expect, the research intensity of the firm within a given industry tends to decrease it.

The implications of these and other results are considered in section 6.6. This section summarises the results and considers their implications for future research.

6.2 THE MEASUREMENT OF DIVERSIFICATION

Measures of industrial diversification for each firm were calculated from Stopford, Dunning and Haberich (1980) using both the tabulated information in the five-year summary and the supplementary descriptive information. Though the majority of firms reported the breakdown of their product range in systematic detail this was not done to a common industrial classification. To derive the aggregated and comparative information reported here it was necessary to reorganise the information for many industries to a common system (see Appendix 6A). It was possible to produce for each firm an estimate of the percentage of its total sales made outside of its main industry, where its main industry is that which accounts for the largest share of its total sales. This information, aggregated by industry and country, is given in Table 6.1. Though the firm-level estimates described above are believed to be sufficiently precise for the information in the table to be of value, it was not felt possible to extend the use of the data in two desirable directions. Though it was possible to locate with some precision the total amount of a firm's sales outside its main industry, it was often not possible to allocate precise percentage shares to each of the firm's 'subsidiary industries'. It was, however, possible to say *which* were the firm's 'subsidiary industries' and to delineate them as either 'major' or 'minor' subsidiary interests. I will return to this shortly.

A second piece of information which cannot be derived (but should become available subsequently) relates to *changes* in the level of diversification. Although for many firms a product breakdown is available for more than one year, it is rarely possible to make the reclassification discussed above with sufficient precision for both years for the change to be estimated reliably.[1]

As suggested above, the type of evidence discussed so far, and presented in Table 6.1, only describes one dimension of industrial diversification. Thus a firm with 45 per cent of its sales outside its main industry, but all in one subsidiary industry, is likely to be a different type of firm from another with 45 per cent of sales spread equally over, say, three or four subsidiary industries. Our approach to this has to be limited to specifying those industries in which a firm has

Table 6.1 *Estimated Percentage of Sample Firms' Total Sales Made outside Their Main Industry, 1978*

	USA	*Canada*	*Europe (Total)*	*EEC (Total)*	*Germany*	*France*	*Italy*	*Netherlands*	*Belgium*	*UK*	*UK/ Netherlands*	*Other Europe (Total)*	*Sweden*	*Switzerland*	*Japan*	*TOTAL*
Aerospace	55	—	0	0	—	—	—	—	—	0	—	—	—	—	—	49
Office Equipment and Computers	17	—	10	10	—	—	10	—	—	—	—	—	—	—	31	17
Petroleum	15	—	18	18	55	11	22	—	7	10	14	—	—	—	38	16
Electronics and Electrical Appliances	47	40	34	34	33	38	—	30	—	41	—	32	23	40	26	37
Chemicals and Pharmaceuticals	31	—	21	22	14	24	38	45	15	23	—	12	—	7	22	26
Industrial and Farm Equipment	26	5	30	36	36	—	—	—	—	32	—	20	20	20	42	30
Rubber	28	—	7	7	0	8	6	—	—	10	—	—	—	—	16	21
Motor Vehicles	12	—	16	16	9	10	34	—	—	24	—	20	20	—	17	14
Metal Manufacture and Products	32	37	29	29	31	44	—	5	5	29	—	27	27	24	11	27
Building Materials	32	—	33	35	—	35	—	—	—	35	—	0	—	0	34	33
Food, Drink and Tobacco	17	11	17	20	—	4	—	0	—	13	40	1	—	1	16	17
Paper and Wood Products	12	10	45	35	—	—	—	—	—	35	—	57	57	—	0	19
Textiles, Apparel and Leather Goods	12	—	25	25	—	—	50	—	—	16	—	—	—	—	29	23
Other Manufacturing	31	—	18	18	17	1	—	30	—	22	—	—	—	—	35	28
TOTAL	22	25	22	23	25	22	29	29	8	20	22	20	28	12	22	22

Note: Table covers all directory firms except De Beers Consolidated Mines
Source: Estimates derived from entries in Stopford, Dunning and Haberich (1980)

a subsidiary interest and categorising those subsidiary interests as 'major' or 'minor'. A firm has a 'major' subsidiary interest in an industry where that industry accounts for over 5 per cent of its total sales or for sales of over $100 million. Obviously a 'minor' subsidiary interest is one of less than 5 per cent of total sales and less than $100 million. Details of this measure of diversification are given in Table 6.2. It will be seen that this table provides not only information on the industrial diversification of the firms from a particular industry but also evidence of the extent to which the industry is 'penetrated' by firms from other industries. Summary diversification and penetration ratios derived from Table 6.2 are included in Table 6.3.

Finally, it is necessary to mention a familiar and intractable problem in measuring industrial diversification, that of industry 'width'. Any industry classification which seeks to be logical along product and/or process lines will end up with some industries covering much more 'industrial space' than others. Other things being equal, such industries would have lower industrial diversification ratios than the more narrowly defined industries. There is, of course, no way in which the full range of industrial space can be operatively divided into a given number of equally wide sub-units. This should be borne in mind throughout, though the discussion of Table 6.3 will suggest that factors other than industry 'width' (these other factors including particular *characteristics* of the industry as defined) do affect industrial diversification.

6.3 EXTENT AND DIRECTION OF INDUSTRIAL DIVERSIFICATION

This section seeks to interpret the pattern of industrial diversification among the sample firms. For this purpose it is useful to distinguish five types of industrial diversification.

(a) *Technological spillover* (T) occurs when a firm from one industry undertakes a subsidiary interest in another industry in order to make use of technology created as a spinoff of R & D aimed at progress in its main industry. Of course the creation of such 'spillover' technology need not inevitably involve the firm in new activity outside its main industry, since it may sell its new knowledge to firms already established in the industry to which it may be appropriate. Nevertheless, we would expect some diversification of this type to have occurred, especially between R & D- and innovation-oriented industries.

Table 6.2 *Estimates of Industrial Diversification of Sample Firms by Subsidiary Industries and Main Industry, 1978*

Main Industry	*No. of firms in Main Industry*	*Aerospace* A	*Aerospace* B	*Office Equipment and Computers* A	*Office Equipment and Computers* B
Aerospace	4	—	—	1	
Office Equipment and Computers	11	3	1	—	—
Petroleum	30			1	2
Electronics and Electrical Appliances	41	11	4	25	1
Chemicals and Pharmaceuticals	69	1	1	6	2
Industrial and Farm Equipment	34	3	5	1	3
Rubber	10	2	1	1	
Motor Vehicles	37	12	2	1	2
Metal Manufacture and Products	62	2	3		
Building Materials	19	1	1		
Food, Drink and Tobacco	58				2
Paper and Wood products	22	1		1	
Textiles, Apparel and Leather Goods	13	1	1		
Other Manufacturing	20		1		
TOTAL	430	37	20	37	12

Main Industry	*No. of firms in Main Industry*	*Metal Manufacture and Products* A	*Metal Manufacture and Products* B	*Building Materials* A	*Building Materials* B
Aerospace	4	3			
Office Equipment and Computers	11				
Petroleum	30	8	2	3	3
Electronics and Electrical Appliances	41	9	4	3	5
Chemicals and Pharmaceuticals	69	14	2	10	6
Industrial and Farm Equipment	34	12	5	9	1
Rubber	10				1
Motor Vehicles	37	6	2	3	4
Metal Manufacture and Products	62	—	—	15	5
Building Materials	19	4		—	—
Food, Drink and Tobacco	58	3	5	2	6
Paper and Wood Products	22	1	4	8	2
Textiles, Apparel and Leather Goods	13	1	1		
Other Manufacturing	20	4	1	2	2
TOTAL	430	65	26	55	35

Petroleum		Electronics and Electrical Appliances		Chemicals and Pharma-ceuticals		Industrial and Farm Equipment		Rubber		Motor Vehicles	
A	B	A	B	A	B	A	B	A	B	A	B
		2	1	1	1	3				2	
		5	3			3	1				
—	—	1	1	24	1	3	2		2	3	1
2		—	—	3	1	24	1			2	0
8	5	9	5	—	—	11	2	2	3	2	1
		11	5	4	4	—	—		1	8	8
			1	5	1	1	—	—		2	3
1		11	3	3		28	1		1	—	—
5	7	8	4	22	13	35	9			7	5
		2	5	8	2	3	3			3	3
3		4	2	20	13	6	7		1	3	
1	3			9	3	3	4				
	1		1	7	1	2	1				1
	1	5	4	3	1	7	1			3	
20	17	58	35	109	41	129	33	2	8	35	23

Food, Drink and Tobacco		Paper and Wood Products		Textiles, Apparel and Leather Goods		Other Manufac-turing		TOTAL	
A	B	A	B	A	B	A	B	A	B
			1			1		13	3
		1				4		16	5
1	3	2	3	2	1	16	4	64	25
3		2	2	2	2	18	1	104	22
14	6	4	2	14	5	21	13	116	53
		2	2	3	2	12	5	65	41
			1	1	3	2	3	14	15
		2				12	3	79	18
2	3	6	3	3	3	28	9	133	64
		6	2	2	2	5	3	34	21
—	—	5	6	7	6	16	11	69	59
1	2	—	—	1	3	8	6	34	27
1	3		1	—	—		5	12	16
1		5	1	2	2	—	—	32	14
23	17	35	24	37	29	143	63	785	383

Note: A—Number of firms from main industry with major subsidiary interest in this industry, where major interest is over 5 per cent of the firm's total sales or over $100 million sales. B—Number of firms from main industry with minor subsidiary interest in this industry, where minor interest is less than 5 per cent of firm's total sales and less than $100 million sales

Source: As Table 6.1

Table 6.3 *Diversification and Penetration Ratios by Industry*

	Diversification Ratios		*Penetration Ratios*	
	Ratio (1)	*Ratio (2)*	*Ratio (1)*	*Ratio (2)*
Aerospace	49	3.6	11.8	0.11
Office Equipment and Computers	17	1.7	3.9	0.10
Petroleum	16	2.6	1.0	0.07
Electronics and Electrical Appliances	37	2.8	1.8	0.19
Chemicals and Pharmaceuticals	26	2.1	1.9	0.36
Industrial and Farm Equipment	30	2.5	4.3	0.37
Rubber	21	2.2	0.6	0.01
Motor Vehicles	14	2.4	1.2	0.12
Metal Manufacture and Products	27	2.7	1.3	0.21
Building Materials	33	2.3	3.8	0.18
Food, Drink and Tobacco	17	1.7	0.5	0.08
Paper and Wood Products	19	2.2	2.1	0.12
Textiles, Apparel and Leather Goods	23	1.5	3.9	0.12
Other Manufacturing	28	2.0	8.7	0.43
TOTAL	22	2.3	2.3	—

Notes:

Diversification Ratio (1): estimated percentage of sales of firms classified to the industry made outside the industry.
Source: Table 6.1.

Diversification Ratio (2): is x/n where x is the total number of diversification points for firms classified to the industry and n is the number of firms in the industry. The number of diversification points is calculated as one point for a major diversification and $\frac{1}{2}$ point for a minor diversification (as defined in Table 6.2).
Source: calculated from Table 6.2.

Penetration Ratio (1): is y/n where y is the total number of penetration points and n is the number of firms classified to the industry. Penetration points are calculated as 1 point for a major interest in the industry by a firm not classified to the industry, and $\frac{1}{2}$ point for a minor interest (defined as in Table 6.2). Note that 'major' and 'minor' are defined with respect to the penetrating firm and not by any criteria relating to the penetrated industry.
Source: calculated from Table 6.2.

Penetration Ratio (2): is $y/(430 - n)$ where y and n are defined as above.
Source: calculated from Table 6.2.

(b) Exploration spillover (E) which is similar to T except that it involves spillover from prospecting activities.

(c) Vertical integration (V) of multi-stage production linking different industries. Thus while several of our industries, e.g. 'metals' and 'petroleum', are defined to internalise a major vertical integration sequence we would expect to find other vertical links which involve

firms diversifying into other industries. Of course we are not arguing that industrial diversification is the only way that firms can secure these vertical links, since they are frequently carried out by contractual or spot market transactions between independent firms from the two linked industries. Nevertheless where quality control or reliability of supply factors are important, the internalising of the link through industrial diversification is to be expected.

(d) *Product complementarity* (P) in which the firm produces a hybrid or multi-component good which uses components from different industries.

(e) *Conglomerate diversification* (C) in which there is no obvious technical connection between the industries. This is regarded as a residual category.

It will be seen that this typology is based on firm behaviour in line with recent theoretical reasoning on MNE motivation. Thus the technological spillover argument rests upon the internalisation of proprietary knowhow generated by the firm, while the exploration spillover involves internalising confidential knowledge to make speculative acquisitions of mineral rights, etc. The vertical integration argument rests upon the internalisation of markets for raw and semi-processed materials. Product complementarity is essentially a synthesis of the earlier arguments. The firm has focused its research on the development or improvement of a hybrid product, and has internalised the exploitation of the knowhow in both the industries involved. It has thereby become responsible for managing a production structure in which components manufactured in different industries are channelled through internal markets to an assembly plant where the final product is made. Conglomerate diversification may rest upon the internal exploitation of very general management skills, or upon the pursuit of 'portfolio gains' of the kind realised by a mutual fund.

Before applying this typology in detail it is appropriate to comment upon some of the outstanding features of diversification revealed by Tables 6.1 to 6.3.

Table 6.1 shows that 22 per cent of the total sales of the sample firms were made outside their main industry in 1978. Industrial diversification was most notably above average for 'aerospace' (49 per cent), 'electronics and electrical appliances' (37 per cent) and 'building materials' (33 per cent). The lowest ratios were recorded by 'motor vehicles' (14 per cent), 'petroleum' (16 per cent), 'office equipment and computers' (17 per cent) and 'food, drink and tobacco' (17 per cent).

Generally there would appear to be little variation between countries in the overall diversification ratio, with US, European and Japanese firms all sharing the sample average of 22 per cent. Though there is clearly more variation between countries within a given industry, there are few cases which suggest that particular countries have a strong general tendency to have firms with consistently above or below average industrial diversification. This is confirmed by the multiple regression analysis reported in Section 6.4.

Table 6.2 presents information on the subsidiary industries into which firms of a particular main industry have diversified, using the classification of major or minor diversifications as outlined in section 6.2. The table also shows the extent to which a particular industry is penetrated by firms of other industries. Thus, for example, 37 firms from other industries have made major diversifications into aerospace and a further 20 firms have made minor diversification into this industry.

Table 6.3 reports summary measures of diversification and penetration at the industry level. Two measures are used in each case: IDR1 and IDR2 for diversification, and PR1 and PR2 for penetration. These measures are explained in the notes to the table, though it should be noted here that PR1 attempts to provide a rough indication of the importance in the total activity of an industry of firms not classified to that industry, whilst PR2 provides some measure of the attractiveness of a particular industry as a direction of diversification for firms of other industries.

At this point we revert briefly to an issue discussed in section 6.2, that of industry 'width'. It was admitted there that the levels of industrial diversification recorded by the firms of a particular industry would be to some extent (perhaps crucially) dependent on how industries were defined. Now if industry 'width' were the preponderant cause of different degrees of industrial diversification between industries there should be a very high (negative) correlation between the diversification ratios and the penetration ratios recorded in Table 6.3. Thus if only industry 'width' affected diversification, then the industry with the widest definition would have the lowest IDR, since it would have the smallest area of industrial space to diversify into. But, on the same assumption, this industry would also have the highest degree of penetration, since it offers the most industrial space to be diversified into.

In fact, the rank correlation coefficient between IDR1 and the two penetration ratios are +0.574 and +0.492, and for IDR2 the corresponding coefficients are −0.035 and +0.079.[2] This suggests that industry definition is far from being the exclusive determinant of levels of diversification and that other factors, including the particular characteristics of industries, have a major influence.

The miscellaneous 'other industries' grouping has an important influence on the aggregate diversification of the remaining industries since it has the greatest number of both major and minor penetrations. We shall, however, not mention this sector in our analysis of diversification and penetration since its diffuse nature precludes the drawing of any helpful conclusions from the extent of its interaction with other groups.

'Aerospace' ranks as the most diversified of the industries. Its most notable diversifications are into 'industrial and farm equipment', 'metal manufacture and products' – each of which receive major diversifications from three of the four aerospace firms – and 'electronics and electrical appliances' and 'motor vehicles'. Of these industries, it is the latter two which have most substantially diversified *into* 'aerospace', though eight more industries have at least one major penetration into it.

Following 'aerospace' among the highly diversified industries is another substantially based on advanced technology, 'electronics and electrical appliances'. Though 'electronics and electrical appliance' firms have some diversification into all industries (except 'rubber'), two predominate. These are 'office equipment and computers' and 'industrial and farm equipment', each of which receive diversification from over 60 per cent of electronics and electrical appliance firms. There is significant diversification by electronics firms into 'aerospace', and diversification of similar magnitude into 'metals'. All industries (except 'paper and wood products') have some diversification into electronics and electrical appliances, with 'chemicals', 'industrial and farm equipment', and 'motor vehicles' predominating.

By contrast 'office equipment and computers', though based on advanced technology, has little diversification. The industry's most substantial diversification is into 'electronics and electrical appliances', followed by 'aerospace' and 'industrial and farm equipment'. The diversification of 'electronics and electrical appliances' into 'office equipment and computers' emerges as the latter industry's major penetration; it accounts for 25 of the 37 major diversifications into the industry. The remaining penetrations of 'office equipment and computers' are spread over eight industries with only one (chemicals) recording more than one major diversification into the industry.

Another research-based industry, 'chemicals and pharmaceuticals', has moderate levels of diversification. The industry has no predominant direction of diversification, but has both major and minor diversifications in every other industry. The only industries to attract significant chemicals diversification were 'food, drink and tobacco' 'metal manufacture and products' and 'textiles, apparel and leather goods'. Similarly penetration of 'chemicals' is spread over all industries (except office equipment and computers), but three industries do clearly predominate: 'petroleum', 'metals' and 'food, drink and tobacco'.

Though 'motor vehicles' has a fairly wide range of diversifications, that into 'industrial and farm equipment' predominates. Thus 28 of 37 motor vehicles firms have major diversifications into 'industrial and farm equipment'. The industry's two other substantial diversifications are into 'aerospace' and 'electronics and electrical appliances'. It is perhaps surprising that motor vehicles has minimal diversification into petroleum and rubber and that diversification into metals is not more significant. 'Motor vehicles' is not one of the most highly penetrated industries, though only two industries have no interest in it. The strongest penetrations come from 'industrial and farm equipment' and 'metals'.

'Industrial and farm equipment' has overall diversification levels above the average but this owes more to a number of fairly substantial links than to any predominant ones. Thus four industries ('electronics and electrical appliances', 'motor vehicles', 'metal manufacture and products', 'building materials') each receive significant diversifications, and no industry receives major diversifications from more than 36 per cent of 'industrial and farm equipment' firms. 'Industrial and farm equipment' is one of the most penetrated industries, with major penetrations from all other industries, though three predominate: 'metals', 'motor vehicles' and 'electronics and electrical appliances'.

Though 'petroleum' has some diversification into all other industries (except aerospace) there is one clearly predominant link, that with 'chemicals and pharmaceuticals': 24 of the 30 petroleum firms have major diversifications into chemicals. 'Petroleum' is one of the least penetrated industries, with diversifications from 'chemicals' and 'metals' predominating.

'Metals' is one of the most substantially diversified industries, with major diversifications in all except two industries. The strongest diversification is into 'industrial and farm equipment'. 71 per cent of the industry's firms have some diversification into 'industrial and farm equipment'. This is a stronger relationship than the, nevertheless significant, one in the other direction as recorded above. Another substantial diversification is into 'chemicals', with 51 per cent of 'metals' firms having some diversification into that industry. 'Building materials' is the third major direction of diversification. All industries, except 'office equipment and computers' and 'rubber', have at least one major penetration into 'metals'. 'Chemicals and pharmaceuticals' and 'industrial and farm equipment' lead, and 'petroleum' and 'electronics and electrical appliances' are also significant.

Like 'metals', 'building materials' is another resource-based industry which has somewhat above-average overall levels of diversification. However, its diversifications are less wide ranging (four industries receive no diversifications) and there are less clearly dominating directions of diversification. Thus, there is no industry in which half building material firms have major diversifications. 'Building materials' also ranks slightly above average in terms of penetration, with 'metals', 'chemicals', 'industrial and farm equipment' and 'paper and wood products' predominating.

Overall, 'rubber' has somewhat below average diversification. This is due partly to a smaller range of diversifications than some industries (five industries receive no major diversifications) and the lack of any major links (only 'chemicals' and 'motor vehicles' receive any form of diversification from half of the 'rubber' firms). 'Rubber' is among the least penetrated industries, receiving only two major diversifications (both from 'chemicals') and no penetrations at all from seven industries.

The remaining three industries are all to some extent resource-based and tend to have low research-intensity, being based on relatively standardised technology. They are all also, to varying degrees, less than averagely diversified.

Though 'food, drink and tobacco' has some diversification into all industries (except 'aerospace') most of these are very small and its overall averages put it among the least diversified industries. Its one notable link is with 'chemicals and pharmaceuticals', in which 57 per cent of its firms have some diversification. 'Food, drink and tobacco' also ranks among the least penetrated industries with 'chemicals and pharmaceuticals' being the dominating source. Only two other industries have more than one major diversification into 'food, drink and tobacco'.

'Paper and wood products' only has more than one major diversification in three industries, of which 'chemicals and pharmaceuticals' and 'building materials' predominate. The industry is about averagely penetrated, with every other industry having at least a minor diversification into the industry.

'Textiles, apparel and leather goods' firms diversify mainly into 'chemicals and pharmaceuticals' which receives diversifications from over 60 per cent of 'textiles, apparel and leather goods' firms. The only other industry to receive more than one major diversification from 'textiles' is 'industrial and farm equipment'. The link with 'chemicals' is again clearly seen in the chemical industry's penetration of 'textiles, apparel and leather goods'. The only other industries to diversify significantly into 'textiles' are 'industrial and farm equipment' and 'food, drink and tobacco'.

The major features of diversification identified above can be readily interpreted using the typology of motivations outlined earlier.

As expected a number of type T – technological spillover – diversifications can be found among the R & D-intensive industries. Predominant examples are 'electronics and electrical appliances' links with 'office equipment and computers' and 'aerospace'; whilst 'aerospace's' links with 'motor vehicles' is also likely to be of this type. Type T diversification is also likely to be a major factor contributing to the links between 'motor vehicles' and 'industrial and farm equipment', though these industries are not quite at the frontiers of R & D-intensity.

The case of type E – exploration spillover – diversification most clearly shown is that linking 'petroleum' and 'metals'.

Examples of type V – vertical integration – diversification can be found in most industries, though (with the exception of 'chemicals') this type seems to be relatively more predominant amongst medium- and low-R & D industries. As noted earlier we are concerned, in type V diversifications, with links outside a major vertically integrated process. Thus although the petroleum industry is defined to run from oil extraction to fuel marketing, a subsidiary vertical link, which involves diversification, is that in which oil serves as the basic input in the manufacture of petrochemicals. The 'petroleum' – 'chemicals' link is predominantly one of forward vertical integration ('chemicals' diversification into 'petroleum' is much less significant, though it is one of the two industries to dominate penetration of 'petroleum'). Similarly, many 'metals' firms have diversified forward into 'industrial and farm equipment' by producing heavy mechanical equipment (e.g. generating plant) based on metal components cast by them, whilst many firms in 'industrial and farm equipment' have diversified back into production of their metal-based components. 'Metals' links with 'motor vehicles' are also likely to be based on type V diversifications. A further link of this type is that between 'paper and wood products' and 'building materials' where the conversion of unprocessed lumber (in the former) into specific housing components (e.g. doors, chipboard, etc.) provides scope for both forward and backward integration. A noteworthy case of vertically integrating diversifications not based on primary productions is the link between 'chemical' firms and 'textiles, apparel and leather goods'. Firms in the latter industry may diversify back into chemicals to produce the basic inputs for the synthetic fibres and industrial fabrics which are included in their final products, while chemical firms may diversify forward to produce fibres incorporating their basic chemical output.

The 'chemicals'– 'food, drink and tobacco' link is similar, as may be the 'chemicals'– 'rubber' link.

Type P – product complementarity – diversifications are, like type T, predominantly found amongst the more R & D-intensive industries. A classic and illustrative example of type P diversifications is that which links the 'electronics and electrical appliances' and 'industrial and farm equipment' industries. Thus here we have two industries, clearly defined by their two distinct types of technology (electrical engineering and mechanical engineering), each of which produces a range of products which is unequivocally based on its own technology. But there also exists quite a range of hybrid products combining considerable elements of both electrical and mechanical engineering, which are nevertheless classified to one or other industry. Where a firm in one industry produces a hybrid product which on balance has been allocated to the other industry, diversification of type P will occur. The 'office equipment and computers' – 'industrial and farm equipment' link is a similar case, as is 'motor vehicles' diversification into 'electronics and electrical appliances'.

Further illustrative links based on type P diversifications are those between 'electronics and electrical appliances' and 'chemicals' (where the chemical industry's role in producing recording tape is complementary to cassette or tape decks); that of 'chemicals' and 'office equipment and computers' (where the chemical industry is involved in the production of copier paper); and 'metals' and 'chemicals' (involving the production of special non-corrosive metal treatment).

Though it is likely that many notable directions of diversification may involve elements both of technological spillover and of product complementarity, the distinction is believed to be useful. The former case frequently involves the unpremeditated – i.e. not predicted before the R & D, from which the diversification flows, was carried out – diversification of a firm into another industry to utilise its newly created technology to make what, from the viewpoint of the penetrated industry also, may be a significant new product or process innovation. The latter type of diversification may take place during, or persist through, the normal process of technological development and refinement of the hybrid products.

Finally the more general type C – conglomerate – diversifications predominate in the less R & D-intensive industries, notably 'building materials', 'food, drink and tobacco', 'paper and wood products' and 'textiles, apparel and leather goods'. Here successful firms may have skills (e.g. management and/or marketing) which provide the basis for expansion but are less likely to dictate the direction of the expansion than more advanced, technologically explicit, forms of advantage.

6.4 DETERMINANTS OF INDUSTRIAL DIVERSIFICATION

Having reviewed the extent and direction of industrial diversification at the industry level we turn now to an attempt to analyse, using a multiple regression analysis, the factors that determine the variation in the level of diversification between firms. Our dependent variable is IDR1, i.e. the proportion of a firm's sales made in industries other than its main industry.

The first explanatory variable included is the size of firm (S), in the form of the total worldwide sales of the multinational group in 1978. The hypothesis is that since industrial diversification is usually considered to be one of the major routes to growth open to a firm there will be a positive relationship between firm size and its extent of industrial diversification. It should be noted that since our equations will include measures of the geographical diversification of markets or production we will be, to some extent at least, normalising for the extent to which a firm has made use of one of the other major avenues of growth. Size is included in quadratic form to detect any non-linearity in the relationship.[3]

To examine the effect on industrial diversification of a firm's industry dummy variables are used. The 'other manufacturing' group is omitted so that the regression coefficient should be interpreted as the *difference* in the dependent variables exhibited by the industry in question from the omitted industry, i.e. if one industry has a significantly positive coefficient then firms in that industry are significantly more industrially diversified than firms in the 'other manufacturing' group. Further we wish to test whether, overall, industry differences are a significant factor determining levels of industrial diversification. This is done using an F-test to determine the combined explanatory power of industry dummy variables. Our hypothesis is that industry differences are a significant determinant of levels of industrial diversification.

As an alternative to the full industry breakdown we test the influence of particular characteristics of industries on industrial diversification. The first of these characteristics, which we believe to be a determinant of industrial diversification, is the level of research intensity. Of our 14 industries 5 are considered to be of High Research Intensity (HRI)[4] and 4 of Low Research Intensity (LRI).[5] The remaining 5 industries are of Medium Research Intensity (MRI) and in our regressions serve the control group functions performed by 'other manufacturing' in the full industry analysis outlined above. The basis for this research intensity classification is the number of scientists and engineers as a percentage of total employment in 1970 in the US.[6] F-tests are again used to find the overall explanatory power of research intensity.

Our hypothesis is that the levels of R & D have a positive relationship with the extent of industrial diversification. So in our regression equations we would expect HRI to be significantly positive and LRI to be significantly negative. At the base of this expectation is the possibility of diversification resulting from technological spillover as discussed in section 6.3. This we would clearly expect to be greater in industries which persistently carry out high levels of research (including much basic research) than in those carrying out lower levels (most of which may be oriented to development and refinement of existing output rather than the creation of potential new innovations). Of course, even if a firm creates knowledge that it suspects may be of value as the basis of an important innovation in another industry, this does not guarantee that it will itself undertake production in that other industry (i.e. diversify). The firm could sell its newly created knowledge to firms already operating in the other industry. However in many cases a firm may be reluctant to adopt this route of obtaining income from its knowledge due to its seller uncertainty, i.e. it will feel insecure in negotiating terms with a buyer from the other industry, since it it will feel that the buyer's vastly superior knowledge of the industry to which the knowledge is appropriate puts it in a significantly stronger (better informed) bargaining position. On the other hand, buyer uncertainty presents similar problems to the firm in seeking income from its new knowledge by diversifying to use the knowledge itself. Perhaps the most logical means of diversification based on technological spillover would be to take over a firm currently operating in the other industry, possibly one that could be obtained cheaply if its current performance is poor precisely because of the need for an injection of new product and process technology. But again the firm's lack of knowledge of the other industry (and thus of the true state and value of the other firm) will handicap its willingness to agree takeover terms. If the firm sought to enter the other industry by a greenfield investment, buyer uncertainty would still persist since the firm would need to buy personnel experienced in the industry (some general management and experienced marketing personnel) and probably some of the existing technology of the industry (including that embodied in any capital equipment it needs to purchase).

This discussion suggests that the link between levels of R & D expenditure and the extent of industrial diversification is less obvious than at first hypothesised. But if we assume that the *choice of route* for obtaining income from knowledge created in one industry but believed to be of value in another is itself *not* determined by the level of R & D intensity of the firm, then we re-establish the relationship that suggests that the level of industrial diversification is positively related to the level of R & D-intensity. The aggregate industry averages discussed earlier would only suggest tentative support for this hypothesis and one function of the multiple regression approach is to see if support becomes stronger once other influences have been allowed for.

The second characteristic of industries that we wish to test concerns vertical integration. Six of our industries[7] are defined to encompass substantial vertically integrated processes running from raw material extraction (or growth) through to final product marketing, and our hypothesis is that firms in such industries will be less diversified than the firms from the other eight industries. Two points should be noted.

Firstly, we are not assuming that any firm in one of these industries is necessarily itself involved at all the stages covered by the complete vertically integrated process. But we do assume that a firm in such an industry is vitally concerned to optimise its links with other stages of the chain even when it has not internalised them into its own activity. Thus, for example, a firm operating in the middle and later stages of the integrated industry will be persistently concerned to obtain security of raw material inputs on the best available terms and to do this will commit considerable resources to the negotiation of suitable contractual agreements or to developing a sophisticated knowledge of the operation of relevant spot markets.

Secondly, we should note that our hypothesis that firms from vertical integration-oriented industries will be less industrially diversified than those from other industries does not inherently contradict our delineation (in Section 6.3) of vertical integration as a mode of industrial diversification. Vertical integrating diversification, as discussed earlier, usually only covers one link in a vertical integration chain and need not include raw materials, so that it can be carried out by firms from other industries.

Bearing these points in mind, our hypothesis is based on the presumption that firms in these vertically integrated industries have committed their major resources of management and knowhow to the optimal functioning of the existing linkages (including those with other firms, upstream or downstream) and prefer to concentrate on retaining competitive efficiency in these industries rather than risk any of the more esoteric forms of diversification. In these terms some lateral vertically integrated diversification (e.g. metals into heavy machinery) is not basically inconsistent with the hypothesis. The fact that three of the six vertically integrated industries are LRI and two others MRI is also consistent with the hypothesis; firms are concerned to perpetuate existing links as effectively as possible at the cost of any sustained interest in R & D as a basis for innovation.

Again, the earlier discussion has not strongly verified this hypothesis and the multiple regression, it is hoped, may clarify the issue by removing other influences.

To examine the effect on industrial diversification of the nationality of the firms dummy variables are again used, with the USA as the omitted nationality. Restricted equations are again run in order to facilitate F-tests of the overall significance of nationality of firm as a determinant of industrial diversification. Our hypothesis is that nationality is of no great significance, certainly less than industry, as an explanation of variations in industrial diversification between firms.

Finally, we seek to test the hypothesis that industrial diversification may be in some way related to the extent to which the firm utilised another major avenue of growth, namely the geographical diversification of production and/or markets. In fact we use in our equations (as alternatives) three measures of a firm's geographical diversification or sourcing behaviour, (for details of the sources of these ratios see Appendix 6B). The three measures are as follows.

Overseas Production Ratio (X) is the sales of foreign affiliates and associated companies divided by the total worldwide sales of the group. Our hypothesis here is that the overseas production ratio and the industrial diversification ratio will be negatively related, with firms tending to commit resources to the development of an expertise in one or other form of growth path. More specifically, it can be suggested that firms that have become widely diversified have done so because they have acquired a particular expertise in innovation, with considerable ability to assess the potential of, and then to effectively market, new products. We would then follow the argument of the product cycle (Vernon, 1966) to suggest that such firms would concentrate on the early phases of a product life, developing it in the context of their familiar domestic markets, and concentrating on exports to service early overseas demand. Such firms will be little concerned to follow through the development of a product to the mature, standardised, phases of its cycle (concentrating rather on the derivation of newer innovations), and thus will not enter upon the cost-competition-based overseas production which occurs later in the cycle.

The *Parent's Export Ratio* (Y) is the parent company's exports divided by the parent company's production. Here we hypothesise a positive relationship between the parent's export ratio and the industrial diversification ratio. We have suggested that overseas production may be negatively related to industrial diversification, but the corollary of that product cycle-based argument is that innovation-based, industrially diversified, firms may be amongst the most successful exporters. Though it is likely that *total* overseas markets will be more substantial for less diversified firms, we have suggested that this will be because of their willingness to pursue these markets through the later stages of the product cycle by overseas production. Widely diversified firms will have substantial overseas markets, nevertheless, and will be more prepared, and more able, to meet these through exports.

The Overseas Market Sourcing Ratio (Z) is the sales of foreign affiliates divided by the sales of foreign affiliates plus parent company exports, i.e. it is the share of overseas production in a firm's total overseas sales. It would follow from our previous discussion that we would expect this ratio to be negatively related to IDR, i.e. widely diversified firms are expected to be strongly oriented to sourcing their overseas market by exports rather than overseas production.

All three of these geographical diversification ratios are tested in a quadratic form to detect any non-linearities.[8]

Our basic full equation then takes the form:

$$IDR = a + bS + cS^2 + \sum_{i=1}^{13} d_i I_i + \sum_{j=1}^{15} f_j N_j + gG + hG^2 + e \qquad (6.1)$$

where S is firm size

I_i takes a value 1 for i and zero otherwise,
N_j takes a value 1 for j and zero otherwise,
G is the geographical diversification ratio,
a is the intercept,
b, c, g, h are regression coefficients,
d_i and f_j are estimated differences from arbitrarily chosen d_{14} (other industries) and f_{16} (USA) respectively, and e is the error term

It should be recalled that in alternative formulations I is replaced by the research intensity division of industries or by the vertical integration division of industries. Further, there are three alternative versions of the geographical diversification/sourcing ratio. Thus there are in effect nine main equations which are reported in Tables 6.4a to 6.6a. As discussed earlier a number of subsidiary (restricted) equations were run in order to facilitate the computation of F-tests. Some of these restricted equations are also reported in Tables 6.4a to 6.6a and the F-tests in Table 6.7.

The regression analysis was carried out for the 387 firms, from

Table 6.4(a) *Multiple Regression Tests of Industrial Diversification: Equations including Overseas Production Ratio (X)*

Equation	*Explanatory Variables*	*Constant Term*	*S*	*S^2*	*X*	*X^2*	*R^2*
X.1.a.	S, S^2, I, N, X, X^2	27.62	0.0003	−9.495 & −9	−0.214	0.002	0.176
			(0.671)	(1.311)	(1.271)	(0.799)	
X.1.b.	S, S^2, HRI, LRI, N, X, X^2	34.83	−0.0002	−4.054 & −9	−0.236	0.002	0.120
			(0.494)	(0.570)	(1.423)	(0.761)	
X.1.c.	S, S^2, VI, N, X, X^2	32.35	−0.00008	−6.856 & −9	−0.198	0.001	0.080
			(0.209)	(0.952)	(1.167)	(0.567)	
X.2.	S, S^2, N, X, X^2	28.28	0.00003	−6.204 & −9	−0.106	0.0002	0.060
			(0.090)	(0.854)	(0.629)	(0.083)	
X.3.a.	S, S^2, I, X, X^2	22.57	0.0001	−5.332 & −9	−0.019	−0.001	0.118
			(0.326)	(0.762)	(0.128)	(0.585)	
X.3.b.	S, S^2, HRI, LRI, X, X^2	30.65	−0.0002	−1.575 & −9	−0.071	−0.0005	0.075
			(0.669)	(0.229)	(0.480)	(0.283)	
X.3.c.	S, S^2, VI, X, X^2	29.50	0.00003	−4.752 & −9	−0.062	−0.0006	0.040
			(0.089)	(0.685)	(0.417)	(0.318)	

Note: * Significant at 10 per cent ** Significant at 5 per cent *** Significant at 1 per cent
& indicates that the coefficient must be multiplied by 10^x where x is the number following &

Table 6.4(b) *Multiple Regression Tests of Industrial Diversification: Equations including Overseas Production Ratio (X) – Sub-samples*

Equations and Samples	*Constant Term*	*S*	S^2	*X*	X^2	R^2
High Research Intensity Sample						
S, S^2, I, N, X, X^2	42.30	0.001*	−1.470 & −8	−0.617*	0.004	0.187
		(1.697)	(1.439)	(1.853)	(0.967)	
S, S^2, N, X, X^2	37.96	0.0004	−9.214 & −9	−0.523*	0.002	0.131
		(0.931)	(0.927)	(1.693)	(0.485)	
S, S^2, I, X, X^2	38.08	0.0006	−1.020 & −8	−0.311	0.002	0.123
		(1.188)	(1.069)	(1.196)	(0.492)	
Medium Research Intensity Sample						
S, S^2, I, N, X, X^2	31.72	−0.001*	1.433 & −8	0.338	−0.004	0.248
		(1.832)	(1.079)	(0.984)	(0.998)	
S, S^2, N, X, X^2	36.13	−0.001**	1.650 & −8	0.232	−0.003	0.226
		(2.160)	(1.267)	(0.691)	(0.752)	
S, S^2, I, X, X^2	25.56	−0.002**	1.896 & −8	0.521*	−0.009**	0.111
		(2.203)	(1.497)	(1.789)	(2.149)	
Low Research Intensity Sample						
S, S^2, I, N, X, X^2	14.88	0.002	−2.510 & −8	−0.353	0.004	0.371
		(0.822)	(0.102)	(1.417)	(1.266)	

S, S^2, N, X, X^2	21.33	−0.001	2.000 & −7	−0.244	0.003	0.221
		(0.549)	(0.840)	(0.902)	(0.719)	
S, S^2, I, X, X^2	21.74	0.0009	6.206 & −8	−0.162	0.0003	0.182
		(0.526)	(0.600)	(0.722)	(0.117)	
Vertically Integrated Sample						
S, S^2, I, N, X, X^2	21.40	−0.0001	−2.440 & −9	−0.082	0.001	0.300
		(0.282)	(0.266)	(0.394)	(0.398)	
S, S^2, N, X, X^2	22.82	−0.0006	4.701 & −9	0.094	−0.001	0.148
		(1.164)	(0.502)	(0.430)	(0.383)	
S, S^2, I, X, X^2	19.14	0.0001	−3.739 & −9	0.139	−0.002	0.156
		(0.206)	(0.405)	(0.748)	(0.966)	
Non-Vertically Integrated Sample						
S, S^2, I, N, X, X^2	31.15	0.0006	−1.663 & −8	−0.307	0.001	0.168
		(1.027)	(1.522)	(1.117)	(0.289)	
S, S^2, N, X, X^2	35.25	0.0008	−2.058 & −8*	−0.385	0.002	0.130
		(1.405)	(1.934)	(1.454)	(0.476)	
S, S^2, I, X, X^2	26.68	0.0001	−7.689 & −9	−0.186	−0.0003	0.082
		(0.218)	(0.737)	(0.785)	(0.083)	

Note: * Significant at 10 per cent ** Significant at 5 per cent *** Significant at 1 per cent

those covered in Tables 6.1–6.3, for which evidence was available on the geographical diversification ratios.[9]

In addition to this 'full sample' regressions were also run for five sub-samples.

(i) A sample including the firms from the highly research-intensive industries. This HRI sample included 147 firms.
(ii) A sample including the firms from the medium research-intensive industries. This MRI sample included 128 firms.
(iii) A sample including the firms from the low research-intensive industries. This LRI sample included 112 firms.
(iv) A sample including the firms from the vertically integrated industries. This VI sample included 178 firms.
(v) A sample including the firms from the non-vertically integrated industries. This non-VI sample included 209 firms.

Regression results from these sub-samples are contained in Tables 6.4b to 6.6b, and F-tests in Table 6.8.

Reference to Tables 6.4a to 6.6a makes it clear that the ability of the variables included in our main equations to explain variation in IDR, at the firm level for the full sample, is very limited. The highest R^2 recorded is 0.181. Amongst the sub-samples delineated by research intensity, explanatory power of the main equations including S, S^2, I, N, G, G^2 tends generally to be greater than for the full sample, with the LRI sample providing the largest R^2 values and the HRI sample the lowest. The VI sample provides larger R^2 values than the non-VI sample.

Similarly disappointing, for the full sample, is the performance of size (as proxied by worldwide sales). Neither S nor S^2 is ever significant and the sign of the S term is unstable. In the sub-samples S does take a significantly positive sign (at 10 per cent) in one case for the HRI sample (the main equation using overseas production ratio as the geographical diversification ratio). On the other hand, for the MRI sample S takes a negative sign and is frequently significant at 10 per cent. There is no significant relationship in the other sub-samples. Generally these results differ notably from those of earlier studies, including those which have been concerned with both industrial and geographical diversification (Wolf, 1977); (Bertin, 1972). However, it is interesting to note that studies by Gort (1962) and Utton (1979) showed that, while firm size and industrial diversification were positively correlated for their full populations of firms, amongst the largest firms the correlation disappeared.

Industry, however, emerges as the strongest influence on IDR. It is consistently significant at 1 per cent in the F-tests recorded in Table

Table 6.5(a) *Multiple Regression Tests on Industrial Diversification: Equations including Parent's Exports Ratio (Y)*

Equation	*Explanatory Variables*	*Constant Term*	*S*	S^2	*Y*	Y^2	R^2
Y.1.a.	S, S^2, I, N, Y, Y^2	24.09	0.0002	−8.259 & −9	0.137	−0.004	0.181
			(0.389)	(1.138)	(0.703)	(1.455)	
Y.1.b.	S, S^2, HRI, LRI, N, Y, Y^2	29.34	−0.0003	−2.384 & −9	0.349*	−0.006**	0.127
			(0.873)	(0.337)	(1.936)	(2.561)	
Y.1.c.	S, S^2, VI, N, Y, Y^2	26.03	−0.0001	−4.323 & −9	0.451**	−0.007***	0.091
			(0.315)	(0.604)	(2.429)	(2.775)	
Y.2.	S, S^2, N, Y, Y^2	23.47	−0.0002	−3.687 & −9	0.562***	−0.008***	0.082
			(0.421)	(0.514)	(3.171)	(3.265)	
Y.3.a.	S, S^2, I, Y, Y^2	22.13	0.00007	−5.805 & −9	0.087	−0.003*	0.134
			(0.193)	(0.819)	(0.564)	(1.667)	
Y.3.b.	S, S^2, HRI, LRI, Y, Y^2	28.68	−0.0004	−3.905 & −10	0.255*	−0.005***	0.088
			(1.089)	(0.056)	(1.769)	(2.638)	
Y.3.c.	S, S^2, VI, Y, Y^2	26.11	−0.0002	−2.822 & −9	0.313**	−0.005**	0.051
			(0.437)	(0.404)	(2.145)	(2.744)	

Note: * Significant at 10 per cent ** Significant at 5 per cent *** Significant at 1 per cent

Table 6.5(b) *Multiple Regression Tests of Industrial Diversification: Equations including Parent's Export Ratio (Y) – Sub-samples*

Equations and Samples	*Constant Term*	*S*	S^2	*Y*	Y^2	R^2
High Research Intensity Sample						
S, S², I, N, Y, Y²	27.66	0.0005	−1.154 & −8	0.668	−0.016**	0.183
		(0.881)	(1.131)	(1.587)	(2.347)	
S, S², N, Y, Y²	20.17	0.0001	−8.045 & −9	1.152***	−0.022***	0.138
		(0.287)	(0.816)	(3.311)	(3.522)	
S, S², I, Y, Y²	30.47	0.0005	−1.095 & −8	0.141	−0.003	0.106
		(0.885)	(1.124)	(0.514)	(1.013)	
Medium Research Intensity Sample						
S, S², I, N, Y, Y²	38.99	−0.001	1.066 & −8	−0.353	0.003	0.253
		(1.570)	(0.808)	(0.963)	(0.542)	
S, S², N, Y, Y²	41.46	−0.001*	1.272 & −8	−0.415	0.003	0.237
		(1.877)	(0.993)	(1.209)	(0.713)	
S, S², I, Y, Y²	38.36	−0.001*	1.123 & −8	−0.343	0.0004	0.180
		(1.685)	(0.892)	(1.349)	(0.106)	

Low Research Intensity Sample						
S, S^2, I, N, Y, Y^2	9.03	0.002	5.427 & −9	0.476	−0.009	0.372
		(0.735)	(0.024)	(1.325)	(1.429)	
S, S^2, N, Y, Y^2	15.38	−0.0009	2.000 & −7	0.642*	−0.011*	0.239
		(0.364)	(0.692)	(1.798)	(1.764)	
S, S^2, I. Y, Y^2	13.33	0.001	−6.929 & −9	0.510	−0.007	0.181
		(0.745)	(0.067)	(1.493)	(1.104)	
Vertically Integrated Sample						
S, S^2, I, N, Y, Y^2	18.67	−0.0002	−1.598 & −9	0.262	−0.006	0.311
		(0.394)	(0.174)	(0.965)	(1.426)	
S, S^2, N, Y, Y^2	22.30	−0.0006	5.338 & −9	0.587**	−0.008**	0.172
		(1.291)	(0.580)	(2.187)	(2.057)	
S, S^2, I, Y, Y^2	20.21	−0.0001	−2.085 & −9	0.201	−0.005	0.171
		(0.132)	(0.224)	(0.926)	(1.527)	
Non Vertically Integrated Sample						
S, S^2, I, N, Y, Y^2	26.21	0.0004	−1.478 & −8	0.145	−0.005	0.167
		(0.794)	(1.343)	(0.486)	(1.247)	
S, S^2, N, Y, Y^2	25.67	0.0005	−1.641 & −8	0.365	−0.008**	0.124
		(0.954)	(1.518)	(1.310)	(1.996)	
S, S^2, I, Y, Y^2	25.66	0.0002	−1.029 & −8	−0.014	−0.002	0.087
		(0.404)	(0.957)	(0.064)	(0.830)	

Note: * Significant at 10 per cent   ** Significant at 5 per cent   *** Significant at 1 per cent

6.7. At the individual industry level,[10] 'food, drink and tobacco' is the only one to emerge consistently as significantly (at either 5 per cent or 10 per cent) less diversified than the 'other industry' control group. 'Metals' and 'electronics and electrical appliances' are consistently more diversified (at 10 per cent), and 'aerospace' (also at 10 per cent) in one case (the equations involving parent's export ratio as the geographical diversification variable). In the sub-samples the effect of industry on IDR is only consistently significant, in F-tests, for the LRI and VI samples (Table 6.8).

In the F-tests the HRI/LRI classification of industries is always significant at 1 per cent as a determinant of IDR. This would seem to be due more to the low industrial diversification of LR firms (significantly negative at 1 per cent in all equations) than to exceptionally high levels of diversification in HRI firms. Thus HRI firms never emerge as having industrial diversification levels significantly different from the control MRI firms. The results are a little less clear cut with the vertical integration classification of industries. In the equations reported in Tables 6.4a to 6.6a, vertically integrated firms were significantly less diversified (at 1 per cent) than non-vertically integrated firms in equations using overseas production ratio as the geographical diversification ratios, but only significant at 10 per cent for the other two cases.

As hypothesised, nationality of firm has less influence on its industrial diversification than does its industry. Of the nine full-sample equations in which it is possible to test the effect of nationality through F-tests significance is (very marginally) achieved once at 5 per cent. The individual nationality results[11] suggest that the USA (the control nationality) has a particularly high level of industrial diversification. In this way the fact that a relatively large number of countries recorded significantly negative levels of industrial diversification is consistent with the fact that nationality differences are not significant overall as determinants of industrial diversification. However Table 6.8 shows that nationality *is* significant as an explanation of IDR for firms in the LRI and VI samples.

Generally the results also give tentative support for our hypotheses relating geographical diversification and industrial diversification. For the overseas production ratio X in the full sample, the combined influence of the quadratic form is not significant when subject to F-tests (see Table 6.7). Further, neither the linear nor the squared term is significant individually in any of the equations reported in Table 6.4a. These full sample equations may perhaps, however, be interpreted as providing some support for our hypothesis of a negative relationship between IDR and X as being the most plausible. The sub-samples (reported in Table 6.4b) provide a variety of experience.

Table 6.6(a) *Multiple Regression Tests of Industrial Diversification: Equations including Sourcing Ratio (Z)*

Equation	*Explanatory Variables*	*Constant Term*	*S*	S^2	*Z*	Z^2	R^2
Z.1.a.	S, S^2, I, N, Z, Z^2	24.65	0.0002	−8.316 & −9	0.097	−0.001	0.173
			(0.419)	(1.151)	(0.602)	(0.845)	
Z.1.b.	S, S^2, HRI, LRI, N, Z, Z^2	30.95	−0.0002	−3.993 & −9	0.178	−0.002*	0.123
			(0.548)	(0.563)	(1.146)	(1.725)	
Z.1.c.	S, S^2, VI, N, Z, Z^2	29.47	0.00002	−6.387 & −9	0.186	−0.002*	0.091
			(0.065)	(0.895)	(1.162)	(1.849)	
Z.2	S, S^2, N, Z, Z^2	26.58	0.00002	−6.285 & −9	0.257*	−0.003**	0.083
			(0.047)	(0.878)	(1.656)	(2.462)	
Z.3.a.	S, S^2, I, Z, Z^2	17.49	0.00008	−5.703 & −9	0.229	−0.002	0.113
			(0.215)	(0.809)	(1.553)	(1.521)	
Z.3.b.	S, S^2, HRI, LRI, Z, Z^2	24.01	−0.0002	−2.259 & −9	0.284**	−0.003**	0.076
			(0.644)	(0.327)	(1.981)	(2.230)	
Z.3.c.	S, S^2, VI, Z, Z^2	23.29	−8.0 & −6	−4.680 & −9	0.282*	−0.003**	0.045
			(0.024)	(0.675)	(1.916)	(2.279)	

Note: * Significant at 10 per cent ** Significant at 5 per cent *** Significant at 1 per cent

Table 6.6(b) *Multiple Regression Tests of Industrial Diversification: Equations Including Sourcing Ratio (Z) – Sub-Samples*

Equations and Samples	*Constant Term*	*S*	S^2	*Z*	Z^2	R^2
High Research Intensity Sample						
S, S^2, I, N, Z, Z^2	34.23	0.0006	−1.217 & −8	0.246	−0.004	0.173
		(1.117)	(1.196)	(0.645)	(1.288)	
S, S^2, N, Z, Z^2	35.66	0.0004	−1.028 & −8	0.237	−0.004	0.154
		(0.888)	(1.055)	(0.677)	(1.655)	
S, S^2, I, Z, Z^2	24.36	0.0004	−8.148 & −9	0.397	−0.004*	0.114
		(0.718)	(0.847)	(1.359)	(1.717)	
Medium Research Intensity						
S, S^2, I, N, Z, Z^2	24.73	−0.001*	1.412 & −8	0.186	−0.0003	0.262
		(1.833)	(1.080)	(0.690)	(0.117)	
S, S^2, N, Z, Z^2	28.61	−0.002**	1.651 & −8	0.153	−0.0002	0.237
		(2.178)	(1.294)	(0.578)	(0.072)	
S, S^2, I. Z, Z^2	20.94	−0.001	1.236 & −8	0.185	−0.0002	0.126
		(1.654)	(0.967)	(0.778)	(0.083)	

Low Research Intensity Sample						
S, S^2, I, N, Z, Z^2	22.50	0.001	9.263 & −8	−0.296	0.002	0.376
		(0.414)	(0.420)	(1.203)	(0.892)	
S, S^2, N, Z, Z^2	27.06	−0.002	3.000 & −7	−0.094	−0.0001	0.231
		(0.825)	(1.233)	(0.367)	(0.025)	
S, S^2, I, Z, Z^2	29.58	0.008	4.335 & −8	−0.240	0.0008	0.206
		(0.518)	(0.433)	(0.998)	(0.407)	
Vertically Integrated Sample						
S, S^2,I, N, Z, Z^2	20.69	−0.0001	−2.076 & −9	0.114	−0.001	0.304
		(0.277)	(0.227)	(0.589)	(0.797)	
S, S^2, N, Z, Z^2	22.74	−0.0004	3.325 & −9	0.338*	−0.004**	0.176
		(0.879)	(0.362)	(1.699)	(2.154)	
S, S^2, I, Z, Z^2	14.92	0.0001	−3.647 & −9	0.285	−0.002	0.162
		(0.132)	(0.396)	(1.541)	(1.482)	
Non-Vertically Integrated Sample						
S, S^2, I, N, Z, Z^2	27.72	0.0004	−1.397 & −9	0.034	−0.0006	0.149
		(0.704)	(1.275)	(0.128)	(0.294)	
S, S^2, N, Z, Z^2	33.34	0.0005	−1.700 & −8	−0.005	−0.0009	0.109
		(0.987)	(1.591)	(0.018)	(0.412)	
S, S^2, I, Z, Z^2	19.43	0.0001	−7.769 & −9	0.185	−0.002	0.056
		(0.171)	(0.725)	(0.766)	(0.781)	

Note: * Significant at 10 per cent ** Significant at 5 per cent *** Significant at 1 per cent

Table 6.7 *F-Tests on Equations using Full Sample*

			Geographical Diversification Ratio used in main equation		
Main Equation	*Variables dropped from main equation*	*Degrees of Freedom*	*Overseas production ratio F-Values*	*Parent exports ratio F-Values*	*Sourcing ratio F-Values*
S, S^2, I, N, G, G^2	G^2	2,354	1.32	2.35	0.58
S, S^2, HRI, LRI, N, G, G^2	G^2	2,365	2.13	3.72*	2.86
S, S^2, VI, N, G, G^2	G^2	2,366	1.68	3.88*	3.88*
S, S^2, I, N, G, G^2	Nationality	15,354	1.69	1.37	1.72*
S, S^2, HRI, LRI, N, G, G^2	Nationality	15,365	1.26	1.10	1.33
S, S^2, VI, N, G, G^2	Nationality	15,366	1.05	1.07	1.22
S, S^2, I, N, G, G^2	Industry	13,354	3.85**	3.31**	2.97**
S, S^2, HRI, LRI, N, G, G^2	(HRI, LRI)	2,365	12.43**	9.58**	8.43**

Note: * Significant at 5 per cent ** Significant at 1 per cent

As might have been predicted, the negative relationship between IDR and X is strongest (and significant at 10 per cent) for the HRI sample, where the quadratic formulation is significant in the F-test (Table 6.8). Though the relationship is very weak for the VI sample (where we might have expected a strongly negative relationship as a result of low levels of industrial diversification, for reasons discussed above, combined with high levels of resource-based overseas production), the sign is only actually reversed in the MRI sample.

Perhaps the most interesting results for geographical diversification ratios are those concerning the parent's export ratios (Y). Though the F-statistic in Table 6.7 on the quadratic form in the first main equation (Y.1.a) is not significant, the F value is notably higher than for any other geographical diversification ratio. Further, once industry is replaced by the HRI/LRI classification (Y.1.b) or the VI classification (Y.1.c), the explanatory power of the Y,Y^2 terms is significant at 5 per cent in F-tests. This tends to suggest that the parent's export ratio here picks up some of the influence of the omitted industry dummies, or more explicitly of some characteristics of industries other than research intensity or extent of vertical integration. This is strongly confirmed in Table 6.5a by comparison of the Y terms in

Table 6.8 *F-Tests on Equations Using Sub-Samples*

		Version of Full Equation		
Sample and omitted variables	*Degrees of Freedom*	S, S^2, I, N, X, X^2 *F-Values*	S, S^2, I, N, Y, Y^2 *F-Values*	S, S^2, I, N, Z, Z^2 *F-Values*
High Research Intensity Sample				
G, G²	2,125	3.78*	3.53*	2.73
Industry	5,125	1.69	1.37	0.60
Nationality	12,125	0.82	0.98	0.75
Medium Research Intensity Sample				
G, G²	2,106	0.51	0.82	1.47
Industry	5,106	0.66	0.43	0.70
Nationality	12,106	1.61	0.86	1.62
Low Research Intensity Sample				
G, G²	2,93	1.02	1.02	1.32
Industry	4,93	5.58**	4.90**	5.35**
Nationality	10,93	2.80**	2.81**	2.51*
Vertically Integrated Sample				
G, G²	2,154	0.08	1.32	0.46
Industry	6,154	5.58**	5.19**	4.67**
Nationality	13,154	2.44**	2.40**	2.40**
Non-Vertically Integrated Sample				
G, G²	2,185	2.27	2.21	0.17
Industry	7,185	1.18	1.38	1.24
Nationality	12,185	1.58	1.49	1.69

Note: * Significant at 5 per cent ** Significant at 1 per cent

Y.1.a with those in Y.1.b and Y.1.c, and also by comparing Y.3.a with Y.3.b and Y.3.c. Also, the greatest significance in Table 6.5a is obtained when all industry characteristics are omitted in equation Y.2. The relationship between IDR and parent exports ratio indicated is that of an inverted U, though if we use the coefficients for those equations where Y, Y^2 are most significant the suggestion is that the inversion will occur at levels of IDR above those of the majority of our sample firms. Generally these conclusions for the full sample are supported by the sub-sample equations of Table 6.5b; though in Table 6.8 F-tests on Y, Y^2 are only significant for the HRI sample. Once again the MRI sample records results in opposition to those of HRI and LRI samples.

The results for the sourcing ratio Z are somewhat inconclusive. This is especially so in the full sample F-tests, where Z, Z^2 have minimal explanatory power in the first full equation, but near significance when industries are replaced by HRI/LRI, and achieve significance (at 5 per cent) when VI replaces industry dummies. The form of relationship suggested by the results reported in Table 6.6a is that of an inverted U, though both Z and Z^2 are only found significant simultaneously in three of the restricted equations. However, the coefficients recorded suggest that the inversion would occur outside the range of values of IDR covered by our sample firms, so that the operative relationship is a positive, but non-linear one. Once again, these full sample results are in general supported by sub-samples (Table 6.6b), though there are no significant results in the main equations and no significant F-tests (Table 6.8). Here the LRI sub-sample runs contrary to the others.

6.5 THE ROLE OF RESEARCH INTENSITY RECONSIDERED

This section reports the results of another sub-sample. In this sample the variables utilised are as described above (and derived from the same sources) except that research intensity is treated at the firm level. Thus for 221 firms from the earlier sample it was possible to obtain an index of the firm's research intensity in the form of R & D expenditure as a percentage of group sales.

Our basic equation for these tests takes the form

$$IDR = a + bS + cS^2 + \sum_{i=1}^{13} d_i I_i + \sum_{j=1}^{12} f_j N_j + gG + hG^2 + k(\mathrm{R\ \&\ D}) + l(\mathrm{R\ \&\ D})^2 + e \quad (6.2)$$

where a, b, c, e, g, h, S, I_i, N_j and G have the same interpretation as before and

R & D is the index of research expenditure,
k, l are regression coefficients, and
d_i and f_j are estimated differences arbitrarily chosen d_{14} (motor vehicles)[12] and f_{13} (USA) respectively.

The three main equations (i.e. one for each of the three main geographical diversification ratios) and various restricted equations are reported in Table 6.9, with F-tests in Table 6.10.

Our major interest in this sample, obviously, is the performance of the R & D index, with the expectation, from our earlier discussion, that industrial diversification would be positively related to a firm's R & D intensity. The three main equations (Table 6.9) and the F-tests (Table 6.10) show that we are clearly disappointed in this. Though significance is only obtained on one occasion, the relationship suggested is a negative one (within the range of values likely to be taken by the R & D index). However it is interesting to note that when the industry dummies are omitted the relationship, though not significant, does become a positive one. We would interpret this as suggesting that, on average, firms in highly research-intensive industries *are* more industrially diversified than firms in less research-intensive industries,[13] but that *within industries* the firm level relationship between IDR and R & D seems to be negative.

A possible interpretation of this might be that the most R & D-intensive firms in an industry are also the firms which feel that their position in the industry is most secure. Thus whilst some of the other firms in the industry may be inclined to pursue industrial diversification based upon research spillover, in order to open up alternative avenues of growth, the most R & D-intensive firms do not feel the need to follow them in this policy. Our result does not imply either that the research of the most R & D-intensive firms is less inclined to produce spillover results, or that these firms ignore the potential returns on such spillover. Rather it may be that, feeling less incentive to create a 'portfolio' of alternative routes to growth, they may be more inclined to obtain their spillover income by marketing the knowledge created, rather than making it a basis of an expansion of their own production.

Possible support for this line of argument may be found in Knickerbocker's (1973) conclusion that there existed, among a sample of large American firms, a negative relationship between R & D intensity and one form of oligopolistic reaction (i.e. the tendency for firms to 'bunch' their initial moves into production in particular foreign

Table 6.9 *Multiple Regression Tests of Industrial Diversification: R&D Expenditure Sub-Sample*

Equation	*Constant Term*	*Sales*	*Sales²*	*R & D*	*(R & D)²*	*G*	*G²*	*R²*
S, S², I, N, R & D, R & D², X, X²	43.22	0.0004	−1.211 & −8	−1.436	0.074	−0.506**	0.005	0.295
		(0.863)	(1.429)	(1.152)	(1.220)	(2.009)	(1.416)	
S, S², I, N, R & D, R & D², Y, Y²	35.58	0.0002	−9.752 & −9	−1.915	0.097	0.329	−0.008**	0.297
		(0.488)	(1.157)	(1.539)	(1.599)	(1.192)	(2.131)	
S, S², I, N, R & D, R & D², Z, Z²	66.09	0.0002	−9.002 & −9	−2.019*	0.101*	−0.774**	0.005**	0.305
		(0.379)	(1.076)	(1.678)	(1.725)	(2.467)	(2.026)	
S, S², I, N, R & D, R & D²	37.63	0.0002	−9.574 & −9	−2.123*	0.102*	—	—	0.275
		(0.471)	(1.129)	(1.743)	(1.707)			
S, S², I, N, X, X²	41.47	0.0004	−1.192 & −8	—	—	−0.578**	0.005*	0.289
		(0.827)	(1.409)			(2.369)	(1.708)	
S, S², I, N, Y, Y²	32.54	0.0002	−9.453 & −9	—	—	0.247	−0.008**	0.287
		(0.431)	(1.121)			(0.907)	(2.007)	
S, S², I, N, Z, Z²	62.75	0.0001	−8.230 & −9	—	—	−0.803**	0.005**	0.294
		(0.260)	(0.982)			(2.561)	(2.144)	
S, S², N, R & D, R & D², X, X²	33.85	0.0001	−5.973 & −9	1.525	−0.009	−0.594**	0.004	0.126
		(0.181)	(0.703)	(1.626)	(0.178)	(2.269)	(1.217)	
S, S², N, R & D, R & D², Y, Y²	21.94	−0.0003	−9.762 & −10	0.327	0.044	0.656**	−0.012***	0.115
		(0.660)	(0.116)	(0.341)	(0.867)	(2.468)	(2.996)	
S, S², N, R & D, R & D², Z, Z²	51.02	−0.0001	−4.165 & −9	0.486	0.032	−0.416	0.001	0.140
		(0.214)	(0.496)	(0.531)	(0.646)	(1:304)	(0.422)	
S, S², I, R & D, R & D², X, X²	41.16	0.0004	−1.001 & −8	−2.081*	0.097*	−0.376	0.003	0.256
		(0.865)	(1.291)	(1.831)	(1.668)	(1.639)	(1.090)	
S, S², I, R & D, R & D², Y, Y²	34.96	0.0001	−7.125 & −9	−2.086*	0.106*	0.175	−0.004	0254
		(0.320)	(0.896)	(1.791)	(1.798)	(0.858)	(1.465)	
S, S², I, R & D, R & D², Z, Z²	53.53	0.0001	−6.439 & −9	−2.636**	0.122**	−0.468*	0.003	0.253
		(0.252)	(0.828)	(2.379)	(2.123)	(1.667)	(1.356)	

Note: * Significant at 10 per cent ** Significant at 5 per cent *** Significant at 1 per cent

Table 6.10 *F-Tests of Equations using R & D Expenditure Sub-Sample*

Main Equation	*Omitted Variables*	*Degrees of Freedom*	*Calculated F Values*
S, S^2, I, N, R & D, R & D^2, X, X^2	XX^2	2,189	2.79
,,	R & D, R & D^2	2,189	0.76
,,	Industry	13,189	3.49**
,,	Nationality	12,189	0.87
S, S^2, I, N, R & D, R & D^2, Y, Y^2	YY^2	2,189	3.05*
,,	R & D, R & D^2	2,189	1.32
,,	Industry	13,189	3.77**
,,	Nationality	12,189	0.97
S, S^2, I, N, R & D, R & D^2, Z, Z^2	ZZ^2	2,189	4.19*
,,	R & D, R & D^2	2,189	1.56
,,	Industry	13,189	3.46**
,,	Nationality	12,189	1.19

Note: * Significant at 5 per cent ** Significant at 1 per cent

locations). It should be noted that Knickerbocker demonstrates this result most clearly at the industry level (i.e. oligopolistic reaction is least prevalent in the most R & D-intensive industries), but is also able to suggest that it persists at the firm level (i.e. within industries). If this is so, the result supports our suggestion that the most R & D-intensive firms in a particular industry do not feel the need to react oligopolistically to the industrial diversification moves of their less R & D-intensive rivals. The F-tests on Table 6.10 show that, for this sample, industry is a persistently significant factor in influencing industrial diversification at the firm level, but nationality is not.

Finally, we see that the results from this sample tend to provide support to our conclusions, from the earlier samples, concerning the relationship between IDR, the overseas production ratio and the parent's export ratio. The results for the sourcing ratio are the surprise here, with Z,Z^2 being significant in F-tests, with a U-shape relationship indicated (but not likely to reach the inversion within the range of values of Z). This is more in line with our hypothesis of this relationship than that found in the earlier samples.

6.6 CONCLUSION

The study shows that the world's leading multinational corporations are extensively industrially diversified, with an estimated 22 per cent of sales outside their main industries. Five main diversification linkages are distinguished. In particular it is found that industrial diversification may be due to 'technological spillover'; to the production of hybrid final products using substantial elements of the basic technology of two distinct industries (e.g. electrical and mechanical or electronic and chemical); or due to vertical integration linkages spread across industries.

Our regression analysis found, somewhat surprisingly, that size of firm was not generally a consistent determinant of the extent of industrial diversification. Nor, to any great extent, was firm nationality an important influence. The industry of a firm does play a major role in determining its industrial diversification, whilst two industry characteristics which to some degree influence industrial diversification are the level of research intensity and whether or not the industry is prone to extensive vertical integration.

The results also provide at least selective support for our belief that industrial diversification will be related to geographical diversification and to the manner in which firms choose to supply overseas markets. We conclude that there is some support for our hypothesis that, within the ranges of values covered by sample firms, industrial diversification tends to be negatively related to overseas production and positively related to exporting. These conclusions are most clearly verified for firms in research-intensive industries.

Our analysis in this paper has, of necessity, been restricted to the exploration of the position of firms at a point in time. It is hoped that when evidence for later years can be added it will be possible to place the information on industrial and geographical diversification more clearly in the context of firm growth.

APPENDIX 6.A: NOTES ON THE INDUSTRIAL CLASSIFICATIONS USED IN THE TABLES

Fourteen industry groups have been used. In the main, the products within each group are self-evident. Nevertheless, there are cases where classification depends upon whether or not a product is directly linked with others sold by the firm, or when a product, such as synthetic fibres, could be considered as belonging to two industries (synthetic fibres are included in 'Textiles' rather than 'Chemicals'). The notes below on 13 of the groups ('Rubber' needing no explanation) are designed to indicate how such cases have been treated.

'Aerospace' includes missile defence systems and related electronics.

'Office Equipment' includes copiers, typewriters, most data processing systems, computers, computer software and services and business equipment (e.g. cash registers).

'Petroleum' includes pipelines and transportation networks for natural gas, oil and gas when they are vertically linked to production and marketing (when independent of production and marketing they are included in 'Other').

'Electronics and Electrical Appliances' includes telecommunications, electric motors, electric lighting systems, electrical products for the residential market (e.g. humidifiers, heating and ventilation equipment). It also includes electrical musical instruments (e.g. organs) but does not include electricity generation (in 'Other'). Electrical parts for motor vehicles are included in 'Motor Vehicles'.

'Chemicals and Pharmaceuticals' includes cosmetics, dyestuffs, photo film stock, and recording tape. It also includes plastics, plastic products (e.g. containers) and paints. It excludes synthetic fibres (in 'Textiles').

'Industrial and Farm Equipment' includes most forms of non-electrical machinery, such as off-highway vehicles (e.g. earthmoving, construction and materials handling machinery). Process plant equipment and railway equipment are also included.

'Motor vehicles' includes trucks, trailers, mobile homes and car rentals when this is integrated with production (otherwise car rental is included in 'Other').

'Metal Manufacture and Products' includes metals trading where this is integrated with manufacturing operations. Also includes metal cans, heavy metal construction products (e.g. bridge parts), simple metal-based wires and cables (more sophisticated composite cables are usually included in 'Electrical' and rubber-based cables in 'Rubber'), metal tubing and piping.

'Building Materials' includes glass and glass products, plumbing fixtures and fittings, prefabricated homes and building merchanting but excludes lumber (included in 'Paper and Wood Products').

'Food, Drink and Tobacco' includes animal and poultry feeds, restaurants which are vertically integrated with food production (other restaurants included in 'Other') and trading in food commodities when integrated with food production.

'Paper and Wood Products' includes paper-based packaging and containers, lumber used in building, and printed business forms where this is part of a vertically linked process including paper production.

'Textiles, Apparel and Leather Goods' includes most synthetic fibres, some industrial fabrics, fabrics used in the home (e.g. draperies, bedspreads, etc.) and footwear.

'Other Industries' includes sports goods (other than clothing and footwear), shipbuilding, leisure craft, marine motors, surgical equipment and other medical equipment, glasses and optical equipment not allocated to 'Chemicals', printing and publishing, bicycles and mopeds, real estate, lawn mowers and garden equipment, gramophone records, radio stations, television networks, motion picture production, furniture not allocated to any other group (e.g. 'Wood' or 'Metal Products'), transportation networks not linked with production, engineering services not linked to machinery production, and retailing not integrated with production.

Note: Each firm has been classified by the industry in which the largest share of its sales to third parties was recorded in 1978.

APPENDIX 6.b: SOURCES OF GEOGRAPHICAL DIVERSIFICATION RATIOS

The information used to compile the three geographical diversification ratios was obtained from the following sources:

(i) a special survey carried out in 1979;
(ii) company reports;
(iii) information given in Table IV–1 of United Nations Commission on Transnational Corporations, *Transnational Corporations in World Development* (New York: UN, 1978);
(iv) *Jane's Major Companies of Europe* (London: Macdonald & Janes, various editions); and
(v) *The Financial Times International Business Yearbook* (London: Financial Times, various issues).

NOTES

1 Thus if the figure for each year was reliable to say 3 per cent or 4 per cent, this would be acceptable for a *static* figure for each year (given that the range of diversification covered by sample firms is from 0 per cent to over 65 per cent), but if a change between years of, say, 5 per cent were recorded in such circumstances the danger of this being totally spurious is very high.
2 The rank correlation between the two IDRs is +0.431 and between the two PRs +0.473.
3 Size was also tested in log form but this gave less explanatory power than the quadratic.
4 'Aerospace'; 'office equipment and computers'; 'petroleum'; 'electronics and electrical appliances'; 'chemicals and pharmaceuticals'.
5 'Building materials': 'food, drink and tobacco'; 'paper and wood products'; 'textiles, apparel, leather goods'.

6 See Dunning and Pearce (1981) p. 10.
7 'Petroleum'; 'rubber'; 'metal manufacture and products'; 'building materials'; 'food, drink and tobacco'; 'paper and wood products'.
8 Tests in log form provided less explanatory power than the quadratic.
9 Firms in the 'Other Manufacturing' sector were allocated, individually, to sub-samples as appeared appropriate.
10 For a full reporting of industry, nationality and other results see Pearce (1982).
11 See Pearce (1982).
12 Note that 'Motor Vehicles' replaces 'Other Industries' as the omitted industry, owing to lack of observations on the latter industry.
13 In other words, when we are not adjusting for industry by the inclusion of the industry dummies.

7 The growth and structure of multinationals in the banana export trade

ROBERT READ

7.1 INTRODUCTION

The export trade in bananas has been active for little more than a century, yet in this time both the structure of the market and the structure of the participating companies have altered greatly. Intense competition characterised the trade initially, with shippers being heavily dependent upon purchases from small growers. Modern-day trade in fresh bananas however, is dominated by vertically and horizontally integrated multinational corporations.

This chapter aims to highlight the principal historical trends in the development of the banana export trade, and in particular to analyse those factors responsible for the emergence of an international oligopoly. The intention is to show that modern theories of corporate and industrial structure (see Chapter 1) provide a satisfactory account of the evolution of an oligopoly dominated by multinational firms.

7.2 MERCHANT CAPITALISM AND COMMERCIAL RISK IN THE EARLY EXPORT TRADE

The North American banana trade began in the ports of the Caribbean, and in particular in Jamaica during the mid-nineteenth century. The occasional enterprising shipper purchased small quantities of locally-grown fruit as deck cargo to be sold on arrival in the USA. The trade in bananas at this time was residual, sporadic, unreliable and, further, unstable because of the perishable nature of the fruit and erratic progress of the slow sailing vessels. Nevertheless, the returns yielded by some of the more successful entrepreneurs encouraged other small shippers and traders to undertake regular importations of bananas. During this period the banana trade began to tap the rapidly growing demand in the USA that had been stimulated by the combination of population growth and increasing real incomes brought about by industrialisation and transatlantic migration. The earliest urban centres to be supplied were those adjacent to the Gulf and East Coast ports to which the highly perishable fruit could be transported without severe deterioration in quality.

The cultivation of bananas on a local or subsistence level was already quite widespread in the Caribbean and on the Central American mainland. The growing export purchases from Jamaica, at first underwritten by a strong indigenous consuming market, encouraged the increased cultivation of bananas as an export crop elsewhere. Small plantations were first established on Roatán, the largest of the Islas de la Bahía (off the northern coast of Honduras), and later on the Atlantic littoral of America from Belice down to Colombia. These plantations were operated by local people or immigrants who developed a regular trade with New Orleans, Tampa and other US Gulf ports.

Cultivation for export in the nineteenth century was seen as a relatively straightforward and inexpensive undertaking; a US government publication concerning Costa Rica put the production costs including clearing, planting, and weeding, at an estimated $8,400 (15.56c per stem) over two years.[1] The estimated gross return of $27,000 (50c per stem) represented a net return of 214 per cent. These figures, however, are rather misleading as they do not imply purchase nor take into account the substantial market risk involved. Very few banana shippers engaged in any form of purchase contract or agreement with planters – the first recorded was transacted in 1878 – but rather growers produced in the hope of being able to sell their produce spot (i.e. without previous guarantees of purchase), and shippers put in at certain frequented ports in the hope of there being fruit available.

The position of an uncontracted grower was difficult. Ships could call for fruit at highly irregular times; only occasionally would a buying agent arrive in advance to inform growers of the amount of fruit required. Once harvested, the fruit perished very quickly. Thus, in the short run, prices were determined under monopsonistic buying conditions, despite the fact that in the long run the market as a whole was highly competitive in terms of the number of firms engaged in trade. Local demand was highly seasonal because of the reluctance of shippers to transport the fruit during the heat of the summer when it would ripen too quickly, and during the colder months to the more northerly ports because of it chilling. The quality of the fruit purchased was strongly influenced by the buyers; if there was an excess of supply, only the premium fruit needed to be acquired, resulting in a high rate of rejection. The planters had the option of accepting either the offered price, counting upon the imminent arrival of another ship, or of selling their fruit locally in competition with the small peasant suppliers.

The banana trade was also difficult for the shippers and there was a rapid turnover of market participants. There was rarely any guarantee of supplies of bananas being available at particular ports. A single consignment from a grower could vary in both quality and maturity. The shipper faced a decision in comparing the potential returns from the fruit currently on offer against the possible returns from proceeding to another port to obtain better fruit. As a result of the lack of refrigeration facilities, healthy returns were dependent upon the speed with which the fruit was shipped to the USA. Losses also resulted from the damage incurred during handling and shipping. The weather and delays experienced by sailing vessels in the Caribbean, together with mishandling at the ports, combined to produce average fruit losses of around 15 per cent.[2]

Between 1885 and 1890 one in seven sailing vessels carrying bananas was lost.[3] Successful arrival in the USA was not always the end of the difficulties; some ports would prevent vessels from landing because of fear of disease (US sanitation and quarantine requirements varied between ports). On landing the fruit many traders lacked purchasers or distribution outlets through which to dispose of the bananas. Local market conditions were affected by the time elapsed since the arrival of the last consignment. If two ships docked within a week some ports experienced gluts, rendering a cargo almost valueless whatever its quality. Markets were restricted to ports and their immediate surroundings, reflecting the slow speed and high cost of inland transport.

One of the first companies to engage in the banana trade was the Frank Brothers' Co., founded by Carl Franc,[4] a steward on a Pacific Mail Co. ship, who brought back several bunches of bananas from Aspinwall (now Colón) in the Panamá Province of Colombia in 1866. The company initiated shipments from Aspinwall into New Orleans which lasted sporadically until around 1900. Unlike many companies who subsequently entered the trade, Frank Brothers' actually grew their own bananas rather than making purchases on the open market.

By 1870, a number of traders were making regular shipments from Jamaica, the Islas de la Bahía and Honduras. New Orleans rapidly became the dominant centre of the banana trade owing to the combination of a large consuming market, its relative proximity to the principal locations of cultivation, and its access via the Mississippi to many of the Mid-West markets further inland. Long-term purchase contracts began to appear after 1886, coupled with experiments in company-owned plantations on a small scale in Jamaica, Costs Rica, Panamá Province, and Colombia; whilst Belice, Guatemala, Honduras, and the Islas de la Bahía remained as markets where spot trading predominated. There was an evident tendency on the part of shippers to specialise in a particular production location from which to service their own domestic market. Very few companies operated to more than one consuming market and many markets were too small to allow more than a single exporter to survive. Purchase contracts were most common where the shipper was servicing a small or isolated final market. Shipments to the highly competitive market of New Orleans tended to have been purchased spot on the Honduran and Guatemalan coast.

This early period of the banana trade was characterised by high levels of risk, reflected in volatile earnings, irregular supplies of fruit, and a lack of control over quality. The large fluctuations in grower and trader incomes were brought about by unpredictable variations in prices – a consequence of imperfect market knowledge, the use of unreliable sailing vessels for transport, and a concentration on short-term profit margins as opposed to long-term market growth. The level of technology was rudimentary and there was a general dearth of vertical links between grower, shipper, importer and consumer.

7.3 THE BOSTON FRUIT CO. AND THE US BANANA TRADE, 1870–99

Between 1870 and 1899 a total of 114 separate banana trading companies were registered in the USA, but by 1899 only 22 had survived, of which only 4 were of any significant size.[5] The two largest of these were the Boston Fruit Co. and its subsidiaries, and the holdings of Minor C. Keith, the assets of both being combined in 1899 to create the United Fruit Co.

The Boston Fruit Co. had its origins in the activities of Lorenzo D. Baker, a Bostonian sailing captain who in 1870 began shipping bananas from Jamaica to Boston, and occasionally to New Orleans and New York. Baker established links with a Boston produce distribution company, Seaverns & Co., who were experienced dealers in perishable fruit. As a result, he met Andrew Preston, a Seaverns employee responsible for marketing Baker's Jamaican bananas in Boston. In 1876, Baker became a minor partner in a new Boston shipping company, the Standard Steam Navigation Co. After moving from Boston to Port Antonio, Jamaica, to organise the production, purchase and shipment of local bananas, he became a major partner in Standard Steam and also established his own firm of L. D. Baker &

Co., operating from Jamaica as a general shipping agent with a specialisation in bananas. Baker thus established a direct link between production and retail in the banana trade. The fruit was purchased by L. D. Baker & Co., shipped on Standard Steam vessels, and marketed by Seaverns & Co. In 1878, Baker negotiated purchase contracts with a number of Jamaican sugar growers on 2,000 acres of good land who were disenchanted with sugar prices on the world market and looked to bananas as a more profitable crop. Baker also investigated some of the more pressing problems of the banana trade, concluding that the fruit should be cut 'thin', i.e. immature, and handled with care if high quality fruit was to reach Boston.[6] Although their sailing vessels were frequently ravaged by the weather on the voyage between Port Antonio and Boston, Baker and Preston estimated that only an average of two out of every three shiploads of bananas needed to arrive in good time and condition to realise substantial profit.

By 1885 the Boston market had grown to such an extent that the Boston Fruit Co. was created as a result of this trade. It was an informal partnership backed by some of the directors of Standard Steam Navigation Co., including Lorenzo Baker who became responsible for the firm's tropical operations, and Andrew Preston who was recruited to take charge of management in Boston. The aim of the company was to supply regular shipments of cheap, consistently good quality fruit, and thereby to stabilise prices. In 1886 Baker purchased some 1,300 acres of plantations in Jamaica for the production of bananas on behalf of the Boston Fruit Co. so as to augment the purchases from the independent planters and thus provide a degree of control over the supply of fruit.

After five quite successful years involving no heavy losses as a result of calamities, the partners in the Boston Fruit Co. had obtained a 3,500 per cent appreciation in their share capital.[7] The company had become the most successful – though by no means the largest – banana firm in the USA during a period when most of its competitors had lost money. The decision was made to incorporate the company legally; some of the original partners sold out and in 1890, after reorganisation, Lorenzo Baker became President as well as Tropical Manager, but he remained in Port Antonio, whilst Preston stayed as Manager in Boston. In 1892, the company increased its land holdings in Jamaica to 3,100 acres, and (as a consequence of the fears of both Baker and Preston) land was also acquired in Santo Domingo (the Dominican Republic) to be developed into a large banana plantation. This new purchase was a consequence of unpredictable weather conditions – a principal cause of liquidation in the trade – since geographic dispersion of cultivation provided a form of crop insurance.

The advent of steam-powered ships replacing old sailing vessels had a profound effect on the banana trade; each ship could now carry between three and five times the cargo on every voyage and could also halve the length of time at sea. The banana trade was able to reach previously distant and thus inaccessible markets in addition to servicing the traditional markets more frequently. Steam power also enabled the trade season to be lengthened, from five to eight months in the case of Boston,[8] besides making fast, regular and reliable shipments possible. The consequences for the Boston Fruit Co. were mixed. More fruit of a better quality could now be sold for a longer period each year with greater quantities of fruit landed each time. Although the local Boston market could absorb more bananas during the extra three months of the year, it was already close to saturation during the normal season. The problem for the company was not only to expand the market around Boston, but also to find major new markets and so diversify its banana trade operation. With this in mind, the company created the Buckman Fruit Co. to import bananas into Baltimore (taking 52 per cent of the equity), the Quaker City Fruit Co. in Philadelphia (taking 50 per cent of the equity), and reorganising the Atlantic Fruit Co. in New York (taking 48 per cent of the equity). The company also acquired 6 per cent of the Banes Fruit Co., which produced bananas in Cuba, and 20 per cent in both the Sama Fruit Co. and the Dumois Fruit Co. who were engaged in the West Indies banana trade.[9] All three companies were shipping bananas to New York, the largest single market in the USA.

The US banana trade at this time was still developing. The major markets of New Orleans, New York, Philadelphia, Boston and Baltimore were responsible for almost 96 per cent of all importations, consumed upwards of 80 per cent of the bananas, yet represented only 16 per cent of the population.[10] The Boston Fruit Co. was merely the largest of five importing companies operating in Boston, the fourth largest market for bananas in the country. The potential Mid-West markets inland were largely untapped, although technological advances in the field of long-distance communication – the telegraph and telephone – and the developments in refrigerated rail transport in the late 1880s and the 1890s made large-scale access a real possibility. The company was losing on its marketing operations in New York, Philadelphia and Baltimore, and it wished to break into the Mid-West to sell the increasing quantities of bananas that it was able to import. With this in mind, a wholly-owned marketing subsidiary, the Fruit Dispatch Co., was formed in the late 1890s to take responsibility for marketing all the bananas imported by the Boston Fruit Co. and its subsidiaries. It was to concentrate on the development of inland markets, converting rail stock for refrigeration and establishing a system of regional offices in the major Eastern cities to provide a distribution network.

By 1898 the Boston Fruit Co. had grown to take a 35 per cent share of the US market. It possessed seven subsidiaries – three producing companies, three banana shipping companies, and the flourishing Fruit Dispatch Co. – making the Boston Fruit Co. the second largest US banana firm and the largest in the Eastern USA. Despite its size, the company and its associated firms produced only about a third of its supplies; much of the fruit was taken on a commission basis for Minor C. Keith's producing companies – the largest producing concern in the industry.

7.4 MINOR C. KEITH'S PLANTATION EMPIRE

Minor C. Keith was a railway construction entrepreneur active in Central and South America during the late nineteenth and early twentieth centuries. In 1870 Keith contracted to build a railway from Puerto Limón to San José in Costa Rica, but after he had constructed more than half the railway he ran out of money. Looking for further finance, he decided to experiment with banana cultivation with rhizomes acquired in Aspinwall, to provide freight income for the completed part of the railway. Discovering that his initial shipments of bananas to New Orleans not only provided freight income, but also generated a good level of profit themselves, he encouraged other landowners in Costa Rica to plant bananas. He formed the Tropical Trading and Transport Co. to ship these bananas from Puerto Limón for sale in New York on joint account with the Atlas Line, and in New Orleans on joint account with the J. L. Phipps Co.

By 1880 Keith had contracted the firm of Hoadley & Co. to market Tropical Trading's Costa Rican bananas in New York, and he was also undertaking extensive plantings of bananas in the Santa Marta area of Colombia through the Colombia Land Co., a British firm of which he had become general manager. The target of the Colombian plantings was the New Orleans market with its high volume of demand which would be advantageous for his relatively low-cost fruit. The J. L. Phipps Co. had become exclusive marketers of the Colombia Land Co. bananas in the New Orleans market by 1885, and by 1891 the company had become the city's largest banana dealer with annual imports of around one and a half million bunches, approximately 16 per cent of the US market. Although the J. L. Phipps Co. were New Orleans' leading dealers, they were never actually profitable because of a combination of glutted markets, poor distribution and heavy spoilage losses. In 1895 they went bankrupt, to be replaced by Hoadley & Co. who had now shifted to the New Orleans market.

Despite the fact that Keith had become the world's leading banana producer in the early 1890s he could not sell his fruit in markets outside New Orleans and New York because of a lack of marketing and distribution connections. To solve this problem he approached the highly successful Boston Fruit Co. in an effort to secure additional market outlets on a commission basis. The result was that the Boston Fruit Co. became the exclusive marketing agent for all of Keith's bananas north of the Carolinas at a commission of 2½ per cent on sales, as opposed to the prevailing rate of 5 per cent. From 1894 Keith was thus assured of markets in both the Southern and Eastern USA.

Keith acquired further banana holdings in 1897 when he purchased a 50 per cent share in the Snyder Banana Co. which produced its own bananas on 6,000 acres of land at Bocas del Toro in the province of Panamá. This was followed in 1898 by a series of catastrophes that brought his venture to the brink of failure: a large New Orleans bank with whom he had taken out loans went bankrupt requiring the repayment of $1½ million at short notice, and only with assistance from the Costa Rican Government was he able to continue trading; epidemics, floods, fires and 'blow-downs' followed which seriously restricted banana production. In October 1898 Hoadley & Co., his southern distributor, went bankrupt. Keith was left with the assets of three banana companies that owned, leased or held concessions for more than 200,000 acres of tropical land, but very little liquidity with which to finance their continued operation. It was to be the second largest company – the Boston Fruit Co. – that he turned for the finance needed to survive.

7.5 INNOVATION IN THE BANANA TRADE, 1870–99

The year of the formation of the United Fruit Co., 1899, is said to mark the beginning of the modern banana industry. Yet the activities of the two principal constituents of this company, the Boston Fruit Co. and the companies of Minor C. Keith, although generally distinct from each other, provided a greater contribution to the eventual success of the United Fruit Co. than they have been credited with by much of the major historical literature.[11] It was these two market participants – and not the United Fruit Co. – which radically transformed the organisation and structure of the banana industry and paved the way for the later commercial success of the United Fruit Co.

The principal innovations during these early years, 1860 – 99, were three-fold: the transition from sail to steam in ocean-shipping; the improvements in communications and railways; and, most significantly, the vertical and horizontal integration of trade within a single company.

(a) Shipping The changeover from sail to steam occurred between 1880 and 1895 and brought with it the first regular and reliable links between ports. For well-known reasons, increasing vessel size afforded technical economies of scale. The consequences for the banana trade were that greater quantities of fruit could be shipped at a single time with a voyage length reduced by up to half, enabling substantial improvements in the quality (it was less prone to damage en route) and maturity of the fruit landed. The speed of the new steam vessels reduced the risk of the cargo freezing in winter and so lengthened the season of the more northerly ports, stimulating additional trade and providing plantation economies from year-round production.

(b) Communication The late nineteenth century was a period of great advance in communications, not only in the coming of steam-powered shipping but also in the development of the telegraph and telephone and the widespread expansion of the US railway network, which permitted rapid dissemination of information and goods on a much larger scale than before. Improvements in communications were essential for the long-run growth and stability of the banana trade.

The telegraph and telephone brought increased market knowledge in the form of accurate and up-to-date information concerning future trends in demand and supply and thereby stabilised prices and earnings. They also improved the coordination of geographically-segmented company operations, increasing corporate efficiency by speeding up decision-making and policy implementation. This enabled managerial responsibility to be centralised in particular functional areas, and led to an overall reduction in market risk.

The railways greatly increased the speed and volume of fruit transported, both in the producing countries and in the US market. The development of refrigerated rail transport improved the condition and overall quality of the fruit delivered in the final markets.

(c) Internalisation The internalisation of banana trading was a result of a continuing process of vertical and horizontal integration. From the earliest days of the trade the stimulus for expansion came from the consuming countries. It was the US shipping companies that initiated the export production of bananas rather than planters searching for new market outlets.

Vertical integration appeared initially as a defensive action ensuring continued supplies, to be observed in the shift from spot purchases to supply contracts and ultimately to production on company plantations.

Control was established over the flow of bananas from the point of production through to the point of final sale. Internalisation of the production, purchase, shipping and marketing processes reduced the associated risks of perishability (risks which were greater then than now). Horizontal integration is apparent in the acquisition of geographically dispersed locations of production linked either by purchase contracts or by plantation ownership. This was an insurance against the major problem of climatic disaster which could devastate a single region, with its severe consequence for undiversified producers.

It was essential that company organisation adjusted to manage this new structure. The role of management increased and there was a tendency towards specialisation and delegation. This resulted in the creation of semi-autonomous regional entities and separate divisions responsible for the different stages in the trade flow.

7.6 THE PERFORMANCE OF THE TWO LEADING FIRMS

Those firms that adopted innovations advantageous to the trade in bananas and engaged in some level of internalisation of the production–distribution flow should have stabilised their prices and earnings, and increased efficiency through economies of scale. The key question therefore is to what extent, if any, did the Boston Fruit Co. and the Keith holdings embody these advantages relative to their competitors, and to what extent were they responsible for their success?

The Boston Fruit Co.

Although inter-company relations were informal, vertical integration was established by 1886 and horizontal diversification undertaken in the mid-1890s. The evidence suggests that it was the only company ever to integrate and diversify on such a scale in this period. From the beginning there was a concentration on fruit quality, reflected in a consistent grading policy, a practice rarely given much thought elsewhere. The changeover to steamers was undoubtedly late, relative to the majority of banana firms, and was a result of the fact that the major partners were sailing captains who were reluctant to innovate. The impetus for change came from the company's manager in Boston, Andrew Preston, who saw evidence of the benefits steam gave to the company's competitors.[12] The coming of steamers required greater quantities of fruit and thus a higher level of capital investment necessitating a reduction of supply risk by location diversification to Santo Domingo. At the same time, the company came to a marketing agreement with Keith that brought about further diversification of supply, but required an expansion of consuming markets. The Boston Fruit Co. formed individual companies for the entry into a number of other Eastern ports and also acquired holdings in companies producing in Cuba and the West Indies.

The Boston Fruit Co. had become the most successful US firm by 1890 and, despite the constant stream of disasters and catastrophes that befell the trade, the company was never at any stage severely affected. The only occasion when the security of its competitive position was imperilled significantly was during the years when it failed to initiate steam shipping. It would seem logical to hypothesise that the initial vertical integration and subsequent horizontal diversification gave the company significant operational advantages, although these alone could not guarantee the long-term survival of the company. This was dependent upon the management's adaptability to innovation and on its decision-making ability, which was generally sound.

Minor C. Keith's Companies

Minor C. Keith expanded his banana cultivations using different producing companies in each location, each oriented towards the large-scale low-cost production of bananas. His activities exhibited a degree of horizontal diversification of location, but little vertical integration. Keith was reliant upon the success or failure of those contracted to ship and market his fruit: J. L. Phipps & Co., Headley & Co. and the Boston Fruit Co. Because of the lack of vertical integration, little control could be exercised over quality – it was not an immediate constraint on sales – and little technological innovation was required in cultivation and transportation to the exporting ports. Keith's major innovation was his large-scale production, coupled with a diversified source of cultivation and access to his own low-cost rail-links with the ports – significant advantages over most producers. His success was in diversifying from railway construction into bananas and taking advantage of production economies of scale. His operations never extended to marketing and distribution; he was content to rely on more specialist firms to undertake this on his behalf. Keith conforms to the traditional view of the entrepreneur: a visionary and an opportunist, but someone lacking in the more mundane management skills.

7.7 THE FORMATION OF THE UNITED FRUIT CO.

The banana interests of the Boston Fruit Co., its seven subsidiaries and the three companies owned by Minor C. Keith complemented each other both geographically and operationally. The Boston Fruit Co. were primarily fruit importers and marketers in the Eastern USA, with some bananas from their own production and purchase operations in the Caribbean. Minor C. Keith's companies grew bananas in Central America from Costa Rica to Colombia for sale to distributors in the Southern USA. There also existed a mutual interest in the Keith fruit handled by the Boston Fruit Co. There were no other firms of such a size operating in the banana trade; by 1898 they possessed between them a 75 per cent share of the US market.[13]

The immediate reason for merger was Keith's liquidity problems which required a quick solution. Preston desired a banana firm that was able to produce simultaneously in several different locations and to ship fruit to all the major US markets. To conduct trade more efficiently he realised that a restructuring of the industry involving substantial new capital investment was required. In time of catastrophe in a specific producing region, the diversified company could recoup its fruit losses from alternative sources of supply.[14] Keith's only assets, possessed through ownership, lease and concession, were 200,000 acres of tropical banana lands in three countries. These assets, when combined with those of the Boston Fruit Co., would create the desired corporate structure.

There must have been a strong realisation of the possible opportunity for monopolising the industry. During the 1880s and 1890s there had been considerable public worry over the development of nationwide 'Big Business'. There had been a tendency for firms to form loose horizontal federations or trusts to fix prices and allocate markets. This led to the passing of the Sherman Antitrust Act of 1890 which imposed legal restraints on monopoly. Laws passed in New Jersey then permitted the creation of holding companies and these were given sanction by a number of key Supreme Court decisions. Whilst prohibiting firms to combine with the purpose of cartelisation, it was permissible to cartelise by consolidation into a single, legally-defined enterprise. These developments, coupled with a buoyant financial market in the late 1890s, led to the emergence of the merger as the principal form of consolidation.

Within the banana trade profits were still unstable, and despite the fact that both firms were taking more than a third of the market there seemed to be gains from further consolidation. It was in this commercial climate that the incorporation of the new United Fruit Co. came about, registered in the state of New Jersey on 20 March 1899 with an authorised (though unsubscribed) capitalisation of $20 million in 200,000 $100 stock. The assets of Boston Fruit Co. were paid for by United Fruit Co. stock at par worth $5,105,000; this comprised $3,177,500 for the company and the Fruit Dispatch Co., and $1,927,500 for its remaining subsidiaries. Keith traded in his shares in the Tropical Trading and Transport Co., the Snyder Banana Co. and the Colombia Land Co. for $3,964,000 of par stock of the new company, enabling him to re-establish his credit and finance his continued operations. Preston became President and Keith First Vice-President. Four of the original Boston Fruit Co. partners were directors, Baker remained as Tropical Manager, and they retained the Head of Shipping and the Cuban Manager.

The new United Fruit Co. now leased or owned more than a quarter of a million acres in Colombia, Costa Rica, Cuba, Honduras, Santo Domingo, Jamaica and Nicaragua, of which 66,000 acres were under cultivation, and 44,000 of those were in bananas. The shipping fleet was made up of 11 steamships supplemented by 12 chartered ships and the company possessed 112 miles of railway, mostly linking the coastal banana properties with the ports. Preston felt that United Fruit's sales establishments needed to be greatly improved. New Fruit Dispatch Co. offices were opened in Baltimore, Philadelphia, New Orleans and Mobile, in addition to those already existing in Boston and New York, and by the end of 1899 the company had sold 11 million bunches – more than half the market. The company management were still not pleased with this performance and looked for ways to better the company's position.

After the merger Preston visited the major banana ports of New York, Mobile and New Orleans, and in return for United Fruit stock and, occasionally, cash, he purchased holdings or secured a controlling interest in at least nine of the competing banana importing companies (see Table 7.1). It has been claimed that Preston always regarded United Fruit as a holding company incorporating independent banana companies and was therefore only interested in the security and continuance of the trade rather than the monopolising of the industry.[15] However, Preston arranged with most of the companies for the Fruit Dispatch Co. to distribute and market their fruit, or else made agreements that eschewed competition. The result of the manoeuvres were that the United Fruit Co. controlled between 80 and 90 per cent of all US banana imports, maintaining full control over the prices and sale of fruit imported by the member companies. Prices were fixed separately for the Eastern US sales area operating from Boston and New York, and the Southern US area centred on New Orleans. The amount of fruit to be imported was restricted at the direction of United Fruit in order to prevent over-supply, and jobbers

Table 7.1 *Corporate holdings acquired by the United Fruit Co. 1899–1906 in exchange for par value $100 United Fruit stock*

Company	*Shares*	*Value*		*Holding (%)*
Boston Fruit Co. (including the Fruit Dispatch Co.)	5,000	3,177,500		100
Banes Fruit Co.	4,550	1,365,000		n.a.
Dominican Fruit Co.	1,000	250,000		100
American Fruit Co.	260	65,000		50+
Quaker City Fruit Co.	250	60,000		50
Buckman Fruit Co.	250	62,500		50
Sama Fruit Co.	600	125,000		n.a.
TOTAL		5,105,000		
Tropical Trading and Transport Co.	389,000	n.a.		50+
Colombia Land Co.	23,400	n.a.		50+
Snyder Banana Co.	500,000	n.a.		50+
TOTAL		3,964,000		
Belize Royal Mail and Central American Steamship Co.	all	400,000		100
Santo Oteri & Son	all	400,000		100
Camors–McConnell & Co.	240	n.a.		86
Orr & Laubenheimer	n.a.	10,000		50
Bluefields Steamship Co.	500	250,000		50
Camors–Weinberger Banana Co.	200	40,000		50
Monumental Trading Co.	126	12,600		50.4
Atlantic Fruit Co.	1,260	46,133	(cash)	50.4
Vaccaro Brothers Co.	n.a.	170,000		50
Hubbard–Zemurray Co.	n.a.	n.a.	(cash)	60
Thatcher Brothers' Steamship Co.	n.a.	4,500	(cash)	60
TOTAL		1,328,733		

Source: Compiled from C. M. Wilson (1947) pp. 107–114, 200–201; and Kepner and Soothill (1935).

were made exclusive handlers of Fruit Dispatch Co. fruit, leaving the independent importers to struggle to find purchasers.[16] These acquisitions were Preston's so-called 'first period' in the creation of United Fruit, a federation working for survival.[17]

7.8 THE TAKEOVER OF ELDERS & FYFFES

In 1904, United Fruit acquired control of the leading firm in the European banana trade. This trade had begun with the shipping of Canary Islands' fruit to Spain and other nearby markets. The first regular shipments to Britain started in 1892, when ships of the Elder Dempster Line on the West African trade route took on bananas as deck cargo from the Canaries, where they were obliged to stop to take on fresh supplies of coal. They very soon faced competition from Fyffes Hudson & Co., a well established firm of fruit importers and distributors, who also began shipping bananas from the Canaries. As in the early days of the US market, prices were high, quality low and earnings unpredictable, leading to little growth in the quantities imported. In 1895 Elder Dempster contracted with Minor C. Keith to import Costa Rican bananas on a shared profit basis, but this venture failed after a couple of seasons. The British government at this time was offering a mail subsidy between Jamaica and Britain which Elder Dempster succeeded in obtaining, forming the Imperial Direct West Indies Mail service with regular connections between the two countries. This led to the establishment of regular shipments of Jamaican bananas to Britain aided by the shipping rate subsidies. Elder Dempster sought to encourage the independent Jamaican planters to increase their production, and in turn attempted to open up new markets in Britain.

In 1901 having acquired Fyffes Hudson & Co., Elder Dempster created a purchasing company, Elders & Fyffes, combining the shipping interests of Elder Dempster and the distribution services of Fyffes Hudson & Co. This was similar to the move that led to the creation of the Boston Fruit Co. The purpose of the new company was to engage in the purchase of bananas in Jamaica, to ship them to Britain, and to supervise their distribution and sale. To this end, the Imperial Direct Service commissioned the construction of a ship built with a mechanical cooling system to prevent the premature ripening of the bananas. The need for this innovation can be seen from the immense distances that the fruit had to travel to reach their final market, and the high risk of loss through premature ripening. The Fyffes Line was formed in 1902 in order to specialise in the banana trade, whilst Imperial Direct eventually failed because of substantial losses.

In 1903 the Fyffes Line ordered three refrigerated steam ships, the first ships ever to be constructed specifically for carrying bananas. Elders & Fyffes faced problems of supply in Jamaica; the United Fruit Co. were a dominant factor in the local market, and the company had to be content with purchasing the residual market supplies. This situation lasted until late 1903, when a violent hurricane devastated the Jamaican banana crop and Elders & Fyffes turned to United Fruit for assistance in procuring alternative supplies. In return for a purchase contract guaranteeing supplies of Costa Rican and Jamaican fruit, United Fruit acquired 45 per cent of the company's stock and in 1904, after a rights issue, United Fruit possessed 50 per cent of the issued capital of Elders & Fyffes.[18]

The influence of United Fruit participation in Elders & Fyffes company policy is evident in the years before the First World War. Elders & Fyffes turned their attention to Europe after 1904 beginning with re-exports of bananas from Hull to Holland and then Scandinavia. By 1914 the company had established some forty branches on the Continent with a European headquarters located in Hamburg and subsequently Rotterdam. In Britain they formed the Fruit Distribution Co., with regional agencies to distribute the fruit. All in all, the activities of the Fruit Dispatch Co. in the US had been replicated in both Britain and Europe. In 1910 United Fruit acquired the remaining Elders & Fyffes stock, and Elders & Fyffes bought 8,000 acres of banana land in the Canaries – their first plantation. Following Andrew Preston's ideas of a federation of banana companies, Elders & Fyffes retained control of its own production, shipping and marketing operations. In 1929 came the introduction of the Fyffes 'Blue Label' – a paper band which appeared around all Fyffes' bananas – and became a symbol in the company's advertising campaigns. It was the first recorded branding of bananas.

The reasons for United Fruit's acquisition of Elders & Fyffes may be found in the combination of four significant factors: their potential threat of competing in the US market; their competitiveness in Jamaica; their possession of refrigerated shipping; and their operation in a different geographical sphere. The possession of refrigeration meant that on arrival the fruit would be of premium quality; it has been claimed that if Elders & Fyffes had turned their attention to the US market, they would have delivered better quality fruit at lower prices,[19] though an alternative source states that refrigeration costs raised prices above those prevailing in the US.[20] United Fruit's action can thus be seen as defensive by preventing the advent of Elders & Fyffes' fruit in the US. Elders & Fyffes' purchasing operation in Jamaica may have removed some of the monopsonistic buying conditions imposed by the presence of United Fruit, and thus precipitated a rise in purchase prices. Finally, horizontal diversification into the markets of Britain and the rest of Europe must have seemed highly desirable to United Fruit; it was now technologically possible to ship fruit efficiently across the Atlantic, to supply the potential market with the increasing quantities of fruit being grown in the Americas.

7.9 THE CONSOLIDATION OF UNITED FRUIT OPERATIONS

Table 7.2 shows that, from its inception, United Fruit continuously expanded its producing lands, although the proportion actually planted to bananas declined constantly. It established plantations at Zent in Costa Rica in 1900, Almirante, Panamá, in 1903, Quirigua (Bananera), Guatemala in 1906, and Trujillo, Honduras, in 1913. The Guatemalan Division was on a much larger scale than any previous cultivation and it became the model for future plantations in terms of its management. The efficiency of the plantation was increased by investment in previously neglected projects: drainage, sanitation and mechanised loading and unloading facilities. To coordinate deliveries and transportation, the company controlled railway and port facilities (often acquired through concessions, and subject to contention in later years). One of the reasons for the large amounts of surplus land acquired was the risk of soil exhaustion and disease. Rapid growth was followed by stagnation or decline; both Costa Rican and Panamanian exports reached their peak in 1913 and then declined because of the abandonment of plantation land. In Guatemala exports increased erratically up until 1929 aided by the initiation of production on the Pacific littoral (a solution also used after 1926 in Panamá with the development of the Armuelles Division). In all three countries, United Fruit were responsible for the majority of banana exports. Production in Honduras increased steadily over the period, and by the end of 1929 United Fruit were responsible for 73 per cent of all banana exports. As Panamá Disease spread, the company switched to purchases from contracted planters, thereby diversifying production risk and avoiding declining returns from the area planted. By 1924 United Fruit were producing only a third of the fruit they exported, and had diversified into sugar, cacao, African oil-palm and coffee in an attempt to utilise abandoned banana lands.

Between 1908 and 1912 United Fruit disposed of their holdings in many of the other banana firms, in response to allegations of monopolising the industry, and consequently faced stiffer competition than before. Their competitors – principally the Atlantic Fruit Co., the Cuyamel Fruit Co. and the Standard Fruit and Steamship Co. – possessed few vertical links, economies of scale, or risk-reducing geographical diversification that had made United Fruit so powerful. These companies concentrated on securing purchase con-

Table 7.2 *Indicators of the growth of the United Fruit Co. 1900–47*

Year	Assets ($m)	Net Income ($m)	Income/ Asset (%)	Assets (1915 = 100)	Land (ha.)	Land (1915 = 100)	Land Used (ha.)	Banana Area (ha.)	Bananas/ All Land (%)	Banana Area (1915 = 100)	Railway (miles)	Ships	
												Owned	Leased
1900	16.950	1.814	10.70	18.85	95,589	20.67	26,829	15,566	16.28	29.86	112	10	40
1905	24.413	1.618	6.63	27.15	129,224	27.95	41,943	22,855	17.69	43.84	174	16	—
1910	45.034	6.553	14.55	50.08	194,394	42.05	68,415	31,293	16.10	60.02	373	27	—
1915	89.916	7.615	8.47	100.00	462,332	100.00	103,430	52,136	11.28	100.00	964	43	40
1920	167.684	43.681	26.05	186.49	659,669	142.68	152,891	55,965	8.48	107.35	1,183	43	19
1925	197.570	21.724	11.00	219.73	742,393	160.58	189,075	69,714	9.39	133.72	1.541	61	18
1930	242.398	13.773	5.68	269.58	1,409,163	304.79	211,669	76,554	5.43	146.84	1,762	90	25
1935	184.909	21.145	11.44	205.65	1,417,276	306.55	182,190	49,225	3.47	94.42	1,795	89	9
1940	186.104	25.528	13.72	206.96	1,254,333[1]	271.31[1]	167,397	49,263	3.87[1]	94.49	1,766	—	—
1945	234.695	43.207	18.41	261.02	—	—	177,097	47,031	—	90.21	1,395	—	—
1947	418.913	87.141	20.80	465.89	—	—	201,279	58,546	—	112.30	1,405	—	—

Source: United Fruit Co. Annual Reports
Notes: [1]Figure given is for 1939; — indicates not available

tracts with private planters subject to intense competition, reflected in the need to ensure minimum prices and purchasing guarantees in return for exclusivity clauses. These were additionally disadvantaged by United Fruits' ownership or control of many rail, port, shipping and distribution facilities.[21]

The 1920s saw the formation of United Fruits' Banana Speciality Co., charged with the discovery of useful banana byproducts, and it also marked the beginning of Federal quality standards with the introduction of inspectors in New Orleans. The intensity of the competition in the trade increased through the gains made by Standard, the Cuyamel Fruit Co. and the Atlantic Fruit Co. (which folded in 1928). The competitive slide of United Fruit in this period can be ascribed to the decline in its productive acreage and the increasing concentration on other crops, the gains made by other firms in attaining economies of scale and establishing vertical links and horizontal diversification, and the loss of experienced managers because of retirement, death and higher salaries elsewhere in the industry. Between 1900 and 1910 United Fruit took 77 per cent of world trade in bananas, but between 1910 and 1930 this slipped to around 60 per cent.

7.10 FACTORS IN THE GROWTH OF UNITED FRUIT, 1899–1929

The years 1899–1929 were years of growth and expansion based on the operational foundations provided by the Boston Fruit Co., which had a significant influence on United Fruit's future market power and position. From being a relatively small but nevertheless multinational trading company at its inception, it had become a multinational corporation of considerable size. The company secured favourable returns from its first years of operation; the average return on investment was 17 per cent.[22] Table 7.2 illustrates a number of important growth indicators over the period. It is possible to identify four factors that provided important contributions to the development of the United Fruit Co. during these years.

(a) Refrigeration United Fruit initiated experiments in the use of refrigerated shipping in 1903 by converting a vessel acquired for that purpose. No ships with refrigeration were available for charter and, despite the holding and subsequent takeover of Elders & Fyffes, the evidence suggests that they were reluctant to use the British firm's technology. A Canadian system utilised only 5 per cent of the cargo space rather than the 20 per cent of Elders & Fyffes' boats, and so worked out less costly. [23] Because of a fundamental lack of research

into the ripening of bananas, perfection of refrigeration techniques required experiments on bananas actually in transit between Central America and the USA and comparisons of the ripening percentages. The first shipments produced no sizeable improvements, but finally by trial and error the rate was reduced from the average of 12 per cent on the steamships to 2 per cent with refrigerating facilities.[24] As soon as refrigeration was a proven success, the company placed orders for more converted ships, and the fleet was painted white to minimise the effects of solar radiation. The resultant improvements in the quality of landed fruit indicated the value of the technique and led to the rapid expansion of the refrigerated banana fleet. In the areas of cultivation the introduction of refrigeration required the overhaul of port and dock facilities, and the building of new railways; it also stimulated further expansion of the banana acreage.

(b) Communications United Fruit made the decision to investigate the possibilities of radio very soon after the first long-distance experiments had been undertaken in 1903. United Fruit had already established telephone and telegraph communications between company farms and regional headquarters in the cultivation areas. However, it was necessary to introduce a reliable system of speedy communication not only between producing divisions, but also between the domestic offices and plantations in order to coordinate shipping, harvesting and loading decisions. At the time there existed only an unreliable communication link via Central America. The lack of proper contact with the producing divisions meant risks in harvesting and transporting fruit to ports which might ripen before the ships arrived. Particularly subject to these costly delays and losses was Bocas del Toro in Panamá which, though efficient in production, was rendered largely unprofitable. Wireless was tried in 1904, but worked for only three months a year because of the weather conditions. In 1906 cables were extended to Managua, Nicaragua, and in 1909 the first shipboard communications were installed. They were very successful although they required a ship to be in the region of Colón for at least six days each week. However, by 1910 improved receivers were installed in all the stations. United Fruit were the first organisation to establish reliable communication links with Central and South America, and in 1913 they formally incorporated their radio offshoot as the wholly-owned subsidiary Tropical Radio Telegraph Co. which still exists today. For the successful operation of such a geographically segmented enterprise, radio communication was indispensable and the need for such technology in the banana trade was recognised at a very early stage.

(c) Concessions The granting of concessions to foreign enterprises

was a practice employed by Central American and other nations for many years before the Second World War as a substitute for national construction programmes, which could not be financed due to the lack of revenue and the poor internal coordination of the countries. In Central America after 1880 many of the principal concessions came into the possession of the banana companies, who used them to expand their producing operations.[25] The idea behind concessions was to provide financial and other incentives in return for the construction of railways, port facilities, telegraph networks and increased banana acreage. The incentives included free use of specified natural resources, the allocation of land – occasionally in alternate lots – exemption from concession-related import duties and levies, long-term exemption from local and national taxes, and the long-term determination of export taxes on bananas. As a result of these concessions, companies often gained complete control of railways and other national resources with long-term consequences for the host countries.

(d) Monopoly There is a lack of adequate data concerning the early period of United Fruit operations which makes it difficult to differentiate between the opportunity to monopolise and actual monopolisation. Monopoly, however, was explicit during Andrew Preston's banana confederacy between 1899 and 1910. During this period United Fruit was the major importer, controlling 80 to 90 per cent of US imports, acting to determine prices and import levels (see the last section of 7.7). Preston's justification lay in the small size of the market relative to the indivisible economies of scale of production and the levels of risk involved. Whether this monopolisation was benign or malevolent is more difficult to determine, although the Antitrust hearings of 1903 imply the latter.

The dissolution of the confederacy during 1908 to 1912 came at a time of continued expansion of the US market and the rapid growth of United Fruit (although its market share began to drop down towards 70 per cent). Whilst United Fruit benefited from the maturing of its communication, refrigeration and distribution developments, competing firms also acquired ships, land and purchase contracts. The monopoly power of United Fruit turned from that of controlling the price and/or supply of bananas, to competing with other firms for the diminishing quantities of potential land and control of purchase contracts. This action often resulted in bankruptcy for the small firm and in United Fruit's monopsonistic demand for the producing area concerned. United Fruit were not averse to acquiring their major competitors – the di Giorgio holdings in 1919, and the Cuyamel Fruit Co. in 1929.

7.11 THE CUYAMEL FRUIT CO.

In December 1929 United Fruit acquired its major competitor, the Cuyamel Fruit Co. This company was formed by Samuel Zemurray (formerly Zmuri) who started business selling low-grade United Fruit bananas in Mobile. In 1903 he formed the Hubbard-Zemurray Co. with the assistance of United Fruit, who acquired 60 per cent of the stock. This company imported fruit purchased in Honduras. In 1905 Hubbard-Zemurray acquired 40 per cent of the ailing Thatcher Brothers' Steamship Co. (United Fruit again acquiring a 60 per cent interest) for the purpose of shipping their fruit. Zemurray then acquired the Cuyamel Co., which operated a small plantation in Honduras, from its founder William Streich, providing Hubbard-Zemurray with an assured supply of fruit. After initial failure and the subsequent withdrawal of United Fruit from stock participation, Zemurray reorganised the firm as the Cuyamel Fruit Co. with the help of a Mobile financier. In 1911 it was capitalised at $5 million. The company engaged in fruit purchases in Vera Cruz, Mexico, and expanded its Honduran operations, establishing the La Lima Division and a Honduran producing company, the Cortés Development Co. The new La Lima Division very quickly became the leading banana division in Central America, specialising in growing large-size bananas of high quality. Using the most advanced methods of drainage and irrigation, and by recruiting skilled engineers and managers (some from United Fruit), Cuyamel possessed the most efficient and productive plantation in operation. In December 1929 United Fruit paid 200,000 shares of common stock (valued at around $32 million) to Zemurray in return for all Cuyamel's stock. They acquired net fixed assets valued at $26 million; a quarter of a million acres of land – including prime banana land in Honduras capable of producing 6 million bunches annually – 15 steamships, railways, port facilities, the Cortés Development Co. and the prized Antichresis Concession.[26] Zemurray thus became the largest single stockholder in United Fruit and took a seat as a director. United Fruit stated that: 'This purchase was warranted by the growing demand for quality fruit by our customers . . . The United Fruit Company . . . has built up a demand for quality fruit in excess of its present supply and can market and distribute to great advantage the increased Cuyamel production.'[27]

As a result of the takeover, United Fruit standardised the fruit as much as was possible and shipped the old Cuyamel fruit to the smaller markets such as Charleston, Galveston and Mobile, where it would not compete with the lower standard United Fruit product. In 1930 United Fruit banana imports to the USA and Canada reached a peak of 65 million bunches. Once United Fruit had acquired its major competitor, the only remaining large company – Standard Fruit – preferred to collaborate rather than compete.

7.12 THE STANDARD FRUIT AND STEAMSHIP CO.

Apart from the Cuyamel Fruit Co., the Standard Fruit Co. was the only one of United Fruit's rivals that was of any significant size. Standard Fruit developed from the activities of the Vaccaro Brothers Co., founded by Salvador d'Antoni and Joseph Vaccaro in 1899 to distribute fruit and other foodstuffs in the Bayou out of New Orleans. The two men built up a trade with the Islas de la Bahia, primarily in coconuts, but after chartering a steamship they began to concentrate on bananas. Finding the quantity and quality of the fruit was inadequate, they shifted their operations to the Honduran mainland around the port of La Ceiba, where they undertook regular purchases. The supervisor of Honduran operations, searching for new growers and developing the trade was d'Antoni, whilst Vaccaro remained in New Orleans to establish a reliable distribution network in the New Orleans area. In 1903 the Honduran government offered a number of concessions to encourage foreign investment in the banana trade; a concession obtained by the Vaccaros allowed them to build a railway inland to facilitate the transport of bananas to La Ceiba. At this stage the United Fruit Co. acquired a 50 per cent interest in the firm for $170,000 to help finance the railway construction.

In 1906, the company was incorporated with a capital of $200,000, and immediately acquired the French Market Ice Manufacturing Co., which made ice for the preservation of bananas shipped by rail. In the same year they undertook their own plantation operation in an attempt to reduce their dependence on the private planters. The company now owned two ships and leased several others; they were second to United Fruit in New Orleans with a market share of between 10 per cent and 15 per cent, but were the most important banana company in Honduras. The years 1908 and 1910 saw the granting of an exclusive rail concession and a concession to construct a wharf at La Ceiba, and the expansion of the plantations to some 25,000 hectares. Between 1913 and 1919 the company organised four Honduran subsidiaries to develop agricultural crop-diversification, the most important being the Aguán Valley Co., a wholly-owned subsidiary which eventually controlled most of the company property in Honduras and was responsible for the major alternative crop, sugar. In 1914 in New Orleans Vaccaros acquired the remaining large ice-making plants and formed the Tropical Ice Co. Panamá Disease appeared for the first time on their lands in Honduras in 1918.

In 1923 the Vaccaro Brothers Co. joined forces with a number of other companies to extend purchase operations to Mexico, Panamá and Cuba – a diversification of supply of their bananas – on account of the increasing ravages of Panamá Disease and the almost perpetual internal political turmoil in Honduras.[28] To facilitate this expansion, the Standard Fruit and Steamship Co. was created in December 1923 and purchased the majority of the assets of the Vaccaro company (which continued to exist), and also acquired a stake in the Mexican American Fruit and Steamship Co., which purchased fruit in Mexico. The company was reorganised in 1926 with the help of a New York bank, and became the Standard Fruit and Steamship Corporation with a capitalisation of $50 million. The management temporarily passed out of the hands of the Vaccaro Brothers Co. until after the onset of the Depression. The new company absorbed a number of smaller banana purchasing concerns including the Frontera Navigation Co. This company's contracts enabled Standard to produce bananas in Mexico for the first time, as foreign ownership of Mexican land was illegal. It also acquired several companies of Joseph diGiorgio (previously of the Atlantic Fruit Co.) who had returned to the banana trade some years after having been bought out by United Fruit. In April 1926 Standard negotiated an agreement with the Cuyamel Fruit Co. to market their fruit jointly so as to compete with United Fruit. This led to the formation of the Banana Distribution Co. and the Gulf Banana Dispatch Co., though the arrangement was dissolved in 1930 after the takeover of the Cuyamel. By the beginning of the 1930s Standard had acquired the majority of the diGiorgio holdings in Jamaica, including a US marketing contract with the newly formed Jamaican Banana Producers' Association. The 1931 Annual Report claimed that Standard now had some 25 per cent of the US market.

The continued existence of Standard within the climate of oligopolistic competition and merger up until the 1930s seems to have been the result of three factors: the company's successful vertical integration and eventual horizontal diversification; the size of the company – it operated under United Fruit's price umbrella and seemed too small to provide any serious threat to the dominant firm; and the absence of any production catastrophes in this period.

7.13 SCIENTIFIC ADVANCES IN THE BANANA TRADE, 1930–68

Until 1968 the world banana trade retained the same oligopolistic structure as in the 1930s: two major firms operating on a geographically diversified basis with a large number of very small firms operating on a regional basis. During this period the industry progressed a great deal in agricultural science and management. Increasing sophistication paralleled by increasing capital intensity had to some extent become a barrier to entry.

(a) Scientific advance in the control of Sigatoka and Panamá Disease Panamá Disease, a disease of banana plants which infects the soil, first appeared in 1906 in Panamá and spread to the rest of Central America during the next twenty years, affecting the productivity of the corporate plantations and wiping out the small growers. No cure for the disease was known and throughout this period there is little evidence of any corporate research efforts into prevention or eradication. Instead, the large companies purchased large reserves of landholdings to which they could move when infected so as to ensure continued production. A number of plantations did have to be abandoned – Bananera (Guatemala), La Lima (Costa Rica), and Almirante (Panamá) – and new ones opened – Tiquisate (Guatemala), Quepos and Golfito (Costa Rica). The infected land could not be re-used for banana production and was therefore diverted into alternative crops. The disease also had implications for the proportion of total banana exports purchased from independent suppliers: there was an increasing trend towards diffusing the production risk by utilising purchase contracts in place of plantation output.

Although both companies had set up plant-breeding establishments (United in the 1920s, Standard in 1931), they tended to be amateurish horticultural experiments rather than professional investigations. The rapid spread of Sigatoka, a virulent air-borne leaf blight, during the mid-1930s wiped out more than 75,000 acres in Jamaica, Mexico and Panamá alone. It threatened to ruin the banana companies, and precipitated a programme of intensive research into its transmission and prevention. The trade was saved from annihilation by quick research results: a preventative solution called Bordeaux Mixture (an expensive chemical spray that required massive investment in piping equipment throughout the plantations) plus the practical development of irrigation channels. Bordeaux Mixture contributed to the emergence of a scientific approach to banana production. The piping was subsequently replaced by overhead sprays, aerial spraying, and back-packs.

The research into Panamá Disease continued through the 1930s and 1940s with increasing emphasis on the development of disease-resistant varieties. Whilst this was in progress, an expensive programme of rehabilitation was carried out on infected land. Flood-fallowing involved the submerging of infected land between artificial dykes for a period of months; the success of the programme was variable. It led to the reopening of United's Almirante Division in 1946, although the loss of the new Tiquisate Division could not be prevented because of geological conditions. The method was only cost-effective if the rehabilitated land could produce well for ten years after fallowing, but increasingly it was found that the infection was reappearing after only five or six years. The cost of Panamá Disease was crippling: it was put at something like $18 million per annum for United Fruit.[29] It was Standard Fruit who were the first to introduce experimental plantings and shipments of the disease-resistant Cavendish-type banana. Their development programme began in 1953, and by 1958 their plantation operations had completely switched from the traditional Gros Michel type although they continued to purchase these bananas from producers in Ecuador and Guatemala.

There were a number of problems associated with the use of the Cavendish: unit costs were higher, it was difficult to transport and process, and it bruised easily, although it did possess a major advantage in having a shorter stem and was therefore less prone to severe wind damage. In order to solve some of these problems, Standard created their Quality Control Department, who developed the idea of de-stemming the bananas on the plantation and packing them into cardboard boxes for transport. Test shipments in 1959 and 1960 indicated that they were delivering a fruit of superior condition that was easier to process, a factor that reduced labour costs and allowed the company greater control over the quality of the fruit to the point of retail. In addition, it was discovered that the yield per plant was substantially higher than that of the Gros Michel, more than covering the initially greater unit costs. United Fruit were more reluctant to switch to the Cavendish-type banana, partly because of the conservatism of the Boston management who ignored the recommendations of the Tropical Managers. By the mid-1960s the bulk of world banana trade was in Cavendish bananas; those producing countries not dependent on the banana multinationals – Jamaica and Ecuador – were slower to change. The companies began to terminate many of their purchase contracts and to divest themselves of the high proportion of reserve lands that they possessed – risk had been reduced substantially and could be better internalised.

With the advent of shipping bananas in boxes, the banana companies constructed manufacturing plants close to some plantations to provide a constant and cheap supply of cardboard boxes. The greater control over quality led United Fruit to perceive the advantages of increased product differentiation and the opportunity to charge a premium price for high quality fruit. In the late 1940s the company had introduced the 'Chiquita' brand of banana, but this brand was never really confined to United Fruit bananas alone. By putting 'Chiquita' marked bands around the bananas and later by applying adhesive labels to each band (very similar to the Elder & Fyffes 'Blue Label' Banana of 1929), it became possible to differentiate bananas. The 'Chiquita' trademark became a symbol of quality to be removed by retailers after a specified length of time awaiting sale – before the quality decline. 'Chiquita' was closely followed by Standard's 'Cabana' which later became 'Dole'. The modern banana market is almost entirely made up of branded bananas, whether they are produced by the big multinational producers or the small independent companies in Ecuador and Colombia.

Scientific improvement first took the form of drainage, followed by the irrigation methods pioneered in the mid-1920s by the Cuyamel Fruit Co. Scientific methods of irrigation, however, were not installed in all of United Fruit's divisions until the late 1930s – Standard Fruit followed on rather later. Modern methods of sanitation, disease control – including the application of Bordeaux Mixture – and phytosanitary control developed slowly. Professionally staffed and funded research into the improvement of cultivation practices was begun in the 1950s and included the development and increasing use of fertilisers.

(b) Management Practices Corporate management structure has changed greatly in the last fifty years, and the banana industry is no exception to this. After the takeover of the Cuyamel Fruit Co. by United Fruit in 1929, Samuel Zemurray retired temporarily but returned as Managing Director in 1934 in an effort to bring the company out of the doldrums of the Depression. His first move was to replace the existing tropical managers with experienced managers both from the tropics and from his old company. He concentrated on improving transport and intra-company communication in order to improve corporate decision-making. This reorganisation gradually led to a specialisation of employees within different parts of the company and the development of a managerial hierarchy. Similarly, within Standard Fruit Co. – still a Vaccaro family-dominated corporation in terms of ownership and decision-making – management was a key problem. The years 1930–53 were difficult: a combination of debts, failures and errors in long-term policy-making had left the

company in danger of folding. Joseph d'Antoni, grandson of the founder and a university medical professor, became President in 1953, and like Zemurray twenty years before he set about reorganising management practices, increasing the emphasis on research, marketing, accounting, advertising and personnel. He saw the need for experimentation and scientific research and believed they should progress, despite the conservatism of the other top managers. In 1956 d'Antoni created the post of Operations Analysis Supervisor with the aim of studying new management practices. Professionals were thus increasingly employed in specialist areas of the company, and there was also an increase in the collection and analysis of financial and operational statistics.

There is evidence of hierarchical delay in both companies, particularly in the case of United Fruit. United Fruit's management was slow to recognise the importance of switching to a new variety of bananas, and also slow to exploit new and expanding markets such as Japan.[30]

The introduction of operations research involving computer analyses of production and marketing revolutionised decision-making. After computers were installed in the late 1960s, United Fruit was able to use production forecasts and analyses of market supply and demand to generate shipment plans and price estimates. Top management had more time to devote to appraisal and policy-making, and were less dependent upon large numbers of managers for information.

In the 1960s there was a trend towards the creation of conglomerates – management and investment companies that owned and formed policy for their subsidiaries. Between 1964 and 1968 Standard Fruit became part of Castle & Cooke, a shipping and food-processing conglomerate, which brought to an end the family control of the Vaccaros. United Fruit became part of United Brands – who also unsuccessfully attempted to purchase one of their competitors, the Del Monte Corporation.

As in many other businesses, the trend in corporate management has been from the traditional family-owned and -operated enterprise towards the development of permanent management structures wherein qualifications, profession and experience are of paramount importance. This has been promoted by the introduction of the large computer processors. Nevertheless, computerisation has failed to eradicate all the decision-making problems of the banana trade.

7.14 DEVELOPMENTS SINCE 1968

The entry of the Del Monte Corporation into the banana trade came about through the acquisition in 1968 of the West Indies Fruit Co., which was involved in banana purchase operations between Ecuador and Tampa. Del Monte (taken over by the R. J. Reynolds conglomerate in 1979) is a large multinational fruit and vegetable processor, whose interest in bananas was the result of United Fruit's attempted takeover. United Fruit were restrained by US antitrust law from acquiring further banana interests and Del Monte avoided absorption by purchasing the West Indies Fruit Co. An additional incentive may have been the desire for product diversification into other fruits, and indeed Del Monte had already initiated experimental banana plantings in the Philippines before 1968.[31]

In December 1971, after the Antitrust Divestiture Suit which had been initially filed in July 1954 alleging violations of the Sherman Antitrust Act and the Wilson Tariff Act, United Brands were ordered to divest themselves of a complete banana-producing division capable of 9 million stems (13 million 40 lb boxes) per year. United Brands first expressed a desire to dispose of the Armuelles Division on the Pacific Coast of Panamá, but this move was blocked by the Panamanian Government. Instead it sold its Guatemalan subsidiary, the Cía. Agrícola de Guatemala, comprising the Bananera Division and its existing purchase contracts, to the West Indies Fruit Co. (Del Monte's banana subsidiary) for a declared sales value of $20 million.

During the 1960s and early 1970s there was a growth of national producer organisations within the banana producing countries, forming a governmental pressure group for the independent planters over the activities of the multinationals.

The effects of the OPEC oil price rises created severe balance of payments problems in many of these countries and put pressure on the governments to improve prices to counter the price rises in oil-based agricultural inputs. OPEC's success had an effect upon the banana producing countries. In March 1974 under the 'Panamá Agreement' they imposed banana export taxes of $1 per 40 lb box in Honduras, Costa Rica and Panamá. This began a drawn-out confrontation between these countries and the banana multinationals from April to September of that year, commonly referred to as the 'Banana War'. The initial levels of the taxes were lowered by degrees, but the continued refusal of the companies to accept the new levy made expropriation the likely solution. On 17 September 1974 these three countries, and also Colombia and Guatemala, formed the Unión de Países Exportadores de Banano (UPEB) to defend the interests of the member countries, re-establish and maintain higher price levels, and adopt common policies. To this end they established an institutional structure based in Panamá City. The formation of the UPEB as a producer union and the later support of the Dominican Republic and Venezuela provided a united front against the banana companies' traditional policy of divide and rule – i.e. threatening to pull out and locate in a neighbouring state (a Sword of Damocles over the individual countries' exports earnings) – although the continued refusal of Ecuador (the world's largest producer) to join has been a major shortcoming.[32]

In terms of market structure, one of the most important outcomes of the UPEB has been the creation of Comunbana S.A. (Commercializadora Multinacional de Banano Sociedad Anonima) a multinational banana company inaugurated in March 1977 with a capital of $10 million, 60 per cent held by member governments and the rest available for nationals and companies. The prospectus for Comunbana was the introduction of operations for the sale of bananas to non-traditional markets, so avoiding immediate competition with the multinationals. Comunbana's potential sources of supply were the state banana corporation in Panamá, producer cooperatives in Costa Rica, Honduras and the Dominican Republic (now a UPEB member), and also the large numbers of independent planters who previously had no alternative purchase outlets apart from the multinationals. The ultimate success of Comunbana depends on the progress made in obtaining assured marketing outlets for the 'Doña Sonia' bananas. The first contract was made with the state marketing organisation of Yugoslavia, followed by Greece, Hungary, Switzerland, Italy and the USA, and all these countries are now supplied from the Dominican Republic. Other potential markets are the Middle East, Eastern Europe and North Africa. It is a structural change that should allow the exporting countries to obtain a larger share of the value added in the production and marketing of bananas, and it may have significant consequences for other commodities in world trade.[33]

7.15 CONCLUSION

The aim of this chapter has been to outline the growth of and major historical developments in the banana trade in such a way as to permit comparison with theories of corporate and industrial structure – specifically the Chandler–Williamson framework. It raises two major questions: does the banana trade as described conform to the Chandler–Williamson perspective, and to what extent if any, have the major banana companies exercised monopoly power?

Chandler's growth through integration is a resource-saving cost-reducing phenomenon which requires organisational reform. Failure to reform, he asserts, will result in collapse.[34] Williamson's internalisation through market displacement follows Coase in that it is a result of the minimisation of transaction costs; a minimisation dependent upon the frequency of transactions, the risk and uncertainty prevalent, and the degree to which it is supported by durable transaction-specific investments.[35]

Banana production is a low-technology product with few economies of integration, illustrated by the large numbers of small non-corporate producers existing in addition to the major companies. It is the coordination of production with the logistics of efficient market servicing that exhibits economies of integration and internalisation. In the early years, significant transaction costs existed at each stage of a then vertically-segmented trade: in production, purchasing, transportation and distribution. Transaction cost-reducing internalisation involved horizontal diversification of production as a hedge against natural catastrophe and the spread of disease, and vertical integration, initially to ensure adequate supplies, but later extended to quality control because of perishability. The control over quality resulted in corporate product differentiation, enabling a premium price to be charged over and above undifferentiated fruit.

Organisational innovation along the Chandlerian lines of multidivisionality gradually developed both vertically and, at plantation level, horizontally. Nevertheless, technological innovation was undertaken as a discrete top managerial response to crises rather than as a continuous divisional programme of experimentation. This organisational inefficiency, though costly to United Fruit and later Standard Fruit, was outweighed by the inherent market advantages of internalisation.

Both Chandler and Williamson identify the pursuit of monopoly gain as only a limited factor in the growth of large firms. The history of the banana trade, specifically that of United Fruit, suggests that monopoly was a significant additional factor. The confederacy at the turn of the century, dominated by United Fruit, was justified then as being vital for the continued existence of the trade. This partly benign monopolisation extended to the acquisition of land through concession and purchase as insurance against soil exhaustion, disease and catastrophe. After the confederacy's dissolution, United Fruit's superior competitive position and corporate power – including its divisionality and internalisation – was used to extend the company's control through the anti-competitive utilisation of concessions, land acquisition and periodic abandonment, with its resultant enhanced bargaining position with host governments. In an effort to maintain the company's market position rival firms were acquired, the most significant being the Cuyamel Fruit Co. in 1929. The Cuyamel can be seen to have embodied an almost similar level of internalisation but a significantly superior managerial organisation to that of its purchaser. After the takeover, United Fruit evolved along the lines of the

Cuyamel Fruit Co.; this included appointing top managerial staff from the latter company. The pre-war position of Standard Fruit was weak, and it acquiesced in the dominance of United Fruit.

In the post-war years evidence of monopoly/monopsony power can be identified – given the greater availability of data – with reference to plantation wages, productivity, retail prices and the value added which was retained by the producing countries. It is important to note that in the period 1950–74 the money price of bananas in consuming countries was static, whilst it declined by 50 per cent in real terms. At the same time, world trade grew from 96 million boxes to 360 million, plantation yields per hectare tripled, as did labour productivity, and money wages doubled but declined by a third in terms of valued added.[36]

The pursuit of monopoly through the advantages derived from integration and internalisation enabled United Fruit to dominate the industry. The significant factor in this dominance was the size of the company *vis-à-vis* its competitors, a result of the initial merger in 1899, the acquisition of the Cuyamel, and the cost barriers to entry. Monopolistic power was the result of the highly internalised nature of United Fruit and the advantages of some early innovations, but the lack of subsequent technological innovation in favour of dominance by acquisition led to the periodic collapse of earning power and an almost continuous post-war decline in market power.

The other major banana companies, Standard Fruit and later Del Monte, immediately upon entry into the market practised internalisation and divisionality, during a period of substantial growth in world trade in bananas. This has changed the market structure from monopolistic to oligopolistic, although direct competition has been limited to the markets of the consuming countries.

NOTES

1 United States (1904). For background information on the early banana industry see Bartlett (1977), Beckford (1967), Jones and Morrison (1952).
2 LaBarge (1960), (1968).
3 C. M. Wilson (1947).
4 Franc *sic*. The difference in the spelling of the company name is probably an Americanisation done purely for commercial reasons.
5 LaBarge (1960), (1968).
6 C. M. Wilson (1947).
7 Ibid.
8 Ibid.
9 Ibid.
10 Ibid.

11 Specifically Adams (1914), LaBarge (1960), Litvak and Maule (1977), May and Plaza (1958), C. M. Wilson (1947), Kepner (1936), and Kepner and Soothill (1935) recognise the importance of the railway enterprises of Keith in establishing the banana trade in its eventual form, but fail to relate this explicitly to corporate structural requirements. Wilson devotes space to both the Boston Fruit Co. (Chapter 4) and Keith (Chapter 6), but makes no attempt to analyse. Much of the modern literature's neglect stems from the lack of historical emphasis placed on the two forerunners of United Fruit.

12 C. M. Wilson (1947).

13 Ibid.

14 Ibid.

15 Ibid.

16 Kepner and Soothill (1935).

17 C. M. Wilson (1947). Preston's first phase is quoted as being the creation of a federation of banana companies aided by United Fruit; the second phase being the withdrawal of majority holdings by United Fruit in these companies; and the third being total withdrawal by the company. See Wilson, Chapter 6.

18 For an account of the history of Elders & Fyffes, see Beaver (1976).

19 Beaver (1976).

20 C. M. Wilson (1947).

21 An account of the early problems of competition can be found in Kepner (1936) and Kepner and Soothill (1935).

22 Ellis (1978).

23 Beaver (1976).

24 C. M. Wilson (1947).

25 The subject is discussed in detail in Kepner and Soothill (1935) and summarised in Ellis (1978).

26 The Antichresis Concession was awarded by the Honduran government in 1920, and turned the National Railway over to the Cuyamel Fruit Co. with certain financial conditions. See Kepner and Soothill (1935) pp. 123–8.

27 United Fruit Company Annual Report (1930).

28 See Karnes (1979, Chapter 3).

29 The true cost of Panamá Disease to the United Fruit Co. is hard to evaluate, although company President T. E. Sunderland stated that an average of 5,000 acres (2,024 hectares) of Gros Michel production was lost each year with an annual replacement cost of some $18 million. At the time it was estimated that United Fruit were spending around $1 million per annum on research into finding a solution.

Table 7.3 *United Fruit Co. earnings, 1958–62*

	Sales ($m)	*Operating Costs ($m)*	*Net Earnings ($m)*
1958	324.386	288.498	22.742
1959	312.921	293.313	12.088
1960	304.421	302.784	2.171
1961	311.321	300.994	8.921
1962	319.787	306.930	11.006

Source: United Fruit Company Annual Reports; Arthur, Houck and Beckford (1969) p. 150

30 See Read (1981).

31 Ibid.

32 For detailed coverage of the export tax and the 'Banana War', see Ellis (1978) and McCann (1976). For additional background material see Organisation of American States (1975).
33 See Gené (1977) and Unión de Países Exportadores de Banano (1977a), (1977b) and *Informe Mensual*.
34 Chandler (1977).
35 Williamson (1981).
36 Ellis (1978) Chapter 5, and also pp. 236–9.

8 Strategic factors in the growth of a multinational enterprise: the Burmah Oil Company 1886–1928[1]

T. A. B. CORLEY

8.1 INTRODUCTION

Mark Casson (Section 1.1) has drawn attention to the boost given to research in international and industrial economics, after a period in the doldrums, by the current lively interest in the multinational enterprise, the analysis of which overlaps both disciplines. Here it is suggested that the third discipline he mentions, business history, is not merely beginning to test the hypotheses being thrown up by the emerging economic theory of business strategy and growth, but is also contributing to the formulation of that theory itself. If one strand in the devising of the present-day transaction costs approach is clearly traceable back to Coase (1937), the other strand owes much to the pioneering historical research of Chandler (1962), (1977), who explored the changes in business organisation that have reduced transaction costs and enabled the present-day giant (domestic and multinational) corporation to evolve. Williamson (1971), (1975), who did so much to adapt Chandler's discoveries to economists' use, has in an important survey article (1981) usefully woven together these and other strands in the rich transaction-cost pattern.

Yet there is one difference of emphasis between some economists and business historians when analysing the corporation. Nowadays the view of economists is that a firm's growth will be stimulated by the prospective benefits of contractual economies, notably the internal exploitation of inventions, but will be constrained by contractual diseconomies: where the costs of increasing the organisation's size will start to outweight the benefits (see Section 1.10). Business historians and some economists – see Calvet (1981) p. 56 – believe that current analysis, by concentrating on the static aspect and not giving enough attention to the underlying forces, tends to validate as efficient responses acts which should properly be studied more critically and in depth. This really means bringing in the entrepreneur: he is considered in Section 8.4 below. One aspect of transaction costs is the problem of communications over long distances, which will be discussed in Section 8.5. Specific questions regarding the progress of internalisation follow in Section 8.6 and a brief summing up is made in Section 8.7.

The discussion in this chapter is put in the context of Britain's oldest surviving oil company, the Burmah Oil Company, which was founded in 1886. Its international production was clearly of the resource-based type, with (i) location advantages (the 'where' of its basic activity) being the possession of resources overseas; (ii) ownership advantages (the 'why' of its activity) being capital, technology, entrepreneurship and marketing skills; and (iii) internalisation advantages (the 'how' of involvement) being to ensure stability of oil supply at suitable prices; see Dunning (1981) p. 49, cf. Teece (1981a) p. 5. Some background facts, to place the company in its institutional setting, are given in Section 8.2. Then in Section 8.3 a narrative of the main events in the company's growth to 1928 is given, starting as far back as the mid-1850s when Burmese crude first became commercially attractive to the British.

8.2 THE BACKGROUND

The Burmah Oil Co. was first registered (as a Scottish company) in 1886 to produce, refine and market oil in the province of Burma, newly absorbed into the Indian empire. Its story is outlined below until 1928, when the old system of operating through managing agencies, in India and Burma, was ended in favour of overseas branches. That year also the marketing of both Burmah Oil's and Shell's oil products in India was integrated into a new organisation, known as Burmah–Shell. Both these events took the company into a new era of consolidation.

By world standards, the quantity of oil it raised in Burma was always minute, as Table 8.1 shows for 1886 and 1928. Although the global volume of oil output was over 26 times as great by the end of the period as at the beginning, the growth in Burma to 130 times the original figure had been from a very low base. By 1928 output there, augmented by some production on the Indian mainland, was not much above a half of one per cent of the world total. The USA throughout played a dominant role, with over 80 per cent of the oil flow coming from the Western Hemisphere but only 1.7 per cent

Table 8.1 *World Production of Oil 1886–1928*

1886			1928		
	Million Barrels	%		*Million Barrels*	%
USA	28.1	59.4	USA	860.2	68.0
Russia	18.0	38.1	Venezuela	103.1	8.1
India (including Burma)	0.05	0.01	Russia	83.7	6.6
Others	1.2	2.5	Mexico	47.8	3.8
TOTAL	47.3	100.0	Persia	40.1	3.2
			India (including Burma)	7.9	0.6
			Others	122.2	9.7
			TOTAL	1265.0	100.0
			(Western hemisphere	1059.1	83.7)
			(British Empire	20.9	1.7)

Sources: 1886, M. Mitzakis (1922) *The Oil Encyclopaedia*, p. 394
1928, W. E. Skinner (1929) *The Oil and Petroleum Year Book*

Table 8.2 *Production and Use of Oil, 1931*

Producing Country	%	*Consuming Country*	%
USA	61.6	USA	66.0
Russia	11.8	Other Europe	9.4
Venezuela	9.1	Russia	6.6
Romania	3.5	Britain	4.3
Persia	3.1	South America	2.8
South America	3.1	Other North America	2.8
East Indies	2.8	Other Asia	2.8
Mexico	2.6	Central America	1.5
Trinidad	0.7	Japan	1.1
India	0.6	India	1.1
Other Europe	0.5	Australasia	0.9
Other	0.6	Africa	0.7
WORLD TOTAL	100.0	WORLD TOTAL	100.0

Source: A. E. Dunstan (ed.) (1938) *The Science of Petroleum*, Vol. I

from the British Empire (India, Trinidad, Sarawak and Canada). By the early 1930s (see Table 8.2) the pattern of world trade in oil was more perceptibly casting its long shadow over the future: the USA was a net importer of oil, and the Middle East was on the brink of assuming its role of massive exporter; it would be contributing 15 per cent of world oil exports by 1938.

In line with its relatively modest supply of oil, the company remained small, compared with the oil giants of the day. In Table 8.3 the relative sizes are set out for 1928, in terms of issued capital. Interestingly enough, all the large companies in the table, apart from Standard Oil of Indiana (Amoco), comprise the 'seven sisters' which in 1949 accounted for 55 per cent of total oil production outside the iron curtain countries[2] and which are considered to dominate the marketing of oil (although no longer, of course, its production) to this day. It was in this industry of giants that Burmah Oil had to survive and prosper.

The extent of the company's own growth is shown in Table 8.4. In the prospectus it issued in 1886 it expected to earn 53 per cent of its profits from kerosene, from a 46 per cent yield in the refinery, and about 20 per cent of profit from the more valuable paraffin wax (the physical yield being 6 per cent). The heavier products, lubricating oil and the like (27–8 per cent), were the remaining saleable products. No later profit breakdowns have survived, but in the 1920s the main products were kerosene (53 per cent yield) and petrol (17 per cent), with wax and lubricants yielding only 8 per cent between them.

Many of these refined products were intermediate goods, such as wax for candles, lubricating oil and fuel oil for ships, and petrol for commercial vehicles and aircraft, which were normally sold to other

Table 8.3 *Leading Oil Firms 1928 (by issued capital, £million equivalent)*

Standard Oil of New Jersey (Esso/Exxon)	126.9
Standard Oil of New York (Mobil)	89.0
Royal Dutch-Shell	74.6
Standard Oil of California (Socal/Chevron)	64.5
Standard Oil of Indiana (Amoco)	47.6
Texas Corporation (Texaco)	43.3
Anglo–Persian Oil (British Petroleum)	23.9
Gulf Oil	23.1
Burmah Oil	10.9

Source: W. E. Skinner (1929) *The Oil and Petroleum Year Book*

Table 8.4 *The Burmah Oil Co. – Selected Indicators 1886–1928*

	Net Assets (£000s)	*Profit from Rangoon (£000s)*	*Investment Income (£000s)*	*Total Profit (£000s)*	*Net Profit (£000s)*	*Oil Production in Burma (000 barrels)*	*Refinery Throughput (000 barrels)*
1886	N/A	—	—	—	—	50	48
1890	80	17	—	17	9	110	64
1903	2034	332	—	332	249	2133	1361
1913	4481	962	42	1004	823	6821	4506
1928	17048	1560	561	2121	1480	6510	4960
(1928 at 1913 prices)	(10270)	(940)	(337)	(1277)	(892)		

Source: Burmah Oil Archives

companies under long-term or annually negotiated contracts. Apart from some petrol for private motorists, only kerosene was a consumption good sold mainly in the spot market. The discussion below will be largely in terms of kerosene.

8.3 THE NARRATIVE

As it happens, the narrative of Burmah Oil's progress to 1928 is only part of a wider story: the winning and commercial exploitation of Burmese oil from the 1850s onwards. There are in fact six phases between then and 1928, which will be considered in turn.

The existence of Burmese oil, and the very primitive indigenous manual methods of scooping it out of shallow wells, were initially brought to Western notice in 1795.[3] Subsequent interest in the oil came chiefly from the British: Burma had a common frontier with Assam and faced the Indian mainland. In the circumstances of nineteenth-century colonialism, Britain made successive moves to annex Burma by force, the first two stages being in 1824 and 1852. It was partly the fear of a bid by France to acquire large interests in what the British considered to be their own economic sphere that led to a third war and the annexation of Upper Burma – where the oil deposits were situated – in 1886.

(a) Initial Demand from Britain, 1856–9

By the 1830s the first experimental analysis of Burmese crude was being carried out in Britain. Two decades later Price's Patent Candle Co., seeking a suitable raw material, namely paraffin wax, to meet the soaring demand for candles, began practical tests in its London refinery.[4] The directors took out a licence on a patent of 1853 for extracting the paraffin wax from Burmese oil, granted to Warren de la Rue, and he participated in Price's own experiments to overcome the practical problems. In about 1855, for the first time anywhere in the world, they succeeded in refining well-oil on a commercial scale.

To supply the crude, in 1856 British merchants in Rangoon, helped by agents specially sent out by the company, organised on Price's behalf its purchase from the agents of the king who held the monopoly. Ships were also chartered for its transport to Britain. This vast and ambitious venture, involving up to 3,000–4,000 tons of crude (valued at about £150,000) annually, was abruptly called off by Price's early in 1858. The refined wax had proved to be too expensive at a time of falling candle prices, while the byproducts, notably kerosene and lubricants, had been more difficult than expected to sell in the Britain of the day, where animal and vegetable substitute oils were still relatively plentiful.

Not surprisingly, transport costs on the 12,000-mile journey accounted for a third of the input price. However, had the venture been successful, Price's would undoubtedly have started up refining in Rangoon to economise on these costs, as it had earlier begun steam crushing of coconuts in Ceylon to extract the oil for candles and save having to export the bulky coconuts to Britain.

(b) First Refining Activities in Burma, 1859–86

Price's thereafter ceased its involvement in Burma, later buying cheaper wax from America. It was the Rangoon merchants who on their own initiative set up a refinery and a marketing organisation there in about 1859. When in 1864 outside capital was required for the refinery, a joint stock company was registered in England. It failed after only four years, and a second (Scottish) company, registered in 1871, went into liquidation during 1876. That same year the assets and goodwill were acquired by a Glasgow merchant, who as sole proprietor ran the refinery and marketing operations in Rangoon. Until 1888 his net returns from there were nil, and he spent £100,000 in all of his own money.

The main reasons for the unprofitability of these successive enterprises after 1864 were the practices of the royal monopolist and the agents who farmed the oil monopoly. The latter created uncertainty over crude supplies by arbitrarily varying the quantities delivered, and the customer firms had to pay up or risk the closure of the Rangoon refinery. Official post-1886 memoranda refer to the constant bribes and extortions that had to be paid to keep deliveries moving. At the same time, technical problems in the refinery, the first of its kind in the tropics, meant that the quality of refined products was far from satisfactory.

(c) Establishment of the Company, 1886–1903

The deposition of the king and the annexation of Burma overcame the problem of crude supplies. In 1886 the Burmah Oil Co. was registered and three strategic decisions were made: (a) to secure from the new British administration licences to prospect for oil, the existing hand-diggers' rights being protected; (b) to begin mechanical drilling once suitable well-sites were located; and (c) to introduce new techniques and machinery into the inefficient Rangoon refinery.

The structure of the oil industry in Burma after 1886 was one of oligopoly. There were no statutory barriers to entry because the local government was ready to issue prospecting licences to all non-foreign comers. However, little competition was thereby generated as most early applicants soon fell by the wayside through inexperience or interest only in quick profits. Not until 1907–9 did two rivals of any note emerge in Burma but, even so, in 1928 Burmah Oil was producing 85 per cent of the province's total and it marketed a further 9 per cent under an agreement with one of the rivals.

As to kerosene, the growth of an indigenous and technically-based oil industry led to a high degree of import substitution, first of all in Burma and later in its neighbouring market of India; see Section 8.3 d.i below. In 1886 no less than 90 per cent of all kerosene used in Burma had been imported, all from the USA. However, as Burmah Oil built up its production, by 1909 imports had fallen to 17 per cent of Burma's kerosene requirements. The company's own kerosene, if smoky and discoloured, was cheap and easily refined, and of better value to the poor of Burma and India than candles or the even less attractive vegetable oils; until 1905 it was unable to make superior (colourless and smokeless) kerosene, and therefore the USA had to make up the shortfall.

(d) Period of Transformation, 1903–5

Four external events, each in its own way an agent for change, affected Burmah Oil in quick succession.

(i) Competition in the Indian Market After 1901 the company had effectively saturated the Burmese kerosene market and was making large inroads into mainland India's market, then dominated by the giants – Royal Dutch, Shell and Standard Oil.[5] As India, with a population of over 300 million, was the most extensive single market for kerosene, apart from the USA, Russia and Britain, these giants sought to knock out Burmah Oil by a prolonged price war from 1903 to 1905. In fact it enjoyed, besides a tenacious management, a 14 per cent tariff advantage and a pledge by the government not to allow outside companies to start up production in Burma; thus a stalemate ensued.

(ii) Admiralty Fuel Oil Contract In 1903 the Admiralty in London asked the company for a long-term contract to supply fuel oil, now that the first oil-burning warships were being laid down. Burmah Oil was of considerable strategic significance as the only producer of note in the British Empire. After prolonged negotiations, the contract was signed in 1905, a war clause guaranteeing an annual supply of 100,000 tons in the event of hostilities. In the event, the Admiralty

drew only small amounts of oil – mainly for consumption in the Far East – because of the heavy transport costs, and for that department the principal value of the contract was as a lever to extract more competitive prices from its regular suppliers, usually Standard Oil and Shell. Burmah Oil itself was out of pocket because it had to install expensive fuel-oil manufacturing plant with no government help over capital costs. However, this contract led to the company becoming involved in Persia: see (iv) below.

(iii) First Indication of Limited Reserves The necessity of ensuring supplies to met its fuel oil commitments – particularly in wartime – forced the company to intensify prospecting outside the proved oil-fields in Burma. Yet by 1905 it was failing to discover worthwhile new reserves, and from that year onwards further internal growth was seriously checked. Whereas in the seventeen years between 1888 and 1905, refinery throughput in Rangoon grew at an annual rate of nearly 27 per cent, in the succeeding twenty-three years to 1928 it increased by only just over $2\frac{1}{2}$ per cent a year.

(iv) The Persian Concession Having gained the Admiralty's goodwill during the fuel oil negotiations, the directors were asked by officials to assume the entrepreneurial and financial burden of seeking oil in Persia.[6] The holder of the concession there, W. K. D'Arcy, was short of funds and planned to sell out to foreign capitalists, which would have gravely harmed British economic (and strategic) interests. Britain looked on southern Persia as in her own sphere of influence and therefore a secure potential source of fuel oil, far nearer to the West than Rangoon was. In 1905 the Burmah Oil directors agreed to provide the necessary resources and, if successful there, to launch a new company to work the deposits. By 1909, when the new company was registered – see Section 8.3.e.ii below – Burmah Oil had spent nearly £400,000 in Persia.

(e) Product Agreements and Diversification, 1905–20

To meet the altered circumstances of new commitments in face of the limited crude reserves mentioned above, the directors made two major decisions, the consequences of which dominated the period from 1905 to 1920:

(i) Agreements with Shell To protect its income, much depleted by the price war, now that it had financial obligations over fuel oil and Persia, the company concluded a kerosene agreement with Shell in 1905. Shell undertook to buy, for resale in outside markets, all surplus

kerosene, over and above an agreed market share for Burmah Oil in India, so as to create an orderly market there. The two companies later made similar agreements on petrol and wax. Standard Oil made secret verbal 'understandings' at the same time, as for antitrust reasons it needed to be able to claim that it had no formal agreements with rivals.

These accords were frankly restrictive, but officials in Whitehall and Rangoon accepted them, partly because in the kerosene agreement Burmah Oil pledged itself – much to the chagrin of Shell – to set a maximum price for the kerosene it sold in the Indian empire.

(ii) Diversification Eight years after the finite nature of oil deposits in Burma became clear, in 1913 total crude production there reached a plateau (see Table 8.4). It is unlikely that the directors would have actively sought opportunities to diversify. The two examples of diversification by the company in Persia and Trinidad between those years were not conscious steps to ensure further growth, but the results of *ad hoc* decisions after carefully considering all propositions put to them. They turned down proposals for Venezuela: the joint venture with Shell in Trinidad during 1911 was a complete flop, from which they pulled out in the 1920s.

Persia, on the other hand, proved a spectacular success. Prospecting there from 1905 onwards took up much of the top management's attention, and the burden if anything increased after oil was struck in 1908. The following year Burmah Oil set up an almost wholly-owned subsidiary, the Anglo-Persian Oil Co., but some years passed before the latter became an efficient and profitable producer. Not until 1917 did it declare its first ordinary dividend, and in the meantime Burmah Oil had to finance its preference dividends. The Admiralty was now looking to Persia for fuel oil, since that country was nearer to Britain than Burma and had far greater oil reserves. Alarmed at the still escalating costs of the Persian operations, the Burmah Oil directors after much debate with the British government induced the government to buy a majority shareholding in Anglo-Persian. The necessary financial agreement, linked with a fuel oil contract, was signed with the government in 1914.

(f) Changes in Strategy, 1920–8

Whereas between 1903 and 1920 most of the impetus towards change and growth had come from outside, in 1920–8 Burmah Oil began to adopt a more positive strategy, most notably in two directions:

(i) Further Diversification In 1921 the company acquired the Assam Oil Co., the only producer of any consequence in India. It had been very underfinanced and poorly managed, and Burmah Oil poured in funds and expertise, sinking no less than £1 million in it by 1928. Not until the mid-1930s, though, did it become a profit-earner and a large producer.

(ii) Scheme of Merger with Shell Potentially far more significant was a plan, devised by Shell in 1915, for a merger with Burmah Oil. As Shell was 60 per cent Dutch-owned, that merger was intended to make the Shell group British-controlled, as the combined shareholding would then secure a majority against the Dutch. For Shell the main economic advantage would be to increase market power in the East, while Burmah Oil shareholders would benefit financially from Shell's worldwide activities. Until 1920 the Burmah Oil reaction was lukewarm, refusing to consider the scheme until Whitehall had given its official approval.

By 1918 Anglo-Persian had to be brought into the scheme as a British counterweight to the now relatively larger Dutch interests. However, that company, by then fully operational and striving to diversify worldwide, opposed the merger, although successive British governments from 1918 to 1924 seemed willing to sell back their shareholdings to the private sector as an integral part of the scheme. After 1920 Burmah Oil became a keen supporter of the scheme, but it was killed off by the combined weight of the Admiralty, fearful of any possible threat to its Persian oil supplies, and British public opinion that was hostile to any oil trust. The first Labour cabinet of 1924 formally rejected it.

As a second-best, in 1928 the two companies set up the Burmah–Shell Oil Storage and Distributing Co. of India, to integrate their marketing operations to save on costs, and also to centralise in London all the policy decisions involved. The managing director of Burmah Oil became a director of Shell, and Burmah Oil purchased a token holding of one million Shell ordinary shares.

These various accommodations with Shell after 1905, which started as alternatives to price wars in India but later went well beyond mere product agreements, were typical of inter-firm relationships to reduce uncertainty; see Richardson (1972). Not surprisingly, the agreements attracted criticisms (Indian Tariff Board, 1928, p. 90) that kerosene prices were consequently far higher than they needed to be: criticisms vigorously rebutted by Watson, who stressed the long-term orderly market argument and also the valuable safeguard of Burmah Oil's maximum price policy.

The Burmah–Shell agreement of 1928 effectively excluded

Burmah Oil from any possibility of diversifying into oil operations elsewhere in the world, even had it wished to do so. Through its shareholdings in Anglo-Persian and Shell, it was now on the way to becoming an investment company with diminishing production interests in the east: in 1928 over a quarter of its gross income was from interest and dividends.

How its top management envisaged the company's eventual future once the oil in Burma finally ran out is not known. In the event, before it did run out, all oil assets in Burma had to be destroyed in 1942 to deny them to the advancing Japanese. After 1945 the company began to rebuild those assets and in 1960 production was back to half the pre-war level. However, by then the company was having to dispose of its interests in Burma and India after those countries achieved nationhood. Only then, at last free from the old pre-war restrictions on expansion, did it begin to diversify into oil and non-oil ventures alike.

8.4 THE ANALYSIS: THE ROLE OF ENTREPRENEURSHIP

The foregoing narrative was set out in terms of events and avoided naming the successive top managers of Burmah Oil. Is it in fact possible adequately to explain the growth of a firm without discussing the part played by the entrepreneurs involved? Penrose (1959), for instance, did so in general terms of unused productive services helping to promote growth and managerial constraints impeding growth. Scherer (1980) sees a firm's relative growth, compared with its rivals, broadly in terms of chance, with only a very minor role given to business acumen: 'Once a firm has, by virtue of early good luck, placed itself among the industry leaders, it can achieve additional market share gains if it should happen again to be luckier than average.'[7]

On the other hand Prais (1976), whose thought in that work is steeped in Marshallian ideas, quotes with seeming approval Marshall's statement (1920, p. 316) that limitations to the inheritance of exceptional ability and wealth could play some part in narrowing the relative size advantage that a successful pioneer may have built up. Somewhat more positively, Williamson (1975) admits that business acumen may have helped a firm to become a dominant one, but a contributing factor could have been the persistent ineptitude of rivals, in failing to use market methods to prevent the pushing firm from getting ahead.[8]

As against these rather tentative views, business historians and others who have studied closely the progress of individual firms are convinced of the important roles that the personal qualities of entrepreneurs have played, whether positively or negatively, not only in the distant past but up to the present day. Chandler (1962, p. 384ff.), while he sees growth in terms of alternatively accumulating and rationalising the use of corporate resources, does specify by name the two American entrepreneurs who pioneered the momentous organisational innovation of the multi-divisional form. Others, such as Hughes (1973) and Silberston (1981), give only a minor role to luck, and concentrate on the concept of the 'great man', one 'who leads his firm to do well in difficult circumstances, or to do exceptionally well in normal circumstances. The more successful his firm is, as compared with other firms in similar circumstances, the 'greater' the man at the top is likely to be'.[9] The weakness of this theory is that it entails a certain amount of circular reasoning, so that a great man is simply one who heads a successful firm. It does nothing to predict the kinds of quality that a successful entrepreneur would need or the circumstances in which he might become successful.

Hopefully, future research will bring about a closer convergence of views by economists and business historians on the causes of corporate growth. Each view in its way has power to enlighten the study of past events. To give one instance on the economists' side, Burmah Oil very soon built up a commanding position in the province's oil industry because the competition-promoting local government was after 1886 generous with concessions to the company, in recognition both of the expense and of the effort incurred earlier and of its current efficiency. Yet before long officials were worrying about its high profits, but could do little to encourage rivals apart from keeping some choice well-sites exclusively for those rivals.

The most effective countervailing measure would have been for officials to accede to the demands of Standard Oil in 1902 and Shell in 1904 for production facilities in Burma. Their refusal to do so would no doubt be regarded as a typical abuse of colonial power to curb investment from other countries (Svedberg, 1981). In fact, however, the two majors, once inside Burma, would have employed price-cutting and other business tactics to bring about the destruction of Burmah Oil and the smaller indigenous companies – see Jones (1979) pp. 360–1.

Those holding business historians' views about entrepreneurship, on the other hand, would be bound to pay much attention to the top managers in Burmah Oil over the period. There were three in all, as follows:

(a) David S. Cargill, 1876–1903 He was the sole proprietor from 1876 to 1886, and then became the first chairman until his death in

1904. The same Glasgow merchant as was mentioned in Section 8.3.b, he had visited Rangoon in 1874–5 and had grasped the long-term and as yet unexploited commercial possibilities of oil in the province. He can thus be seen as a 'gap-filler' and input completer (Leibenstein, 1978), able to back his judgement with ample funds from a very lucrative emporium ('the Harrods of the East') in Ceylon and some tea plantations there. Being extraordinarily tenacious and far-seeing, he even carried out costly investment before 1886, despite the unprofitability of the operations at that time.

From the Glasgow head office after that date, he worked in tandem with the managing director Kirkman Finlay, who had been an employee of the former company's agency house in Rangoon and had in 1874–5 first suggested to Cargill that he should purchase the oil interests. Finlay set up the London office and dealt with day-to-day affairs, including negotiations with government departments such as the India Office. Their joint running of the firm was undoubtedly 'coordination by anticipation', to use Casson's phrase. From 1889, when the company was fully established, until 1928 and beyond, it had no problems in raising whatever outside funds were required: finance was never a constraint on growth.

(b) (Sir) John Cargill, 1903–20 In 1903 Finlay died suddenly, not being permanently replaced in the London office until 1912, nor as managing director until 1920. As David Cargill was by 1903 mortally ill, his son John took over, succeeding as chairman the following year. A painfully diffident man, John Cargill was, in the conditions of rapid change in 1903–5 (see Section 8.3.b), fortunate in being able to rely on a series of very competent and strong-minded advisers in London: Sir Boverton Redwood (d. 1919) the oil consultant, C. W. Wallace (d. 1916) who was on the London side of the company's Indian sub-agency Shaw Wallace & Co., and R. I. Watson (see (c) below).

According to Casson's definition, John Cargill and his advisers made up a consultative bureaucracy, with Wallace as a director and running the London office intermittently on an *ad hoc* basis (he refused on health grounds to become managing director) until Watson came home in 1912. This decentralised and delegated management system that Cargill evolved, or allowed to develop, worked moderately well, with the donkey work – particularly day-to-day liaison with Shell over the product agreements – falling on a scratch team from Shaw Wallace & Co. As it happened, because there was no one else, that scratch team after 1904 more or less took charge of the non-technical side of the Persian operations, and then did most of the work of setting up Anglo-Persian.

The fact that those who took over the running of Anglo-Persian were non-Burmah Oil-bred men made it easier for that company to develop policies that were independent of Burmah Oil; Cargill and later Watson were no more than non-executive directors on their subsidiary's board. The terms of D'Arcy's original concession with the Shah had required the formation of an entirely new company to work any oil discovered in Persia, and in 1915–17 the two companies finally separated those functions (such as plant and stores) which had been run jointly.

(c) Robert I. Watson, 1920–8 Watson was from the Burmah Oil agency in Rangoon and joined the London office in 1912. He differed from John Cargill in many ways, notably in actively promoting change rather than merely adapting to it, and he used a rational rather than a pragmatic approach to problems. When he became managing director in 1920 he virtually took full charge of the company, Cargill being happy to become an elder statesman (honoured with a baronetcy) well above the hurly-burly. Watson saw his task as one of converting the company from an entrepreneurial to managerial one.

Whereas Cargill as entrepreneur had run the firm in loose association with his advisers, Watson now established a hierarchy of management and set about centralising decision-making. He was well qualified to do this, having a marked capacity for logical thought, a phenomenal memory and great physical and mental stamina. He was able to benefit from the more advanced technology of management then becoming available: more efficient telephones, office machinery for the better keeping of records (particularly statistical ones), cost accounting methods, management consultancies and so on. Some of the reforms he introduced into the company will be discussed in subsequent sections.

8.5 THE PROBLEM OF EXTENDED COMMUNICATIONS

As Casson pointed out in Section 1.6, in a world where information is scarce and its sources localised, the better the organisation has adapted itself to use whatever information there is, the more beneficial the impact on the firm's conduct and growth. It is therefore worth studying the actual mechanisms whereby the entrepreneur reaches his decisions and ensures that they are carried out. These mechanisms are likely to involve incompletely specified contracts (Williamson, 1975; Leibenstein, 1976; Teece, 1981a), and the nature of these contractual relationships is even more important when operations have to be carried out over considerable distances. The trade-off between effectiveness and cost is particularly crucial.

Over frontiers, the form that a multinational organisation has to take will depend on international communication costs, which themselves will be affected by the technology of communication at the given time (cf. Buckley and Casson, 1976, especially Section 2.2). In contrast with the enormous improvements in our own time, until 1928 aids to communications were limited. In the 1860s it took three to four months to get a message to Burma, but during that decade two technological developments took place:

(a) the opening of the Suez canal in 1869 and the replacement of sail by steam which progressively reduced the surface communications lag with Britain to twenty-three days by the 1920s, and
(b) the installation of the electric telegraph, which linked Britain with Rangoon from 1865 onwards and with Mandalay, capital of the oil-supplying Upper Burma, a few years later.

Thereafter the entrepreneurs in Britain could send fairly brief messages to Burma one day and expect a reply during the next day's working hours. Even so, some reliable system of delegated responsibility in the host country was required.

An early system was to use a trusted relative or senior employee who could be relied on to act in accordance with the anticipated wishes of the people in Britain: cf. 'a person of proven ability and integrity' (Section 1.8). When some more formal arrangement was needed, the managing agency grew up.[10] In essence a British system, it was found mainly in the East and extensively in India. The managing agent overseas contracted to take responsibility for the home-based organisation's affairs for, say, ten or twenty years at a time, the arrangement being terminated only in the event of 'incapacity or wilful default'. The agent was furnished with overall instructions but had the final powers of decision within the scope of those instructions. He was in no sense running a branch, for his agency typically dealt in a variety of other activities as well, sometimes even acting for rival companies at the same time.

Since service contracts were drawn up in the broadest terms, success or failure of the managing agency system depended on how the relationship with home worked out in practice. As stated in Section 8.3.b, two British-registered companies in succession – in 1864 and 1871 – were set up to refine and market Burmese oil; yet none of the home directors had specialist knowledge of oil and they maintained an arm's-length relationship with the managing agents in Burma.

The first company's investment in refining plant can be described as expatriate (using Stopford's distinction between types of capital exports)[11] since little strategic control seems to have been exercised from Britain. However, the second, founded in 1871 by some shipowners with interests in Anglo-Burmese trade, was more than a financial 'shell' and undoubtedly maintained entrepreneurial supervision by telegraph. Only when David Cargill took over in 1876 was a close relationship built up with the managing agents, for his personal friend Kirkman Finlay was the first general manager of Finlay Fleming & Co. of Rangoon.

From an organisational point of view, that agency was far closer to the principals at home than its predecessors had been. It was largely owned by Cargill, who appointed all the European staff, the most successful often eventually returning to managerial posts in the company at home. Until 1904 the Rangoon general managers were unimaginative, commercially-educated Scots. From then on, all in turn were public school men, two having university degrees and two legal or accounting qualifications; all but one were knighted for public services. A few years later the company began recruiting its overseas assistants from among Cambridge graduates. That followed the practice of Shell, but although the Shell directors expected their agents to carry out instructions without argument, there was an incessant dialogue with Rangoon which usefully complemented the up-to-date knowledge of the Finlay Fleming & Co. men with the mature experience of the Burmah Oil directors, all but one of whom had years of Eastern service behind them.

Despite this fruitful information-sharing relationship, Watson on his return to the London office from Burma in 1912 sought to introduce more effective monitoring of the agency by reorganising the correspondence along systematic lines and building up specialist staff – including a statistical section – in his office. Not until he became managing director in 1920 could he move to the next stage. Most of the company's departments had been transferred from Glasgow to within his control, so that he had both the executive power and the technical advisers such as an advisory chemist (see Section 8.6) and an engineer. He instructed Rangoon to provide regular income and expenditure analyses, broken down into detailed categories, of all operations from production to sea transport and marketing; he also personally scrutinised all proposals for capital expenditure. On one occasion, he even sent out a consultant, a man from Price Waterhouse & Co., to study on the spot the organisations in both the refinery and the oilfields, and also the costing systems, which led to some limited reforms.

His long-term plan was to transfer direct supervision of as many functions as possible from Rangoon's hands to his own in London: those moves would both reduce the expense of duplication and provide more effective monitoring from his specialist (in Williamson's terms, elite) head office staff. Between 1920 and 1925 he took away from the agency responsibility for all functions except marketing. In 1928, with the establishment of Burmah–Shell, marketing as well came under London; Finlay Fleming & Co. then ceased to be the company's agency and a branch office was set up in Rangoon. Clearly improvements in office methods, and in communications, allowed him to centralise in this way; but the entrepreneurial aspect, of having both the vision and the will for change, should not be overlooked.

8.6 THE ANALYSIS: INTERNALISATION

As was suggested above, when British interests sought to turn Burmese oil to commercial use from the 1850s onwards, they were – in terms of multinational enterprise analysis – productively combining location-specific endowments in the host country with ownership- and, later, firm-specific factors in the home country. The former was the oil waiting to be raised efficiently and turned into saleable refined products, while the latter comprised entrepreneurship, capital, technical (geological, drilling, refining) expertise and so on.

Among the areas where the participation of multinational enterprises is most pronounced in host countries is that of export-oriented primary goods sectors requiring large amounts of capital. Moreover, these are all sectors in which firms have a high propensity to internalise activities, so as to come to terms with market imperfections, including uncertainty (see Dunning, 1981, pp. 28–9, and Teece, 1981a, p. 5).

In the 1850s, when Price's Patent Candle Co. required Burmese crude for paraffin wax, the fact that it had to send out inexperienced agents and then use brokers limited its influence over the purchasing and shipping operations, and may have contributed to the venture's collapse. When refining began in Rangoon and was combined with local marketing, as long as crude oil had to be bought from Upper Burma, there was no real control from home. Not until 1886 could production, refining and marketing all be looked at in unison and the company begin to lay down for its agents a coordinated programme, requiring from the oilfields enough output to keep the refineries at full capacity and from the refineries the correct mix of products to satisfy demand. Marketing was still largely decentralised. In Burma kerosene distribution was run (on an arm's-length basis) by a Chinese agent, since the retail stores were all Chinese-owned, while in the subcontinent of India the sub-agents Shaw Wallace & Co. sold through Indian merchants.

Once drilling and refining improvements allowed output both of crude and of refined products to soar, the first bottlenecks to appear were in transport facilities. Deliveries to the main Indian ports could only be made by deck cargo in general merchant ships; from the late 1890s onwards the company acquired its own tankers and tank installations. Then in 1908 it completed a pipeline to bypass the monopolistic Irrawaddy Flotilla Co., which had hitherto conveyed the crude downriver from the oilfields to Rangoon. These steps appreciably reduced freight costs, protected the company from the inefficiencies and exploitation of outside undertakings, and enabled Finlay Fleming & Co. to match both crude and refined product requirements with transport resources. A further integrating move was a response to the first indications of difficulties over future crude supplies. Until 1904 it had relied for evidence of possible oil finds on the mapping by the government-run Geological Survey of India, but that year it began to recruit geologists who would be under its exclusive control and concentrate on the most promising exploration areas.

The technology of refining was still very simple, with only a few patented processes acquired on licence. Then in 1906–8 the company set up two subsidiaries to develop patents it had bought. One was for an early form of cracking; that failed and was quickly wound up, but the other, for improving the colour of kerosene and wax, proved very successful. After 1912 Watson began an intensive search for new refining methods, bringing home the Rangoon refinery manager to be a full-time advisory chemist with a laboratory in London, and sending him out to investigate certain continental discoveries. Watson also set up a system for acquiring copies of all relevant patent specifications for vetting in London and Rangoon. Not until after 1918 was Watson able to take tighter control of research and development in this area, by encouraging the senior refinery staff to devise an improved method (later patented) of refining, which gave far better yields of some of the more profitable products. Once the method was perfected, he masterminded a complete refinery reconstruction and the installation of appropriate new plant which was laid out more logically than in the past.

For any multinational enterprise, an organisation chart may show that a certain department is subordinate to, say, some authority, but if that department is in an out-of-the way location and run entirely by a close-knit group of foreign technical people, then any sort of effective control may be very difficult. So it proved in the Burmese oilfields, three hundred miles away from Rangoon, as the drillers and field management staff were all Americans. At the outset Finlay Fleming & Co. more or less left them to their own devices, as long as enough oil continued to flow. Then in 1905, when the limited quantity of oil in Burma became clear and the company began to be cost-conscious, it inserted the thin end of the agency control wedge by appointing an office man as fields agent, ostensibly to help with the paper work. It took eighteen years, some reverses (including a drillers' strike which successfully got rid of an over-zealous fields agent) and two changes of fields manager before proper office control was imposed.

The X-inefficiency can be illustrated by two examples: the fields manager building himself a lavish official bungalow without the agency realising it; and much plant being left about to rust and consumables being squandered. The managerial cost of imposing control was in making effective arrangements to obtain first hand information (which had earlier been rather sparse) as to what was happening in the oilfields. Moreover, there also had to be the will to carry the reforms through. Once achieved, these reforms did yield considerable economies in costs.

Watson, especially after his appointment as managing director in 1920, was strong on furthering internal changes, and three important ones in that decade can be mentioned: the refinery reconstruction to provide up-to-date plant and more systematic layout (as already described); the electrification of the oilfields, powered by otherwise useless natural gas; and a joint venture, with an Indian steel firm, to make tinplate for kerosene and petrol tins as a substitute for the more costly imports. These changes were all very expensive but well costed, the first running to £1 million, the second to well over £800,000 and the third requiring £1 million of Burmah Oil money to be sunk in it. Watson's greater professionalism was seen in the fact that instead of keeping suppliers of plant and machinery at arm's length and simply telling them what they should produce (or alternatively just asking for a catalogue from which to choose), he brought them actively into the planning process so as to provide expertise as well as hardware. In the electrification case, he hired an expert from each of the two main electrical suppliers, keeping one in London and sending one to Burma; there was constant bickering, but he felt the creative tension to be a bonus rather than the reverse.

He was meanwhile carrying out some important organisational changes. One in the early 1920s was to fire the total unsatisfactory Chinese marketing agent for Burma and then set up a network of branches, staffed by Finlay Fleming & Co. assistants, to control sales (still by local Chinese shopkeepers) in each district of the province. This helped to diminish both costs and uncertainty. As was mentioned in Section 8.5, by 1928 he had centralised all the main functions of the company in the head office. It was basically a unitary firm (Williamson, 1975), although the Assam Oil Co. could be classed as a quasi-firm, being the only subsidiary with considerable funds, management and technical expertise locked up in its lengthy reshaping. Watson's highly integrated and centralised organisational system remained virtually intact until the diversification of the 1960s, when the acquisition of oil and non-oil interests led to a multi-divisional structure being set up.

8.7 CONCLUSIONS

Why did the Burmah Oil Co. grow as it did? The crucial date here seems to be 1886, when the authorities in Burma granted it the initial well concessions, to acknowledge past endeavour and entrepreneurial promise for the future. These liberal concessions, linked with vigorous production and marketing policies, put the company so far ahead that, despite free entry for indigenous applicants, other entrants never stood a chance of mounting an effective challenge. Hence by 1928 it was marketing all but 7 per cent of the oil produced in Burma.

Thus the most basic precondition for substantial growth was present. On top of this, Casson (Section 1.9) has pointed out that the simplest reason for a firm's growth is that it has a monopoly of a product for which there is an expanding demand. Here Burmah Oil enjoyed two supreme advantages. The first was in its staple product of cheap kerosene, and the second was in having a natural and near-at-hand market, in Burma and also mainland India. The kerosene was easy to refine, was inexpensive, carried no tariff nor (until 1921) excise duty, and was subject to the company's voluntary maximum price code. The outlets in Burma and India meant that, in contrast with the 1850s, transport costs were low and could be reduced even further by internalisation, whether setting up a tanker fleet, a pipeline or one's own Indian port storage facilities.

As against the overwhelming advantages of plentiful concessions, a cheap and easily marketable staple product, and a natural outlet in the amply populated Indian empire, the company had two disadvantages. One was that it came late to mainland India, where Shell and Standard Oil had well-established markets for their kerosene. Thus its incursion into that market inevitably provoked counter-measures such as a price war and efforts to secure concessions in Burma itself. The only way of ensuring continued growth, without debilitating conflicts, was to accept market-sharing agreements.

The second disadvantage was the fact that the oil resources in Burma turned out to be finite, at least in the existing state of geological knowledge. The company did take the logical step of diversifying, but only after outside pressure, and John Cargill seems early to have accepted that he could play no part in the day-to-day running of

Anglo-Persian, the first subsidiary. By the 1920s that subsidiary, while providing its parent with good dividends, was largely being managed independently. The second subsidiary, Assam Oil, tied up almost as many resources as the first had done and took almost as many years (thirteen in all) to become fully viable, but was ideal material to work on as it was within Burmah Oil's home territory of the Indian empire.

In short, the company's successive entrepreneurs do seem to have made much of its advantages and were not too rash in their schemes, such as diversification, to offset its disadvantages. Their reward was therefore a very reasonable if not spectacular record of growth.

NOTES

1 Information regarding the company is from my forthcoming History of the Burmah Oil Company, Vol. I (1886–1924). Thanks are due to the directors for permission to use this information. Much valuable material was destroyed in 1940 when the Glasgow office archives (including all original accounts and related financial documents) were sent for salvage. However, most of the London correspondence between 1897 and 1928 has survived.
2 International Petroleum Cartel (1952) p. 24.
3 The 1795 and later descriptions of oil raising in Upper Burma are fully discussed in Noetling (1898) pp. 4ff., and the early chemical analyses in ibid. pp. 143ff.
4 For the use of Burmese oil for candle-making in the 1850s see Price's (1947), supplemented by Wilson (1876) and Price's (1891).
5 Royal Dutch and Shell merged in 1907, but from 1903 onwards they marketed jointly in the East, the sales organisation being the Asiatic Petroleum Co. Ltd. For simplicity, these various organisations are referred to in this chapter as Shell.
6 The first volume of a history of British Petroleum, up to the early 1930s, by Dr R. Ferrier, is to be published in 1982, but some aspects of its relationship with Burmah Oil are covered in Ferrier (1976).
7 Scherer (1980) p. 146.
8 Williamson (1975) pp. 212ff.
9 Silberston (1981) p. 346.
10 For the managing agency system see Anstey (1929) pp. 113–14 and Rungta (1970) pp. 219–55.
11 Stopford (1974) p. 305.

9 The growth of transnational banking

GEORGE N. YANNOPOULOS

9.1 INTRODUCTION

This chapter traces the growth of transnational banks (TNBs) and attempts to explain the transnationalisation of banking by drawing upon theories of foreign direct investment. Sections 9.1 to 9.3 chart the recent growth of TNBs, while Sections 9.4 to 9.7 examine the economic rationale of the TNB. The conclusions are summarised in Section 9.8.

It is useful at the beginning to distinguish between transnational banking and international financial intermediation. In the theory of international financial intermediation (Freedman, 1977), the concern is with the movements in a bank's net spot position in foreign currencies irrespective of the form of the bank's involvement in the international money market. The theory of transnational banking is concerned with the choice of alternative forms of involvement in the international money market and the consequences of such choices. Banks have always carried on international business – such as foreign lending from their home offices using domestic funds or accepting foreign currency deposits with their domestic offices (Einzig, 1970). Such international banking business was – and still is – carried out from a bank's domestic offices through a network of correspondents in different foreign financial centres (Revell, 1974). Whilst international banking is concerned with dealings from a home base with foreign customers or in foreign currencies, transnational banking implies the physical presence of a bank outside its home territory through a branch agency, a wholly owned or a majority owned subsidiary, or through the development of links with other banks internationally. Transnational banking should not be exclusively identified with the activities of Eurobanks. Eurobanks are TNBs located in external markets where banking transactions such as deposits, loans, etc., are denominated in a currency other than the currency of the host country. However, TNBs can also operate in foreign markets by dealing with credit denominated in the currency of the host country. Eurobanks are thus a special category of TNBs which enjoy the advantage of not being subject to home banking regulations (Dufey and Giddy, 1978). TNBs are banks which supply banking services through offices located outside the country in which they are incorporated.

Whilst for our purposes the ownership of banking facilities in one country by a bank domiciled in another suffices to characterise the bank involved in this transborder move as a TNB, other authors qualify the definition by imposing restrictions either on the number of countries in which a TNB has to own banking facilities or on the number of banking offices that it operates outside its home territory. Wellons (1976) defines a TNB as a deposit-taking institution operating in more than five countries through branches or subsidiaries. Brimmer and Dahl (1975) consider that transnational banking comes into being when the bank operates three or more branches. The rationale for imposing these restrictions either in terms of country coverage or in terms of the units operated abroad is to emphasise the importance of a globally integrated network of banking facilities that respond to a common strategy. The importance that some writers attach to the ability to operate on the basis of a global strategy leads them to disregard forms of representation abroad other than branches. S. W. Robinson (1972) maintains that only branch representation can serve the aims of a TNB. Emphasis on a globally integrated network of branches is very much related to the attention that these writers wish to focus upon the ability of a TNB to mobilise financial resources located in many countries in full or partial independence of the policies of those countries. However, any discussion about transnational banking should be able to explain not only how TNBs acquire this ability but also how they choose among different forms of international involvement.

The involvement of a bank in the international money market (in short, international involvement) can take place in a number of ways. The simplest method through which a bank can supply banking services beyond the national borders of its country of domicile is through correspondent bank connections. A correspondent connection acts as a kind of sales agency for the bank that wishes to engage in international banking activities. This type of involvement is the equivalent to the exporting activities of commodity producing firms. Once the bank decides to move from international banking to transnational banking, it has five main options: a representative office, an agency, a branch, a joint venture or a majority-owned subsidiary.

The first move towards transnational banking comes usually through the establishment of a *representative office*, which opens up new sources of local information and facilitates the generation of additional business. But the establishment of a representative office constitutes only a transitional move to transnational banking proper. An *agency* is a banking office that lends and transfers funds but cannot accept deposits from domestic sources of the host country (Terrell and Key, 1978). Agencies are organisational forms most suited to the financing of foreign trade (handling letters of credit, bills of exchange, etc.). A *branch* can offer a full range of banking services. Both agencies and branches form an integral part of the parent bank. A *joint venture* offers participation in an already functioning financial institution in the host country. The most preferred form of joint venture in the 1970s has been the consortium bank. Subsidiaries that are wholly owned are a less popular form.

It is often the case that the choice of organisational form open to a bank contemplating the establishment of some presence abroad is limited by the legislative requirements of both host and home countries. Legal restrictions in Mexico, for example, make the subsidiary the only organisational form of foreign presence in that country's financial market. But other factors relating to a bank's global strategy decisively influence this choice. A branch permits the maximum degree of parent control whilst it provides a very effective means of tapping foreign funds, since the branch enjoys the full backing of the resources of the parent. Participations require a more moderate amount of investment, limit the risks to which the parent bank is exposed, and require a limited commitment on manpower. The same is true for the subsidiaries, which have the additional advantage of enabling a bank to diversify and to engage abroad in activities beyond those permitted to overseas branches by the law of the country of the parent bank.

Table 9.1 *Main Forms of Foreign Presence of Thirty Largest US Banks, 1974*

	Overseas Offices		*Assets*	
	Number	%	*Amount (in $m)*	%
Branches	616	66.5	132,546	85.4
Bank Subsidiaries	122	13.2	19,910	12.8
Finance company subsidiaries	156	16.8	2,650	1.7
Other subsidiaries	33	3.6	678	0.1
TOTAL	927	100.0	155,238	100.0

Source: FINE (1976)

Table 9.2 *Main Forms of Presence of Foreign Banks in the US Market, 1972–80*

	November 1972				*March 1980*			
	Number	*Percentage of Total*	*Total Assets ($m)*	*Percentage of Total*	*Number*	*Percentage of Total*	*Total Assets ($m)*	*Percentage of Total*
Agencies	50	50	13,635	59.3	165	50.1	62,227	35.6
Branches	26	26	5,302	23.0	127	38.6	85,889	49.4
Subsidiaries	25	25	4,064	17.7	37	11.3	25,788	15.0
TOTAL	101	100	23,001	100.0	329	100.0	173,904	100.0

Source: Goldberg and Saunders (1981a) p. 367

Given the importance that TNBs attach to their ability to mobilise financial resources on a worldwide basis, it is not surprising to find that the most preferred forms of presence in a foreign market have been the branch and the agency. This strong preference is noticeable among both the US banks operating abroad and the non-US transnational banks with a presence in the US market (see Tables 9.1 and 9.2).

9.2 THE GROWTH OF TRANSNATIONAL BANKING

Contrary to what is widely believed, the growth of transnational banking is not an exclusively post-Second World War phenomenon.

The earliest TNB can be traced back to the end of the fourteenth century. It was the Medici Bank based in Florence. Following the institutionalisation of international fairs in Europe, the Medici Bank established affiliated companies not only in other Italian cities, but also in Geneva, Avignon, Bruges and London. Each of these banking affiliates was a separate legal entity with its own capital and set of accounts (de Roover, 1948).

The first modern TNBs appeared during the second half of the nineteenth century with the emergence of the British Overseas Banks. These banks started by financing import and export trade with funds raised from their headquarters in the UK. They soon moved into retail banking overseas to tap the colonial markets where indigenous banks were rare (Nwankwo, 1971; Channon, 1977). Familiarity with the colonial administrations, the dominant position of sterling as an international trading and reserve currency and specialisation by region, enabled these banks to expand and to become before the Second World War net exporters of short-term capital from the overseas territories to London. The breaking up of the empire did not wipe out these banks. Their experience in international finance, their innovative capacity and versatility, enabled them to adjust and redirect their business towards the provision of specialist banking services (e.g. leasing) and technical banking assistance to the developing countries, and also to the establishment of worldwide banking facilities to service the growing financial needs of the multinational corporations. They have thus entered into the third stage of their life-cycle, moving from mainstream international banking to transnational retail banking and then into the transnational wholesale banking market.

Already at the beginning of the twentieth century, the 32 British Overseas Banks had a network of 2,104 branches, predominantly in the colonies. At about the same time, similar 'colonial' banks with headquarters in France, Germany and Holland operated a network of about 242 branches in their own overseas territories (Vollmer, 1974). US banks had very few foreign branches at that time, though by 1902 three New York banks had opened offices in London. During the first two decades of this century, US banks tried to expand in Latin America but with little success. Lack of experience and overestimation of the potential size of the Latin American market led to disappointments (Kelly, 1977). Thus, during the third decade of this century, US banking institutions embarked upon a contraction of their transnational activities. The number of US banks with an overseas presence dropped from 20 in 1920 to only 8 in 1933. In any case, the period between the two world wars was an era of disintegration of the world economy as a result of widespread protectionism and growing rivalries among the European nations. Thus at the start of the second half of the twentieth century (1954) the total world figure of foreign banking offices was reported to be 1250: 40 per cent of these offices were branches of UK banks, 30 per cent of banks from Continental Europe, 9 per cent of US banks and 10 per cent of Canadian Banks (Vollmer, 1974).

The pattern of transnational banking that evolved during the second half of the twentieth century is distinctly different from that of the previous periods. This is not simply a question of growth rates; it is related to a number of qualitative characteristics. The predominance of transnational corporations and official institutional actors in the international financial markets brought about a change of emphasis from retail banking overseas to international wholesale banking. The role of the US dollar in the post-war international monetary system and the growth of American foreign direct investment facilitated a spectacular expansion in the overseas operations of the US banks and enabled them to become the dominant group amongst TNBs. Thus whilst in 1954 the USA accounted for only 9 per cent of world foreign banking offices and the UK for about 40 per cent, in the late 1970s the US accounted for about one-third of such offices and the UK for approximately 15 per cent.

A third qualitative difference is related to the geographical orientation of the activities of TNBs. In the pre-war period most of the moves of the TNBs were directed towards the developing countries. True, several US banks, the Swiss Bank Corporation and a few other TNBs of developed countries had established their presence in London. But by and large the direction of TNB moves were from the developed economies to the developing areas of the world. By contrast, the current pattern involves an increasing interpenetration of developed countries' TNBs into each other's territory, with the significant exception of the offshore centres located in developing countries. Parallel to this trend is the emergence of third world TNBs Stimulated by the post-war international labour migrations, third world TNBs tend to follow their migrant workers into provincial centres of the UK, into the ethnic districts of New York, or near to the ghetto areas of the large European cities where the guest workers reside (Moran, 1975). The phenomenal post-war growth of tourism and business travel is a further factor in the changing international scene that has influenced the development of transnational banking.

Apart from structural changes, growth rates have been very high during the last two decades. As the most comprehensive data are those pertaining to the international operations of US banks and to the activities of non-US TNBs in the US markets, I shall concentrate on this data. Table 9.3 shows that between 1960 and 1978 the number of overseas branches of US banks increased by almost six times. During the decade 1965–74 the number of US TNBs increased from 11 to 125 and their branches (extending over 59 countries) from 181 to 732. Asset growth has been impressive both over time and in comparison with asset growth from the domestic operations of US banks. The Federal Reserve Bank of New York estimates that the claims on foreigners of the foreign branches of US

Table 9.3 *Growth of the Overseas Branches of US TNBs and Subsidiaries, 1960–78*

	Number of Branches	*Assets ($ billion)*	*Number of Subsidiaries**	*Assets ($ billion)*
1960	131	3.5	15	—
1964	181	6.9	38	0.9
1965	211	9.1	42	1.0
1966	244	12.4	49	1.4
1967	295	15.7	53	1.5
1968	375	23.0	63	2.5
1969	459	41.1	71	3.5
1970	536	52.6	77	4.6
1971	583	67.1	85	5.5
1972	627	77.4	92	6.0
1973	699	118.0	104	6.9
1974	732	151.9	114	—
1975	762	175.9	—	—
1976	731	219.4	—	—
1977	738	258.9	—	—
1978	761	305.8	—	—

Note: * Includes only Edge and Agreement Corporations
Source: FINE (1976) p. 812 and Khoury (1980) p. 10

banks have grown at an annual rate of 33 per cent during the period 1969–78, while their liabilities to foreigners have increased at 22 per cent per annum. By comparison, assets of domestic offices of the so-called weekly reporting banks in the United States have grown much more slowly, at only 9 per cent per year. Both the assets of overseas branches and their deposits constitute an ever-increasing share of the total assets and liabilities of US TNBs. Data for the years 1971–4 (FINE, 1976) for the twelve largest US TNBs show that assets and liabilities of foreign branches as a percentage of their total asset/liabilities varied on the average from 28.6 to 34.1 per cent. However, for all US commercial TNBs, their foreign branches and assets were equal to 22.2 per cent of the assets of their domestic offices in 1978 (Khoury, 1980). The growth of the foreign branch network of US TNBs raised substantially the importance of foreign earnings in their total net income. The net foreign income of the twelve largest US TNBs as a percentage of their total net income rose steadily from 22.7 per cent on the average in 1971 to as high as 63.0 per cent in 1975 (FINE, 1976).

The rapid growth of transnational banking is also evident from the expansion of foreign banks (non-US TNBs) in the US market (Table 9.4). The fast expansion of the non-US TNBs in the US market started several years later than the accelerated growth of US TNBs in the international market. Between 1972 and 1978 foreign banking offices in the USA multiplied approximately three-fold and their assets almost five-fold. In 1977 the then existing offices were controlled by 96 different non-US TNBs. During the same period the share of the US offices of foreign banks in total US domestic banking assets increased more than 2½ times, indicating a faster rate of asset growth in comparison with US domestic banks.

Table 9.4 *Growth of Foreign Banks in the US, 1972–78*

	*Number of Offices**	*Assets ($ million)*	*Share of total banking assets (all offices) (%)*
1972	110	26,795	3.6
1973	124	37,345	4.5
1974	165	55,866	6.1
1975	184	64,300	6.7
1976	202	75,694	7.3
1977	253	93,684	8.0
1978	305	129,528	9.5

Note: * Includes branches, agencies, investment companies and agreement corporations
Source: Goldberg and Saunders (1981a)

A comparison of the performance of European and US TNBs in each other's territory (Table 9.5) shows that US TNBs have more than twice the assets in their European branches than European TNBs have in the USA. With the exception of Canada and Japan, non-US TNBs have a much lower level of operation in the USA than US TNBs have in other developed countries. It is interesting to note that the bulk of the foreign branch activity of US TNBs (75 per cent) is carried on in unregulated and reserve-free banking markets in London (44 per cent), the Bahamas and the Cayman islands (25 per cent), and Luxembourg, Singapore and Panama.

The growth of the non-US TNBs, and particularly their increasing presence in the US financial markets, demonstrates the fallacy of the view that the transnational activities of banks can be solely explained by international differences in banking regulations and exchange controls. This type of explanation has been advanced, especially in connection with the spectacular surge in the numbers of foreign branches of US TNBs since 1964 – the year that the interest rate equalisation tax was introduced by the Federal government, to be followed in 1965 by the Voluntary Credit Restraint Programme. Differential regulation regimes exert an impact not only on the availability of funds but also on the cost of acquiring such funds. Differences in the costs of acquiring deposits influence, no doubt, a bank's choice of type of international involvement. This can further be shown by the decision of the German banks during the period 1968–73 to transfer a significant proportion of their business to their foreign branches since the liabilities of German non-bank residents to the foreign branches of German banks were not subject to the minimum reserve

Table 9.5 *Branch Assets of Foreign Banks in the US from Selected Areas and US Banks Overseas in Selected Areas, 1975*

Country	*Foreign Banks in US ($ million)*	*US Banks Overseas ($ million)*
United Kingdom	3,090	72,455
Continental Europe	11,463	24,738
(of which Luxembourg)	(—)	(1,424)
Japan	19,762	10,341
Canada	6,049	—
Bahamas	—	35,678
Cayman Islands	—	5,595
Other countries	2,635	16,677
TOTAL	42,999	165,484

Source: FINE (1976) p. 745

requirement imposed by the capital controls programme of that period (Hewson and Sakasibara, 1977).

However, TNBs do not move abroad just to take advantage of inter-country differences in the cost of acquiring deposits. Banks engage in finance to industry for development and export support and it is in this area that a presence abroad is regarded as essential for the provision of speedy and reliable services to clients. Banks tend to follow their trade flag, although cases can be found where they appear to have travelled in advance of that flag. Banks, like large enterprises in other industries, may expand abroad as part of a strategy to exploit under-utilised resources which derive from large firm size and technical (financial) expertise. Banks are often obliged to follow their big customers abroad in order not to lose them to their foreign competitors. Robinson (1972) has demonstrated how the three waves of overseas post-1945 expansion of US TNBs were motivated by different factors. The first wave (mid-1945 to 1953) was essentially related to the trade finance business of US TNBs. This view is supported by the listing of the principal businesses of the overseas banks operating in London in the 1950s given in the report of the Radcliffe Committee (1959). According to the Radcliffe Report, foreign and overseas banks in London were principally engaged either in foreign exchange dealings or in the granting of credits to finance the movement of goods between the UK and the other countries in which they operated.

The second wave of US TNB expansion (1959 to mid-1963) was related to the multinationalisation of the major industrial clients of the large US banks. Second wave US branch banks were thus established during that period in order to serve directly their customers located in or near the host countries and thus compete effectively with the first wave US branch banks already present there. It is interesting to note that ten years after the Radcliffe Committee published its report, the Monopolies Commission (1968) found that servicing the UK activities of US multinational corporations had become the staple business of US banks in London. Four-fifths of their sterling advances and two-fifths of their sterling deposits were with UK branches or UK subsidiaries of US multinational corporations. A more recent study (Dunning and Norman, 1979) has found in the course of a survey of the factors influencing the location of offices of multinational enterprises in the UK that the majority of the original (and current) business of all of the respondents (which included – although not exclusively relating to – US branch banks) was (and is) derived from US contacts.

The third wave of expansion (which is traced by Robinson after mid-1963) was motivated by the need for a foreign branch which could tap Eurodollar deposits for lending directly to foreign borrowers without violating the US balance of payments legislation. The pattern of growth of the US TNBs clearly indicates that differences in banking and exchange control regimes are one of a host of factors that explain the transnationalisation of banking. The problem is to determine the interplay of these factors, to show the way they interacted to produce the present pattern of TNB growth. This issue is taken up in Sections 9.4 to 9.7.

9.3 THE GEOGRAPHICAL ORIGIN OF TNBs

The data in Table 9.6 confirm the picture emerging from the discussion in the previous section. The post-war TNB scene is dominated by the TNBs domiciled in the USA. In 1977, 34 per cent of the world's international banking offices were controlled by US TNBs. The UK's share in this total declined substantially from its estimated level in 1954. But when all the European Community nations are taken as a whole, the share of TNBs with an EEC home base is most probably at the same level as that of the US domiciled TNBs. The data in Table 9.6, by omitting the agency form of foreign presence, underestimate the share of TNBs with an EEC home base, as this form of representation is almost exclusively used in the North American market. The same table confirms the rising importance of Third-World TNBs. Their share of international banking offices – at 9.7 per cent in 1977 – exceeds that of Japanese TNBs. Data stated in terms of numbers of international banking offices probably exaggerate the importance of TNBs domiciled in developing countries. The latter's share in terms of assets or deposits would have most certainly been lower, as these TNBs tend to do business primarily with ethnic groups in developed countries rather than with the large corporate and institutional clients. The rise in the transnational activities of banks with a home base in the developing oil-exporting countries will tend to redress this imbalance. The share of US TNBs in the world's international banking offices stands above the US share in world trade, but is probably less than the US share in the stock of direct investment abroad.

The picture which emerges from Table 9.6 is essentially static and does not reveal the trend that has developed during the 1970s towards a considerable diversification in the countries generating transnational banking activities. For evidence on this, it is necessary to look at the changes in the geographical breakdown of the international banking offices and in the size of their assets over time. This can be done by utilising the more reliable and consistent data published in the USA and the UK about the activities of foreign banks in

Table 9.6 *Geographical Breakdown of Transnational Bank Offices* by Home Country*

		Home Country										
Host Country	*Total*	*USA*	*Canada*	*UK*	*France*	*Germany*	*Holland*	*Italy*	*Switzer-land*	*Japan*	*Other DMEs***	*LDCs*
Africa	277	51	1	68	51	25	4	24	5	4	24	20
Asia	685	218	38	99	28	32	22	12	8	97	53	78
Latin America	371	193	23	38	21	8	17	11	3	30	8	19
Caribbean	294	124	67	49	6	8	9	5	9	3	8	6
Western Europe	666	237	37	56	50	16	15	19	10	45	89	92
North America	143	9	12	22	13	13	3	8	14	21	7	21
TOTAL	2436	832	178	332	169	102	70	79	49	200	189	236
Percentage	(100.0)	(34.2)	(7.3)	(13.6)	[	(17.2)		]	(2.0)	(8.2)	(7.8)	(9.7)

Note: * Includes branches, subsidiaries and affiliates, but excludes agencies and representative offices ** Developed Market Economies
Source: Banker Research Unit

Table 9.7 *Total Assets of US Offices of Foreign Banks by Nationality of the Parent Bank, 1972–78*

	November 1972		*May 1978*	
Nationality of Parent Bank	*$m*	*%*	*$m*	*%*
Japan	10,778	46.7	31,829	33.3
Canada	5,032	23.6	12,397	13.1
Europe	5,784	25.1	42,053	43.9
Rest of the world	1,050	4.6	9,333	9.7
TOTAL	23,031	100.0	95,611	100.0

Source: Terrell and Key (1978)

these markets. Data from the UK indicate that since 1975 the proportional growth of advances, both in sterling and in foreign currency, of the non-US foreign banks with branches and/or subsidiaries in the UK has been faster than the corresponding growth of the offices of the US TNBs. The share of the US-based TNBs in total assets of overseas banks with a UK presence still remains high (38.8 per cent in December 1978), but it did show signs of decline during the 1975–9 period.[1] Data from the US market (Table 9.7) give further evidence of the growing diversification in the origin of TNBs. Between November 1972 and May 1978 the share of the Japanese TNBs in the total assets of US offices of foreign banks declined from 46.7 per cent to 33.3 per cent whilst the share of European-based TNBs increased from 25.1 per cent to 43.9 per cent.

Data from the *Banker*'s list of leading banks show even more clearly the growing significance of non-US banks. In 1965, 9 of the world's top 20 banks (i.e. 45 per cent) were American. In 1980 their

Table 9.8 *The World's Leading Twenty Banks by Nationality, 1965–80*

Nationality	*1965*	*1976*	*1980*
American	9	4	4
British	4	2	3
Canadian	3	0	0
Italian	1	1	0
French	1	4	4
German	0	3	3
Japanese	2	5	6
Brazilian	0	1	0

Source: The Banker

number went down to 4 (20 per cent). In contrast the number of Japanese, French and German banks has steadily risen (Table 9.8).

9.4 THE SEARCH FOR AN EXPLANATION

The post-war pattern of growth of transnational banking is often explained as a response by the TNBs to the multinationalisation and geographical diversification of the activities of their home country clients (Hendley, 1973; Fieleke, 1977; Khoury, 1980; Goldberg and Saunders, 1980, 1981a, 1981b). The establishment of foreign branches is seen either as a problem in the choice of a profit-maximising location or, alternatively, as a defensive investment strategy aiming at the preservation of the TNB's share in the market of its home country (Koszul, 1970). The TNB's presence abroad is thus explained in terms of the location of markets for banking services. This location-theoretic approach is not sufficient in explaining the transnationalisation of banking, since markets for banking services can be supplied by indigenous rather than foreign banks. In other words, the theory must explain the ownership-specific advantages that enable the TNBs through their internalisation to compete successfully with indigenous banks in an unfamiliar environment and especially in credit markets where equal treatment with the nationals is rarely offered to foreign financial institutions.

Grubel (1977) was the first to address himself to the problem and put forward a three-stream theory providing alternative explanations for the development of multinational retail banking, multinational service banking and multinational wholesale banking. The existence of different kinds of surplus entrepreneurial resources (such as management technology, marketing knowhow and commercial intelligence) provides the explanation for the multinationalisation in retail and service banking, whereas the presence of imperfections in the currency markets explains the development of wholesale banking. The existence of surplus entrepreneurial resources as such fails to provide a convincing theory, unless one explains the way these surplus entrepreneurial resources are combined with others in order to take advantage of the production of joint products. Furthermore, it always seems to be more useful to have a unified theory which is able to predict the emergence of different forms of multinational banking as special cases of a more general model. Gray and Gray (1981) make an interesting attempt to apply the eclectic theory of international production (Dunning, 1981a) – originally developed to explain the multinationalisation of non-financial corporations – to multinational commercial banking. This is an extremely useful approach and in what follows I try to build upon it and explore its advantages in explaining the pattern of growth of transnational banking. The value of the approach adopted in this chapter is that it shows that different forms of transnational banking and different strategies of international involvement in the financial markets follow as special cases of a more general theory. There is thus no need to seek alternative explanations for different forms of transnational banking development as Grubel (1977) and Gray and Gray (1981) do.

A theory of transnational banking should be able to explain the postwar patterns of development of transnational banking, including the increasing interpenetration of the developed countries' credit markets by each other's TNBs, the increasing number of different countries generating transnational banking activities, the rise of the Third World TNBs as well as the preponderance of very large firms among TNBs. It should be able, furthermore, to explain why some TNBs start at the wholesale end of the markets while others start at the retail end and why, irrespective of which end they start, TNBs may find it necessary to universalise their services. Finally, it should be able to explain why some TNBs can take advantage of the favourable banking rules of offshore centres whilst others can not.

The eclectic theory of international production predicts these outcomes from the particular combination of location-specific, ownership-specific and internalisation advantages that prevail at a given time and place. The theory suggests that the extent to which a bank provides particular types of services through offices located outside its home country will depend on its comparative ownership advantages *vis-à-vis* host country banks and the comparative location endowments of home and foreign countries. To judge the predictive ability of the theory when applied to transnational banking it is essential to specify the nature of the location endowments in banking, the nature of ownership specific advantages that are required by financial corporations and the scope of internalisation that can take place within banking firms. It is to these questions that we now turn. As it will be shown, the nature of the markets for banking services and the special characteristics of the financial institutions and the international credit markets strengthen the eclectric theory in its application to transnational banking.

9.5 THE GEOGRAPHICAL REDISTRIBUTION OF THE MARKETS FOR BANKING SERVICES

Banking is on balance a market-oriented rather than a footloose industry. Differences in the distribution of location-specific endowments between countries form a necessary, although not a sufficient, condition for the transnational operations of banks. What, then, are the factors, specific to banking, that differentiate between the location endowments of the host and home country? Countries acquire location-specific advantages for a number of reasons.

(a) Differences in the regulatory framework of banking and in the fiscal treatment of income from deposits and banking influence the cost of the provision of banking services from different jurisdictions. Requirements for non-interest-bearing reserves effectively impose a 'tax' on banking activities. Differences between jurisdictions in this implicit tax enable banks with offices in countries where minimal reserve requirements are imposed to supply services at more competitive interest rates. This differential regulation of banking is basic in the emergence of external currency markets (Aliber, 1980). The growth of the external ('Euro') financial intermediation markets is not, however, exclusively determined by differences in the cost structures of banking services. Differences in the risk perceptions relative to domestic financial intermediation (Dufey and Giddy, 1978) are also important and put limits to the extent that demand for deposits shifts from the domestic to the external (offshore) market.

(b) An important factor in the geographical redistribution of the demand for deposits has been the desire on the part of some investors to separate currency risk from the political risks associated with the currency's country. It is well known that the attempt to separate political risk from currency risk led to the emergence of the Eurodollar market when at the beginning of the Cold War the USSR, fearing that the dollar balances she accumulated during the war would be confiscated if placed with banks in the USA, decided to deposit them instead in London with British banks.

(c) The multinationalisation of the activities of the world's major manufacturing enterprises produced locational shifts in the traditional markets of the banks domiciled in the home country of the MNEs and created new business opportunities for the banks in both the home and the host countries of the non-financial MNEs (Klopstock, 1973). The geographical redistribution of the banks' clientele is accompanied by the generation of new types of services in response to the requirements of MNEs in foreign exchange management, arbitraging between funding and financing, etc. Thus the geographical redistribution of the markets for the traditional banking services brought about by the multinationalisation of the non-financial corporations also gives rise to service diversification with the creation of new forms of banking business. However, the demand for these new forms of banking services does not become so geographically dispersed as the demand for the traditional banking services of deposit-taking and lending. Many non-financial MNEs tend to centralise their currency risk management operations and monitor this activity from their headquarters. The multinationalisation of a bank's clientele does not merely imply that the expected increase in the bank's market from the growth of a home MNE will shift to another jurisdiction. If the home bank fails to supply the services required by the world operations of its home MNE customers, then it may lose to host country TNBs part of the domestic business of the home MNEs.

(d) The extensive international labour migration that took place in the post-war period (Commonwealth migration to the UK, the influx of guest workers in Europe, the continuing immigration into North America) produced similar locational shifts in the traditional markets of the banks of the labour exporting countries. Of course, the banking services involved are qualitatively different and the size of the relevant markets considerably smaller.

(e) There are differences among countries in the availability of information inputs characterised by high communication costs. A number of the services supplied by banks dealing with transnational customers require intermediary information inputs which are acquired only through orientation contacts that entail a physical presence near to the source of the relevant information. Examples are the clearing of international currency settlements and foreign exchange management. Unlike programmed contacts, which are part of a routine, repetitive process and can be handled through the ordinary telecommunications media, orientation contacts require quick interaction and are associated with face to face contacts (Yannopoulos, 1973). Even when communication by telephone or telex can provide useful information, such communication must be simultaneous. Some banking services require communication that has to extend itself over many time zones. In such cases simultaneous communication involves dislocation of the working day for at least one partner (Kindleberger, 1974). To overcome these high costs of dealing in finance at a distance, proximity to source of information is essential.

(f) Difference in location-specific advantages are generated by the differential availability of pools of skilled personnel with expertise in foreign exchange management and in international credit analysis. Certain banking services can thus be supplied competitively only from offices located in places with a sizeable pool of skilled personnel.

Thus differences in the distribution of location-specific endowments among countries are generated by government interventions – cases (a) and (b) above – by the growth of the non-financial MNEs and international labour migrations – cases (c) and (d) above – and by the economics of agglomeration – cases (e) and (f) above.

9.6 THE SOURCES OF OWNERSHIP-SPECIFIC ADVANTAGES

As Dunning (1981, p. 77) points out, the location-theoretic approach is not sufficient by itself to explain why it is that the foreign owned banks can out-compete indigenous banks in serving their own markets. To explain this we have to trace the sources of the net ownership advantages that foreign banks possess *vis-à-vis* banks of other nationalities in supplying services to particular markets.

One reason why foreign-owned banks could out-perform indigenous banks in supplying their own market might be the result of peculiarities of national legislation systems which through various loopholes may confer upon foreign banks advantages that are not made available to indigenous ones. For example, before the recent (1978) International Banking Act in the USA, foreign owned banks – which were then chartered under state law only – could obtain charters to conduct full-service banking operations in more than one state. Here, however, our concern is primarily with the sources of ownership-specific advantages that are associated with the structure of the banking firm and the structure of the market in which this firm operates.

A major source of comparative advantages over local banks is the extensive product differentiation in banking. Product differentiation in banking derives essentially from two sources. The first is a consequence of the international monetary system and derives from the different role of national currencies in the settlement of international payments. The second is a consequence of the predominance of non-price competition in the markets for banking services.

Banks operating from a 'vehicle currency' source of domestic funds acquire an advantage over other banks, because the use of vehicle (or 'key') currencies reduces transaction costs. Thus the 'real' yield of maintaining a deposit in a vehicle currency and the 'real' advantage of borrowing in such a currency tend to be higher. The dollar has become in the post-war period the dominant currency and more than a half of world trade is priced in dollars (Page, 1981). The Deutsche Mark is used for about 14 per cent of the total, followed by sterling and the French franc at around 7.5 and 6 per cent respectively. The dominant role of the US dollar in international trade invoicing and payments, and the required access to clearing facilities in New York, provides a number of US banks with distinct advantages in certain kinds of banking business over both the indigenous banks and banks with a non-dollar source of domestic funds. The diversification of the currency structure of the international trade invoicing and payments systems reduces the intrinsic service value of the dollar arising from its use as a vehicle currency and permits other banks with sources of domestic funds in emerging key currencies to compete on better terms with US banks. But the fact is that only four currencies can be used as 'vehicle' currencies. This will confer on banks whose source of domestic funds is in such currencies a comparative advantage *vis-à-vis* local banks in countries whose currencies are either non-convertible or have limited use in international trade invoicing and payments.

Product differentiation based on the differences in the 'vehicle' role of currencies is one of the sources of ownership-specific advantages in banking. There are, however, considerable additional differences among banks regarding their ability to sell deposits and buy loans, arising from the importance of service quality in banking competition. Here we must distinguish between *apparent differentiation* and *perceived differentiation*. Apparent differentiation is associated with the terms which are offered on loans and deposits; it is differentiation which is visible. Perceived differentiation is associated with either the risks (political or default risks) investors attach to deposits held in banks with different endowments or the probability of credit renewal and loan extension when the borrower needs it. Depositors, for example, perceive foreign currency deposits at banks of one nationality to be imperfect substitutes for foreign currency deposits at banks of another nationality. Differences among banks regarding their ability to sell deposits and buy loans are determined by such factors as country of domicile of the parent, the parent's capital–deposit ratio and above all the size of the bank.

Apart from the gains in perceived product differentiation, size may bring other advantages. The evidence of scale economies in banking is not strong (Moullineaux, 1978), but most of the literature has not clearly differentiated between wholesale and retail banking in this respect. Foreign exchange management, for example, is an activity characterised by high fixed costs. The larger the share of a bank's international activities and the more diverse its linkages the lower will be, in relative terms, the cost of acquiring information on currencies and of management of exposure to exchange risks. Thus size determines the ability of a bank to satisfy the special needs of MNEs for multi-currency multi-country lines of credit and for the management of their international funds. The provision of financial services to MNEs requires a presence in overseas markets which must be not so much extensive, as in units of sufficient size to provide adequate operating capability. Thus, both size and multinationality create ownership-specific advantages in banking. There exist, therefore, considerable non-legal entry barriers to transnational banking stemming from the substantial organisation and resources required to provide full scale transnational banking services, from the reduced marginal costs of uncertainty associated with each new venture, from the increased learning experience to scan the international environment for new business and from the mere possession of an internationally recognised name (e.g. the American Express name in the travellers' cheques market).

An advantage possessed by foreign banks' branches over domestic banks is their access to the resources and the stock of information and commercial intelligence possessed by the banking network of the parent organisation. The global relationship that exists between TNBs and MNEs enables the local branch through its access to the endowment in knowledge and other resources of the parent bank to make a more accurate assessment of the risks involved in lending and doing business with foreign subsidiaries of MNEs domiciled in the country of the parent bank's headquarters. Thus branches of foreign banks have not only access to markets that are not available to local competition but also a zero or very low marginal cost of acquiring knowledge inputs. All this leads to a further advantage in the sense that it makes the cost of innovative banking techniques lower for TNBs. By utilising the credit ratings of their head offices, foreign banks' branches may expand their leading operations on the basis of quasi guarantees (like the so-called 'monkey letters') instead of demanding the formal guarantees required by local competitors (Hendley, 1974).

9.7 THE SCOPE OF INTERNALISATION IN BANKING

The exclusive possession of proprietary information is one of the major sources of ownership-specific advantages. Whereas the acquisition of proprietary information is through R & D in most non-financial MNEs, in the case of banking it is based on commercial intelligence and contacts. As Casson (1979) has shown, industries which rely heavily on proprietary information enjoy considerable advantages from internalisation. Banking is an activity where information is a vital intermediate input. Information is produced through a constant stream of contacts, through financial analyses and project appraisal; but whatever production method is used, markets for information are characterised by important imperfections. Information inputs are difficult to obtain through arm's length transactions (Buckley and Casson, 1976). Information is not an exhaustible product and there may be advantages in not sharing it with others or indeed in passing misinformation to others. Because information is subject to rapid obsolescence, its effective transfer among unrelated decision makers is seriously impeded. There are inherent difficulties of specifying contractual arrangements in arm's length transactions and the reliability of information cannot be judged until one possesses it. Furthermore, returns from the production of information cannot be fully appropriated. It is evident, therefore, that the economics of information production are characterised by scale advantages and learning effects. So on the one hand, the nature of information markets give rise to what Cruise O'Brien and Helleiner (1980) call 'opportunism' (i.e. incentives to gain through lack of honesty or candour in transactions) and, on the other hand, they make those involved in information production over wider areas and longer periods of time constantly better and better at acquiring more – i.e. better in terms of reliability and quality of the information flows. There are thus clear advantages in internalising one's information sources.

Banks make extensive use of information as an intermediate product in the supply of banking services. They will thus enjoy considerable advantages from the internalisation of this market. There is, however, another important reason why the propensity to use internal markets will be high in banking. Internalisation will permit a bank to reap the advantages from maturity transformation. If banks are large enough relative to their customers then they can use stochastic principles in order to raise their gains from maturity transformation. To obtain the advantages from maturity transformation, a bank servicing large transnational clients must either develop a local deposit base or develop an extensive branch network with a presence in several financial centres or, in case neither of the above options are open, participate in the inter-bank market. But the inter-bank market is an inferior facility because it forces the bank to share the advantages from maturity transformation with other banks. Banks involved in wholesale lending will require a sizeable and stable retail deposit base to be able to apply the stochastic principles that bring about gain from maturity transformation. Banks will tend to develop a judicious mix of wholesale and retail business to enable them either to reduce risks or to increase returns (Artis and Lewis, 1981, Ch. 5). This partly explains the attempts of TNBs to strengthen their capacity to raise local funds in local markets (Hindley, 1981). A further explanation for such attempts is that the lack of a local deposit base will strengthen the links of the multinational clients of the foreign bank with local banks. The links that local banks develop with host MNEs may then be further exploited through the establishment of some form of presence in the MNE's country of origin, thereby seriously eroding the market share of the TNB with no local deposit base.

9.8 CONCLUDING COMMENTS

This chapter argues that the eclectic theory of international production can successfully explain the growth and the pattern of growth of transnational banking. It demonstrates this by tracing the sources of location-specific endowments, ownership-specific advantages and internalisation advantages in banking. As Dunning (1977) and Buckley and Casson (1976) demonstrate, firms will have no reason to engage in international production without a strong incentive to internalise market imperfections. Because of the nature of the intermediate inputs used in banking (information) and the nature of the banking business (maturity transformation) these incentives will be as strong and perhaps even stronger than in enterprises with high R & D activities. Perhaps as a result of these strong incentives to internalise, banking has become transnational at an earlier stage (late nineteenth and early twentiety century) than manufacturing. Rather than limit the applicability of the eclectic theory to the explanation of certain types only of transnational banking (Gray and Gray, 1981), the analysis in this paper suggests that the explanatory power of the theory is at its strongest when applied in banking.

NOTE

1 Terrell and Key (1978) estimate that between May 1977 and May 1978 total assets (minus claims on related institutions) of foreign branches of US TNBs increased by approximately 15 per cent compared to a much faster growth rate of about 30 per cent in the standard banking assets of the US offices of non-US TNBs (p. 10).

Bibliography

Adams, F. U. (1914) *Conquest of the Tropics* (New York: Doubleday Page).

Aharoni, Y. (1966) *The Foreign Investment Decision Process* (Boston, Mass.: Graduate School of Business Administration, Harvard University).

Aliber, R. Z. (1970) 'A Theory of Direct Investment', in C. P. Kindleberger (ed.), *The International Corporation* (Cambridge, Mass.: MIT Press).

Aliber, R. Z. (1980) 'The Integration of the Offshore and Domestic Banking System', *Journal of Monetary Economics*, 6, 509–26.

Allen, G. C. and Donnithorne, A. G. (1954) *Western Enterprise in Far Eastern Economic Development: China and Japan* (London: Allen & Unwin).

Anstey, V. (1929) *The Economic Development of India* (London: Longmans Green).

Archibald, G. C. (ed.) (1971) *The Theory of the Firm* (Harmondsworth: Penguin).

Arpan, J. S., Flowers, E. B. and Ricks, D. A. (1981) 'Foreign Direct Investment in the United States: the State of Knowledge of Research', *Journal of International Business Studies*, 12, 137–54.

Arrow, K. J. (1962) 'Economic Welfare and the Allocation of Resources for Invention', in National Bureau of Economic Research, *The Rate and Direction of Inventive Activity: Economic and Social Factors* (Princeton, NJ: Princeton University Press).

Arrow, K. J. (1969) 'The Organisation of Economic Activity', *The Analysis and Evaluation of Public Expenditure: the PPB System*, Joint Economic Committee, 91st Congress, 1st Session, 59–73.

Arrow, K. J. (1975) 'Vertical Integration and Communication', *Bell Journal of Economics*, 5, 173–83.

Arthur, H. B., Houck, J. P. and Beckford, G. L. (1969) *Tropical Agribusiness Structures and Adjustments: Bananas* (Cambridge, Mass.: Graduate School of Business Administration, Harvard University).

Artis, M. J. and Lewis, M. K. (1981) *Monetary Control in the United Kingdom* (Deddington, Oxon: Philip Allan).

Bagchi, A. K. B. (1972) *Private Investment in India 1900–1939* (Cambridge: Cambridge University Press).

Bain, J. S. (1956) *Barriers to New Competition* (Cambridge, Mass.; Harvard University Press).

Bandera, V. N. and White, J. T. (1968) 'U.S. Direct Investments and Domestic Markets in Europe', *Economia Internazionale*, 21, 117–33.

Barlow, E. R. and Wender, I. T. (1955) *Foreign Investment and Taxation* (Englewood Cliffs, NJ: Prentice-Hall).

Bartlett, W. (1977) 'L. D. Baker and the Development of the Banana Trade between Jamaica and the U.S., 1881–1890', Ph.D. thesis, The American University.

Baumol, W. J. (1959) *Business Behaviour, Value and Growth* (New York: Macmillan).
Beaver, P. (1976) *Yes We have Some: A History of Fyffes*, private publication.
Beckford, G. L. (1967) *The West Indies Banana Industry* (Jamaica: Institute of Social and Economic Research, University of West Indies).
Bennett, W. B. (1943) *The American Patent System: An Economic Interpretation* (Baton Rouge, La: Louisiana State University Press).
Bentham, J. (1793) 'Manual of Political Economy', in W. Stark (ed.), *Jeremy Bentham's Economic Writings*' Vol. 1 (London: Allen and Unwin) pp. 221–73.
Berle, A. A. and Means, G. C. (1932) *The Modern Corporation and Private Property* (New York: Macmillan).
Bertin, G-Y. (1972) 'Foreign Expansion and Diversification of Multinational Firms', in G. Paquet (ed.), *The Multinational Firm and the Nation State* (Toronto: Collier-Macmillan).
Black, D. (1958) *The Theory of Committees and Elections* (Cambridge: Cambridge University Press).
Boddewyn, J. J. (1979) 'Foreign Divestment: Magnitude and Factors', *Journal of International Business Studies*, 10, 21–7.
Boulding, K. E. (1950) *A Reconstruction of Economics* (New York: Wiley).
Bowman, W. S., Jr (1973) *Patent and Antitrust Law* (Chicago, Ill.: University of Chicago Press).
Brash, D. T. (1966) *American Investment in Australian Industry* (Canberra: Australian National University Press).
Brimmer, A. F. and Dahl, F. R. (1975) 'Growth of American International Banking: Implications for Public Policy', *Journal of Finance*, 30, 341–63.
Brooke, M. Z., Black, M. and Neville, P. (1977) *International Business Bibliography* (London: Macmillan).
Buckley, P. J. (1981) 'A Critical Review of Theories of the Multinational Enterprise', *Aussenwirtschaft*, 36, 70–87.
Buckley, P. J. and Casson, M. C. (1976) *The Future of the Multinational Enterprise* (London: Macmillan).
Buckley, P. J. and Casson, M. C. (1981) 'The Optimal Timing of A Foreign Direct Investment', *Economic Journal*, 91, 75–87.
Buckley, P. J. and Roberts, B. R. (1982) *European Direct Investment in the U.S.A. before World War I* (London: Macmillan).
Calabresi, G. (1968) 'Transactions Costs, Resource Allocation, and Liability Rules: a Comment', *Journal of Law and Economics*, 11, 67–73.
Callis, H. (1942) 'Foreign Capital in South East Asia', New York: New IPR International Research Series (*mimeo*).
Calvet, A. (1981) 'A Synthesis of Foreign Direct Investment Theories and Theories of the Multinational Firm', *Journal of International Business Studies*, 12, 43–60.
Cassel, G. (1928) *Foreign Investments* (Chicago, Ill.: University of Chicago Press).
Casson, M. C. (1979) *Alternatives to the Multinational Enterprise* (London: Macmillan).

Casson, M. C. (1981) Foreword to Alan M. Rugman, *Inside the Multinationals* (London: Croom Helm).

Casson, M. C. (1982a) *The Entrepreneur: An Economic Theory* (Oxford: Martin Robertson).

Casson, M. C. (1982b) 'Transaction Costs and the Theory of the Multinational Enterprise', in A. M. Rugman (ed.), *New Perspectives in International Business* (London: Croom Helm).

Casson, M. C. (1982c) 'The Theory of Foreign Direct Investment', in J. Black and J. H. Dunning (eds) *International Capital Movements* (London: Macmillan).

Caves, R. E. (1971) 'International Corporations: the Industrial Economics of Foreign Investment', *Economica*, New Series, 38, 1–27.

Caves, R. E. (1980) 'Investment and Location Policies of Multinational Companies', *Zeitschrift für Volkswirtschaft und Statistik*, 3, 321–327.

Caves, R. E. and Porter, M. E. (1977) 'From Entry Barriers to Mobility Barriers: Conjectural Decisions and Contrived Deterrence to New Competition', *Quarterly Journal of Economics*, 9, 241–61.

Chamberlain, N. W. (1962) *The Firm: Microeconomic Planning and Action* (New York: McGraw-Hill).

Chandler, A. D., Jr (1962) *Strategy and Structure* (Cambridge, Mass.: MIT Press).

Chandler, A. D., Jr (1977) *The Visible Hand: The Managerial Revolution in American Business* (Cambridge: Harvard University Press).

Chandler, A. D., Jr (1981) 'Global Enterprise, Economic and National Characteristics: an Historical Overview', Harvard University (*mimeo*).

Chandler, A. D., Jr and Daems, H. (1974) 'The Rise of Managerial Capitalism and Its Impact on Investment Strategy in the Western World and Japan', in H. Daems and H. Van der Wee (eds) *The Rise of Managerial Capitalism* (Louvain: Louvain University Press).

Channon, D. F. (1977) *British Banking Strategy and the International Challenge* (London: Macmillan).

Clark, J. B. (1907) *Essentials of Economic Theory* (New York: Macmillan).

Coase, R. H. (1937) 'The Nature of the Firm', *Economica*, New Series, 4, 386–405, repr. in G. J. Stigler and K. E. Boulding (eds) *Readings in Price Theory*, (Homewood, Ill.: Richard D Irwin, 1952).

Cole, A. H. (1962) 'What is Business History?' *Business History Review*, 36, 90–106.

Commission of the European Communities (1976) *Survey of Multinational Enterprises*, Vol. 1 (Brussels and Luxembourg: EEC).

Conan, A. R. (1960) *Capital Imports into Sterling Countries* (London: Macmillan).

Coram, T. C. (1967) 'The Role of British Capital in the Development of the United States', M.Sc. thesis, University of Southampton.

Cournot, A. (1838) *Researches into the Mathematical Principles of the Theory of Wealth* (ed. I. Fisher) (London: Hafner, 1960).

Cruise O'Brien, R. and Helleiner, G. K. (1980) 'The Political Economy of Information in a Changing International Economic Order', *International Organisation*, 34, 445–70.

Curhan, J., Davidson, W. and Suri, D. (1977) *Tracing the Multinationals* (Cambridge, Mass.: Harvard University Press).
Cyert, R. M. and March, J. G. (1963) *A Behavioural Theory of the Firm* (Englewood Cliffs, NJ.: Prentice-Hall).
Davidson, W. D. and McFetridge, D. G. (1979) 'International Technology Transactions and the Theory of the Firm' (*mimeo*).
Deane, R. S. (1970) *Foreign Investment in New Zealand Manufacturing* (Wellington, N.Z.: Sweet & Maxwell).
Dixit, A. (1979) 'A Model of Duopoly Suggesting a Theory of Entry Barriers', *The Bell Journal of Economics*, 10, 20–32.
Dufey G. and Giddy, I. H. (1978) *The International Money Market* (Englewood Cliffs, NJ: Prentice-Hall).
Dunning, J. H. (1958) *American Investment in British Manufacturing Industry* (London: Allen & Unwin).
Dunning, J. H. (1971) 'United States Foreign Investment and the Technological Gap', in C. P. Kindleberger and A. Shonfield (eds) *North American and Western European Economic Policies* (London: Macmillan).
Dunning, J. H. (1972) *The Location of International Firms in an Enlarged EEC: An Exploratory Paper* (Manchester: Manchester Statistical Society).
Dunning, J. H. (1973) 'The Determinants of International Production', *Oxford Economic Papers*, 25, 289–336.
Dunning, J. H. (1977) 'Trade, Location of Economic Activity and the Multinational Enterprise: a Search for an Eclectic Approach', in B. Ohlin, P. O. Hesselborn and P. M. Wijkman (eds) *The International Allocation of Economic Activity* (London: Macmillan).
Dunning, J. H. (1979) 'Explaining Changing Patterns of International Production: In Defence of the Eclectic Theory', *Oxford Bulletin of Economics and Statistics*, 41, 269–95.
Dunning, J. H. (1980) 'Towards an Eclectic Theory of International Production; Some Empirical Tests', *Journal of International Business Studies*, 11, 9–31.
Dunning, J. H. (1981a), *International Production and the Multinational Enterprise* (London: Allen & Unwin).
Dunning, J. H. (1981b) 'Explaining the International Direct Investment Position of Countries: Towards a Dynamic or Developmental Approach', *Weltwirtschaftliches Archiv*, 117, 30–64.
Dunning, J. H. (1982) 'Non-equity Forms of Foreign Economic Involvement and the Theory of International Production', *University of Reading Discussion Papers in International Investment and Business Studies*, no. 59.
Dunning, J. H. and McQueen, M. (1981) 'The Eclectic Theory of International Production: a Case Study of the International Hotel Industry', *Managerial and Decision Economics*, 2, 197–210.
Dunning, J. H. and Norman, G. (1979) *Factors Influencing the Location of Offices of Multinational Enterprises in the U.K.* (London: Economists Advisory Group).
Dunning, J. H. and Pearce, R. D. (1981) *The World's Largest Industrial Enterprises* (Farnborough: Gower).
Einzig, P. (1970) *The Eurodollar System*, 5th edn (London: Macmillan).

Ellis, F. (1978) 'The Banana Export Activity in Central America 1947–1976', Ph.D. thesis, Institute of Development Studies, University of Sussex.

Ellis, F. (1981) 'Export Valuation and Intra-firm Transfer in the Banana Export Industry in Central America', In R. Murray (ed.) *Multinationals Beyond the Market* (Brighton: Harvester Press) pp. 61–76.

Ferrier, R. W. (1976) 'The Early Management Organisation of British Petroleum and Sir John Cadman', in L. Hannah (ed.), *Management Strategy and Business Development* (London: Macmillan).

Fieleke, N. J. (1977) 'The Growth of US Banking Abroad: an Analytical Survey', in *Key Issues in International Banking*, Federal Reserve Bank of Boston (Boston, Mass.: Ballinger).

FINE (1976) *Financial Institutions and the Nation's Economy: Compendium of Papers Prepared for the FINE Study*, Book II, Washington, DC: Committee on Banking, Currency and Housing, House of Representatives, 94th Congress, 2nd Session.

Forsyth, D. J. C. (1972) *U.S. Investment in Scotland* (New York: Praeger).

Frankel, S. H. (1938) *Capital Investment in Africa* (London: Oxford University Press).

Frankel, M. (1955) 'Obsolescence and Technological Change in a Maturing Economy', *American Economic Review*, 45, 296–319.

Franko, L. G. (1976) *The European Multinationals* (London: Harper & Row).

Franko, L. G. (1978) 'Multinationals: the End of U.S. Dominance', *Harvard Business Review*, 56, 93–101.

Freedman, C. (1977) 'Micro Theory of International Financial Intermediation', *American Economic Review, Papers and Proceedings*, 67, 172–9.

Galambos, L. (1966) 'Business History and the Theory of the Growth of the Firm', *Explorations in Entrepreneurial History*, 2nd series, 4, 3–16.

Gené, F. C. (1977) 'Comercializadora Multinacional del Banano (Comunbana)', *Troquel*, 1(8), 4–7.

Giddy, I. H. (1978) 'The Demise of the Produce Cycle Model in International Business Theory', *Columbia Journal of World Business*, 13, 90–7.

Gilman, M. (1981) *The Financing of Foreign Direct Investment* (London: Frances Pinter).

Goldberg, L. G. and Saunders, A. (1980) 'The Causes of U.S. Bank Expansion Overseas: the Case of Great Britain', *Journal of Money, Credit and Banking*, 12, 630–43.

Goldberg, L. C. and Saunders, A. (1981a) 'The Growth of Organisational Forms of Foreign Banks in the United States', *Journal of Money, Credit and Banking*, 13, 365–74.

Goldberg, L. G. and Saunders, A. (1981b) 'The Determinants of Foreign Banking Activity in the United States', *Journal of Banking and Finance*, 5, 17–32.

Gordon, R. A. (1945) *Business Leadership in the Large Corporation* (Washington, D.C.: Brookings Institution).

Gort, M. (1962) *Diversification and Integration in American Industry* (Princeton, N.J.: Princeton University Press).

Graham, E. M. (1978) 'Transnational Investment by Multinational Firms: a Rivalistic Phenomenon', *Journal of Post-Keynesian Economics*, 1, 82–99.

Gray, J. M. and Gray, H. P. (1981) 'The Multinational Bank: A Financial MNC?', *Journal of Banking and Finance*, 5, 33–63.

Greenhut, J. G. and Greenhut, M. L. (1975) 'Spatial Price Discrimination, Competition and Location Effects', *Economica*, New Series, 42, 401–19.

Grubel, H. G. (1977) 'A Theory of Multinational Banking', *Banca Nazionale del Lavoro Quarterly Review*, 30, 349–63.

Heal, G. M. (1973) *The Theory of Economic Planning* (Amsterdam: North Holland).

Hendley, J. (1973) 'Multinational Companies and the Banks', *Midland Bank Review*, May, 3–7.

Hendley, J. (1974) 'Financial Institutions and the Growth of the Multinational Corporation', in J. S. G. Wilson and C. F. Scheffer (eds) *Multinational Enterprises — Financial and Monetary Aspects* (Leiden: Sijthoff).

Hewson, J. and Sakasibara, E. (1977) 'The Effectiveness of German Controls on Capital Inflow', *Review of World Economics*, 4, 660–70.

Hindley, T. (1981) 'Modest Impact in the Retail Banking Market', *The Banker*, 131, 125–33.

Hirsh, S. (1976) 'An International Trade and Investment Theory of the Firm', *Oxford Economic Papers*, 28, 258–70.

Hood, N. and Young, S. (1980) *European Development Strategies of U.S.-owned Manufacturing Companies Located in Scotland* (Edinburgh: HMSO).

Horst, T. (1971) 'Theory of the Multinational Firm', *Journal of Political Economy*, 79, 1059–72.

Horst, T. (1974) 'American Exports and Foreign Direct Investments', *Harvard Institute of Economic Research Discussion Paper* 362.

Hou, Chi-ning (1965) *Foreign Investment and the Economic Development of China* (Cambridge, Mass.: Harvard University Press).

Houston, T. and Dunning J. H. (1976) *U.K. Industry Abroad* (London: Financial Times).

Hughes, J. (1973) *The Vital Few* (London: Oxford University Press).

Hymer, S. H. (1971) 'The Multinational Corporation and the Law of Uneven Development', in J. N. Bhagwati (ed.) *Economics and World Order* (New York: World Law Fund).

Hymer, S. H. (1976) *The International Operations of National Firms: A Study of Direct Investment* (Cambridge, Mass.: MIT Press; previously unpublished Doctoral Dissertation, 1960).

Hymer, S. H. and Rowthorn, R. (1970) 'Multinational Corporations and International Oligopoly: the Non-American Challenge', in C. P. Kindleberger (ed.) *The International Corporation: A Symposium* (Cambridge, Mass.: MIT Press), pp. 57–91.

Indian Tariff Board (1928) *Report of the Indian Tariff Board Regarding the Grant of Protection to the Oil Industry* (Calcutta: Government of India Central Publication Branch).

International Petroleum Cartel (1952) *The International Petroleum Cartel:*

Staff Report to Federal Trade Commission (Washington, DC: U.S. Government Printing Office).

Iremonger, D. S. (1972) *New Commodities and Consumer Behaviour* (Cambridge: Cambridge University Press).

James, J. (1981) 'Structural Changes in American Manufacturing', 1850–90 (*mimeo*).

Johnson, H. G. (1970) 'The Efficiency and Welfare Implications of the International Corporation', in C. P. Kindleberger (ed.) *The International Corporation*, (Cambridge, Mass.: MIT Press).

Johnson, H. G. (1975) *Technology and Economic Interdependence* (London: Macmillan).

Jones, C. F. and Morrison, P. C. (1952) 'Evolution of the Banana Industry of Costa Rica', *Economic Geography*, 28, 1–19.

Jones, G. G. (1979) 'The State and Economic Development in India 1890–1947: the Case of Oil', *Modern Asian Studies*, 13, 353–75.

Kaldor, N. (1934) 'The Equilibrium of the Firm', *Economic Journal*, 44, 60–76.

Kamien, M. and Schwartz, N. (1982) *Market Structure and Innovation* (Cambridge: Cambridge University Press).

Karnes, T. L. (1978) *Tropical Enterprise: The Standard Fruit and Steamship Company in Latin America* (Baton Rouge, La: Louisiana State University Press).

Katrak, H. (1981) 'Multinational Firms' Exports and Host Country Commercial Policy', *Economic Journal* , 91, 454–65.

Kay, N. M. (1979) *The Innovating Firm* (London: Macmillan).

Kelly, J. (1977) *Bankers and Borders* (Cambridge, Mass.: Ballinger).

Kepner, C. D. and Soothill, J. H. (1935) *The Banana Empire, A Case Study in Economic Imperialism* (New York: Vanguard).

Kepner, C. D. (1936) *Social Aspects of the Banana Industry* (New York: AMS; reprinted 1967).

Khoury, S. J. (1980) *Dynamics of International Banking* (New York: Praeger).

Kidron, M. (1965) *Foreign Investment in India* (London: Oxford University Press).

Kindleberger, C. P. (1960) *American Business Abroad* (New Haven, Conn.: Yale University Press).

Kindleberger, C. P. (1964) *Economic Growth in France and Britain, 1851–1950* (Cambridge, Mass.: Harvard University Press).

Kindleberger, C. P. (1974) 'The Formation of Financial Centres: a Study in Comparative Economic History', *Princeton Studies in International Finance*, no. 36.

Kirzner, I. M. (1973) *Competition and Entrepreneurship* (Chicago, Ill.: University of Chicago Press).

Kirzner, I. M. (1979) *Perception, Opportunity and Profit* (Chicago, Ill.: University of Chicago Press).

Klein, B., Crawford, R. C. and Alchian, A. A. (1978) 'Vertical Integration in the Oil Industry, *Bell Journal of Economics*, 21, 297–326.

Klopstock, F. H. (1973) 'Foreign Banks in the United States: Scope and

Growth of Operations', *Monthly Review of the Federal Reserve Bank of New York*, 55, 140–54.

Knickerbocker, F. T. (1973) *Oligopolistic Reaction and Multinational Enterprise* (Boston, Mass.: Graduate School of Business Administration, Harvard University).

Knight, F. H. (1921) *Risk, Uncertainty and Profit* (ed. G. J. Stigler) (Chicago, Ill.: University of Chicago Press, 1971).

Kojima, K. (1980) 'Japanese Direct Foreign Investment in Asian Developing Countries', *Rivista Internationale di Science Economiche e Commerciale*, 27, 630–40.

Kopits, G. (1979) 'Multinational Conglomerate Diversification', *Economia Internationale*, 32, 99–111.

Koszul, J-P. (1970) 'American Banks in Europe', in C. Kindleberger (ed.) *The International Corporation* (Cambridge, Mass.: MIT Press).

Koutsoyiannis, A. (1979) *Modern Microeconomics*, 2nd edn (London: Macmillan).

Krugman, P. (1979) 'Increasing Returns, Monopolistic Competition and International Trade', *Journal of International Economics*, 9, 469–79.

Krugman, P. (1981) 'Intra-industry Specialisation and the Gains from Trade', *Journal of Political Economy*, 89, 959–73.

Kumar, K. and McLeod, M. G. (1981) *Multinationals from Developing Countries* (Lexington, Mass.: Lexington Books).

LaBarge, R. A. (1960) 'A Study of the United Fruit Company Operations in Isthmian America 1946–1956', Ph.D. thesis, Duke University.

LaBarge, R. A. (1968) 'The Impact of the United Fruit Company on the Economic Development of Guatemala 1946–1954', Tulane University: *Studies in Middle American Economics*, no. 29.

Lake, A. W. (1979) 'Technology Creation and Technology Transfer by Multinational Firms', in R. G. Hawkins (ed.) *The Economic Effects of Multinational Corporations* (Greenwich, Conn.: Jai Press).

Lall, S. (1979) 'The International Allocation of Research Activity by U.S. Multinationals', *Oxford Bulletin of Economics and Statistics*, 41, 313–32.

Lall, S. (1980) 'Monopolistic Advantages and Foreign Involvement by U.S. Manufacturing Industry', *Oxford Economic Papers*, 32, 102–22.

Lall, S. and Streeten, P. (1977) *Foreign Investment, Transnationals and Developing Countries* (London: Macmillan).

Lancaster, K. (1979) *Variety, Equity and Efficiency* (Oxford: Basil Blackwell).

Lavington, F. (1927) 'Technical Influences on Vertical Integration', *Economica*, Old Series, 7, 27–36.

Leibenstein, H. (1976) *Beyond Economic Man* (Cambridge, Mass.: Harvard University Press).

Leibenstein, H. (1978) *General X-Efficiency Theory and Economic Development* (New York: Oxford University Press).

Leibenstein, H. (1979) 'A Branch of Economics is Missing: Micro-Micro Theory', *Journal of Economic Literature*, 17, 477–502.

Lewis, C. (1938) *America's Stake in International Investment* (Washington, DC: Brookings Institution).

Lewis, C. (1945) *Debtor and Creditor Countries, 1938–1944* (Washington, DC: Brookings Institution).

Lewis, C. (1948) *The United States and Foreign Investment Problems* (Washington, DC: Brookings Institution).

Litvak, I. A. and Maule, C. J. (1977) 'Transnational Corporations and Vertical Integration: the Banana Case', *Journal Of World Trade Law*, 11, 537–49.

Luce, R. D. and Raiffa, H. (1957) *Games and Decisions* (New York: Wiley).

Magee, S. P. (1977a) 'Information and the Multinational Corporation: an Appropriability Theory of Direct Foreign Investment', in J. N. Bhagwati (ed.) *The New International Economic Order* (Cambridge, Mass.: MIT Press).

Magee, S. P. (1977b) 'Multinational Corporations, Industry Technology Cycle and Development', *Journal of World Trade Law*, 11, 297–321.

Magee, S. P. (1981) 'The Appropriability Theory of Multinational Corporation Behaviour', *University of Reading Discussion Papers in International Investment and Business Studies*, no. 51.

Malmgren, H. B. (1961) 'Information, Expectations and the Theory of the Firm', *Quarterly Journal of Economics*, 75, 399–421.

Mansfield, E. S., Teece, D. J. and Romeo, A. (1979) 'Overseas Research and Development by U.S.-based Firms', *Economica*, New Series, 46, 187–96.

Marris, R. L. (1964) *The Economic Theory of Managerial Capitalism* (London: Macmillan).

Marschak, J. (1968) 'The Economics of Inquiring, Communicating, Deciding', *American Economic Review*, 58, 1–18.

Marshall, A. (1920) *Principles of Economics*, 8th edn (London: Macmillan).

Marshall, H., Southard, F. A., Jr and Taylor, K. W. (1936) *Canadian-American Industry* (New Haven, Conn.: Yale University Press).

Mason, R. H. (1980) 'A Comment on Professor Kojima's 'Japanese Type' versus 'American Type' of Technology Transfer', *Hitotsubashi Journal of Economics*, 20, 42–52.

May, S. and Plaza, G. (1958) *The United Fruit Company in Latin America* (Washington, DC: National Planning Association, Study No. 7).

McCann, T. P. (1976) *An American Company: The Tragedy of United Fruit* (New York: Crown).

McGuiness, A. (1979) 'A Critical Assessment of Markets and Hierarchies in Terms of Neo-Austrian Economic Method', University of Sheffield (*mimeo*).

McKay, J. P. (1970) *Pioneers for Profit: Foreign Entrepreneurship and Russian Industrialisation 1885–1913* (Chicago, Ill.: University of Chicago Press).

McLelland, D. C. (1967) *The Achieving Society* (New York: Free Press).

McManus, J. (1972) 'The Theory of the International Firm', in G. Paquet (ed.) *The Multinational Firm and the Nation State* (Toronto: Collier-Macmillan).

Mill, J. S. (1848) *Principles of Political Economy*, new edn (ed. W. J. Ashley) (London: Longmans, 1909).

Monopolies Commission (1968) *Barclays Bank, Lloyds Bank and Martins Bank: A Report on the Proposed Merger* (London: HMSO, HC319).

Monteverde, K. and Teece, D. J. (1982) 'Supplier Switching Costs and Vertical Integration in the Automobile Industry', *Bell Journal of Economics*, 13, 206–13.

Montias, J. M. (1976) *The Structure of Economic Systems* (New Haven, Conn.: Yale University Press).

Moore, E. S. (1941) *American Influence in Canadian Mining* (Toronto: University of Toronto Press).

Moran, P. (1975) 'Les Banques Etrangères en France', in J. Soufflet *et al. L'activité des Banques Etrangères en France* (Paris: Presses Universitaires de France).

Moss, S. J. (1981) *An Economic Theory of Business Strategy* (Oxford: Martin Robertson).

Moxon, R. W. (1974) 'Offshore Production in Less Developed Countries', *The Bulletin*, Institute of Finance, New York University, July 8–9.

Moullineaux, D. J. (1978) 'Economies of Scale and Organisational Efficiency in Banking: a Profit-function Approach', *Journal of Finance*, 33, 259–80.

Mueller, D. C. (1972) 'A Life Cycle Theory of the Firm', *Journal of Industrial Economics*, 20, 199–219.

Mueller, D. C. (1979) *Public Choice* (Cambridge: Cambridge University Press).

Neumeyer, F. and Stedman J. C. (1971) *The Employed Inventor in the United States* (Cambridge, Mass.: MIT Press).

Newbould, G. D., Buckley, P. J and Thurwell, J. (1978) *Going International: The Success of Smaller Companies Overseas* (London: Associated Business Press).

Nicholas, S. J. (1982a) 'British Multinational Investment before 1939', *Journal of European Economic History* (forthcoming).

Nicholas, S. J. (1982b) 'Transaction Cost Approach to Institutional Change', London: Business History Unit (*mimeo*).

Noetling, F. (1898) 'The Occurrence of Petroleum in Burma, and its Technical Exploitation', *Memoirs of the Geological Survey of India*, no. 27 (Calcutta: Government of India Printing Office).

Norman, G. (1981) 'Spatial Competition and Spatial Price Discrimination: An Extension', *University of Reading Discussion Papers in Urban and Regional Economics*, no. 7.

Norman, G. and Nichols, N. K. (1982) 'Dynamic Market Strategy under Threat of Competitive Entry: an Analysis of the Pricing and Production Strategies open to the Multinational Company', *Journal of Industrial Economics* (forthcoming).

North, D. C. (1981) *Structure and Change in Economic History* (New York: Norton).

Nwankwo, G. D. (1972) 'British Overseas Banks in the Developing Countries', *Journal of the Institute of Bankers*, 93, 148–58 and 253–61.

OECD (var. dates) *Investing in Developing Countries* (Paris: OECD).

Oi, W. Y. and Hurter, A. P., Jr (1965) *Economics of Private Truck Transpor-*

tation (Dubuque, Iowa: William C. Brown) repr. as 'A Theory of Vertical Integration in Road Transport Services' in B. S. Yamey (ed.) *Economics of Industrial Structure* (Penguin, Harmondsworth, 1973).

Organisation of American States (1975) *Sectoral Study of Transnationals in Latin America: The Banana Industry* (Washington, DC).

Page, S. A. B. (1981) 'The Choice of Invoicing Currency in Merchandise Trade', *National Institute Economic Review*, 78, 60–72.

Pamuk, S. (1981) 'A Note on the Portfolio-Direct Composition of Private Foreign Investment in the Ottoman Empire in 1914', Ankara: University of Ankara (*mimeo*).

Papandreou, A. (1952) 'Some Basic Problems in the Theory of the Firm', in B. F. Haley (ed.) *A Survey of Contemporary Economics*, Vol. 2, (Homewood, Ill.: Richard D. Irwin).

Paterson, D. G. (1976) *British Direct Investment in Canada: Estimates and Determinants* (Toronto: University of Toronto Press).

Pavitt, K. and Soete, L. (1981) 'International Differences in Economic Growth and the International Location of Innovation', Brighton: Sussex University (*mimeo*).

Pearce, R. D. (1982) 'Industrial Diversification amongst the World's Leading Multinational Corporations', *University of Reading Discussion Papers in International Investment and Business Studies*, no. 61.

Penrose, E. T. (1956) 'Foreign Investment and the Growth of the Firm', *Economic Journal*, 66, 220–35.

Penrose, E. T. (1959) *The Theory of the Growth of the Firm* (Oxford: Basil Blackwell).

Pigou, A. C. (1938) *Economics of Welfare*, 4th Edn (London: Macmillan).

Plant, A. (1934) 'The Economic Theory Concerning Patents for Inventions', *Economica*, New Series, 1, 30–51.

Polanyi, M. (1958) *Personal Knowledge: Towards a Post Critical Philosophy* (Chicago, Ill.: University of Chicago Press).

Porter, M. E. (1980) *Competitive Strategy* (New York: Free Press).

Prais, S. J. (1976) *The Evolution of Giant Firms in Britain* (Cambridge: Cambridge University Press).

Price's (1891) *A Brief History of Price's Patent Candle Co. Ltd.;* private publication.

Price's (1947) *Still the Candle Burns*, private publication.

Pugel, T. A. (1978) *International Market Linkages and U.S. Manufacturing: Prices, Profits, and Patterns* (Cambridge, Mass.: Ballinger).

Quirin, G. D. (1980) 'Changes in the Parameters of Comparative Advantage: the Multinational Corporation', Toronto: Faculty of Management Studies, University of Toronto, *Working Paper* 80–04.

Radcliffe Committee (1959) Committee on the Working of the Monetary System, *Report* (London: HMSO, Cmnd 827).

Read, R. A. N. (1981) 'Corporate Foreign Direct Investment Strategies and Trade Liberalisation in the Japanese Market for Bananas 1960–1976', *University of Reading Discussion Papers in International Investment and Business Studies*, no. 60.

Reddaway, W. C., Potter, S. J. and Taylor, C. T. (1968) *The Effects of U.K.*

Direct Investment Overseas: Final Report (Cambridge: Cambridge University Press).

Remer, C. F. (1933) *Foreign Investment in China* (New York: Macmillan).

Revell, J. (1974) 'Financial Centres, Financial Institutions and Economic Change', in H. G. Johnson (ed.) *The New Mercantilism* (Oxford: Basil Blackwell).

Richardson, G. B. (1972) 'The Organisation of Industry', *Economic Journal*, 82, 883–96.

Rippy, F. J. (1959) *British Investment in Latin America* (Hamden, Conn.: Archon Books).

Robertson, D. H. (1923) *The Control of Industry* (London: Nisbet).

Robinson, E. A. G. (1931) *The Structure of Competitive Industry* (London: Nisbet).

Robinson, E. A. G. (1934) 'The Problem of Management and the Size of Firm', *Economic Journal*, 44, 242–57.

Robinson, S. W., Jr (1972) *Multinational Banking* (Leiden: Sijthoff).

Ronstadt, R. (1977) *Research and Development Abroad by US Multinationals* (Praeger: New York).

de Roover, R. (1948) *The Medici Bank: Its Organisation, Management, Operation and Decline* (New York: New York University Press).

Rossman, J. (1931) *The Psychology of the Inventor* (Washington, DC.: Inventor's Publishing Co.).

Royal Institute of International Affairs (1937) *The Problem of International Investment* (London: Oxford University Press).

Rugman, A. M. (1979) *International Diversification and the Multinational Enterprise* (Lexington, Mass.: Lexington Books).

Rugman, A. M. (1981) *Inside the Multinationals* (London: Croom Helm).

Rungta, R. S. (1970) *The Rise of Business Corporations in India 1851–1900* (Cambridge: Cambridge University Press).

Safarian, A. S. (1966) *Foreign Ownership of Canadian Industry* (New York and Toronto: McGraw-Hill).

Say, J. B. (1803) *A Treatise on Political Economy: Or, the Production Distribution and Consumption of Wealth* (New York: Augustus M. Kelley, 1964).

Scherer, F. M. *et al.* (1975) *The Economics of Multi-Plant Operation* (Cambridge, Mass.: Harvard University Press).

Scherer, F. M. (1980) *Industrial Market Structure and Economic Performance*, 2nd Edn. (Chicago, Ill.: Rand McNally).

Schumpeter, J. A. (1934) *The Theory of Economic Development* (Cambridge, Mass.: Harvard University Press).

Sekiguchi, S. (1979) *Japanese Foreign Direct Investment* (London: Macmillan).

Shackle, G. L. S. (1979) *Imagination and the Nature of Choice* (Edinburgh: Edinburgh University Press).

Shubik, M. (1980) *Market Structure and Behaviour* (Cambridge, Mass.: Harvard University Press).

Silberston, Z. A. (1981) 'Factors Affecting the Growth of the Firm in Theory and Practice', in D. Currie, D. Peel and W. Peters (eds) *Microeconomic*

Analysis: Essays in Microeconomics and Economic Development (London: Croom Helm).

Simon, H. A. (1947) *Administrative Behaviour* (New York: Macmillan).

Simon, H. A. (1957) *Models of Man* (New York: Wiley).

Simon, H. A. (1980) *Models of Thought* (New Haven: Yale University Press).

Sornarajah, M. (1981) 'The Myth of International Contract Law', *Journal of World Trade Law*, 15, 187–217.

Southard, F. A., Jr (1931) *American Industry in Europe* (Boston, Mass.: Houghton Mifflin).

Stamp, J. (1929) *Some Economic Factors in Modern Life* (London: P. S. King).

Stewart, C. F. and Simmons, G. B. (1964) *A Bibliography of International Business* (New York: Columbia University Press).

Stobaugh, R. B. *et al*. (1976) *Nine Investments Abroad and Their Impacts at Home* (Boston, Mass.: Graduate School of Business Administration, Harvard University).

Stone, I. (1977) 'British Direct and Portfolio Investment in Latin America Before 1941', *Journal of Economic History*, 37, 690–722.

Stopford, J. M. (1974) 'The Origins of British-based Multinational Manufacturing Enterprises', *Business History Review*, 48, 303–35.

Stopford, J. M., Dunning, J. H. and Haberich, K. O. (1980) *The World Directory of Multinational Enterprises* (London: Macmillan).

Stopford, J. M. and Haberich, K. O. (1976) 'Ownership and Control of Foreign Operations', *Journal of General Management*, 3, 3–20.

Streit, C. (1949) *Union Now: A Proposal for an Atlantic Federal Union of the Free* (New York: Harper).

Stubenitsky, F. (1970) *American Direct Investment in Netherlands Industry* (Rotterdam: Rotterdam University Press).

Stuckey, J. A. (1981) 'Vertical Integration and Joint Ventures in the International Aluminum Industry', Ph.D. thesis, Harvard University.

Svedberg, P. (1978) 'The Portfolio-direct Composition of Private Foreign Investment in 1914 Revisited', *Economic Journal*, 88, 763–77.

Svedberg, P. (1981) 'Colonial Enforcement of Foreign Direct Investment', *Manchester School*, 50, 21–38.

Teece, D. J. (1976) *The Multinational Corporation and the Resource Cost of International Technology Transfer* (Cambridge, Mass.: Ballinger).

Teece, D. J. (1977) 'Technology Transfer by Multinational Firms: the Resource Costs of Transferring Technological Know-How', *Economic Journal*, 87, 242–61.

Teece, D. J. (1980) 'Economies of Scope and the Scope of the Enterprise', *Journal of Economic Behaviour and Organisation*, 1,223–47.

Teece, D. J. (1981a) 'The Multinational Enterprise: Market Failure and Market Power Considerations', *Sloan Management Review*, 22, 3–17.

Teece, D. J. (1981b) 'Delineating Efficient Enterprise Boundaries for a Regime of Rapid Technological Change', Stanford, Ca.: Stanford University (*mimeo*).

Teece, D. J. (1981c) 'The Market for Know-How and the Efficient International Transfer of Technology', *The Annals of the Academy of Political and Social Science*, 458, 81–96.

Teichova, A. (1974) *An Economic Background to Munich* (Cambridge: Cambridge University Press).

Terrell, H. S. and Key, S. J. (1978) 'U.S. Offices of Foreign Banks: The Recent Experience', *Princeton International Finance Discussion Papers*, no. 124.

Tsurumi, Y. (1976) *The Japanese are Coming: The Multinational Spread of Japanese Firms* (Cambridge, Mass.: Ballinger).

Tucker, K. A. (1972) 'Business History: Some Proposals for Aims and Methodology', *Business History*, 14, 1–16.

Union de Paises Exportadores de Banano (1977a) *Ley No. 8 Por la Cual se Autoriza la Constitucion y Funcionaria de la Comercializadora Multinacional del Banano S.A.* (Panama: UPEB).

Union de Paises Exportadores de Banano (1977b) *Minuto de Pacto Social de la Sociedad Anonima Denomindada Comunbana* (Panama: UPEB).

Union de Paises Exportadores de Banano, *Informe Mensuel* (Panama: UPEB, various issues).

United Brands, *Annual Report* (New York: various issues).

United Fruit Company, *Annual Report* (Boston, Mass.: various issues).

United Nations (1949) *International Capital Movements during the Interwar Period* (New York: UN).

United Nations (UNCTC) (1978) *Transnational Corporations and World Development: A Re-examination* (New York: UN, E/C. 10/38).

United Nations (UNCTC) (1981) 'Salient Features and Trends in Foreign Direct Investments' (*mimeo*).

United States (1904) *Costa Rica* (Washington, DC: Bureau of the American Republics).

Utton, M. A. (1979) *Diversification and Competition* (Cambridge: Cambridge University Press).

Vaitsos, C. V. (1974) *Intercountry Income Distribution and Transnational Enterprises* (Oxford: Clarendon Press).

Vaupel, J. W. and Curhan, J. P. (1969) *The Making of Multinational Enterprise* (Cambridge, Mass.: Graduate School of Business, Harvard University).

Vaupel, J. W. and Curhan, J. P. (1974) *The World's Multinational Enterprises* (Geneva: Centre for Education in International Management).

Vernon, R. (1966) 'International Investment and International Trade in the Product Cycle', *Quarterly Journal of Economics*, 80, 190–207.

Vernon, R. (1974) 'The Location of Economic Activity', in J. H. Dunning (ed.) *Economic Analysis and the Multinational Enterprise* (London: Allen & Unwin).

Vernon, R. (1979) 'The Product Cycle Hypothesis in a New International Environment', *Oxford Bulletin of Economics and Statistics*, 41, 255–67.

Vernon, R. (1981) 'Organisational and Institutional Responses to International Risk', Boston, Mass.: Graduate School of Business Administration (*mimeo*).

Vollmer, D. D. (1974) 'Financial Institutions and the Growth of Multinational Corporations – an American Point of View', in J. S. G. Wilson and C. F. Scheffer (eds) *Multinational Enterprises–Financial and Monetary Aspects* (Leiden: Sijthoff).

Wellons, P. A. (1976) *Transnational Banks: Report to the Centre on Transnational Corporations* (New York: UN).

Wilkins, M. (1970) *The Emergence of Multinational Enterprise: American Business Abroad from the Colonial Era to 1914* (Cambridge, Mass.: Harvard University Press).

Wilkins, M. (1974a) *The Maturing of Multinational Enterprise: American Business Abroad from 1914 to 1970* (Cambridge, Mass.: Harvard University Press).

Wilkins, M. (1974b) 'Multinational Enterprises', in H. Daems and H. Van der Wee (eds) *The Rise of Managerial Capitalism* (Louvain: Louvain University Press).

Wilkins, M. (1976) 'Multinational Companies and the Diffusion of Technology to Africa: a Historical Perspective' in D. Thomas Babatunde, *Importing Technology into Africa* (New York: Praeger).

Wilkins, M. (1977a) 'Modern European Economic History and the Multinationals', *Journal of European Economic History*, 6, 575–95.

Wilkins, M. (1977b) 'Cross-currents: American Investments in Europe, European Investments in the United States', in P. Uselding (ed.) *Business and Economic History*, 6, 22–35.

Williamson, O. E. (1971) 'Managerial Discretion, Organisation Form and the Multi-division Hypothesis', in R. L. Marris and A. Wood (eds) *The Corporate Economy* (London: Macmillan).

Williamson, O. E. (1975) *Markets and Hierarchies: Analysis and Antitrust Implications* (New York: Free Press).

Williamson, O. E. (1979) 'Transaction Cost Economics: the Governance of Contractual Relations', *Journal of Law and Economics*, 22, 233–61.

Williamson, O. E. (1981) 'The Modern Corporation: Origins, Evolution, Attributes', *Journal of Economic Literature*, 19, 1537–68.

Williamson, O. E. and Teece, D. J. (1983) 'European Economic and Political Integration: The Markets and Hierarchies Approach', in P. Salmon (ed.) *New Approaches to European Integration* (forthcoming).

Wilson, C. (n.d.) 'The Multinational in Historical Perspective', in K. Nakagawa (ed.) *Strategy and Structure of Big Business* (Tokyo: Tokyo University Press).

Wilson, C. M. (1947) *Empire in Green and Gold: The Story of the American Banana Trade* (New York: Henry Holt).

Wilson, G. (1876) *The Old Days of Price's Patent Candle Company*, private publication.

Wolf, B. N. (1977) 'Industrial Diversification and Internationalisation: Some Empirical Evidence', *Journal of Industrial Economics*, 26, 177–91.

Yannopoulos, G. N. (1973) 'Reasons for London's Dominance', *Built Environment*, 1, 413–7.

Index

DATE DUE

DEC 16 1983			
MAY 10 1993			